For Jim
without him I would not be in Cable

5/19/2012

Dream Chaser

A TRUE STORY

BY

Maqbool Qurashi

ISBN: 1456456172
ISBN - 13: 9781456456177
LCCN: 2010919415

"Wishing is not enough, one must do."
Johann Wolfgang von Göthe

TO

Reinhild, my wife, my friend, who made my dream into
our dream and stood by me without hesitation
and to Nina, Alexandra, Taylor Sage, Luci and Finn.

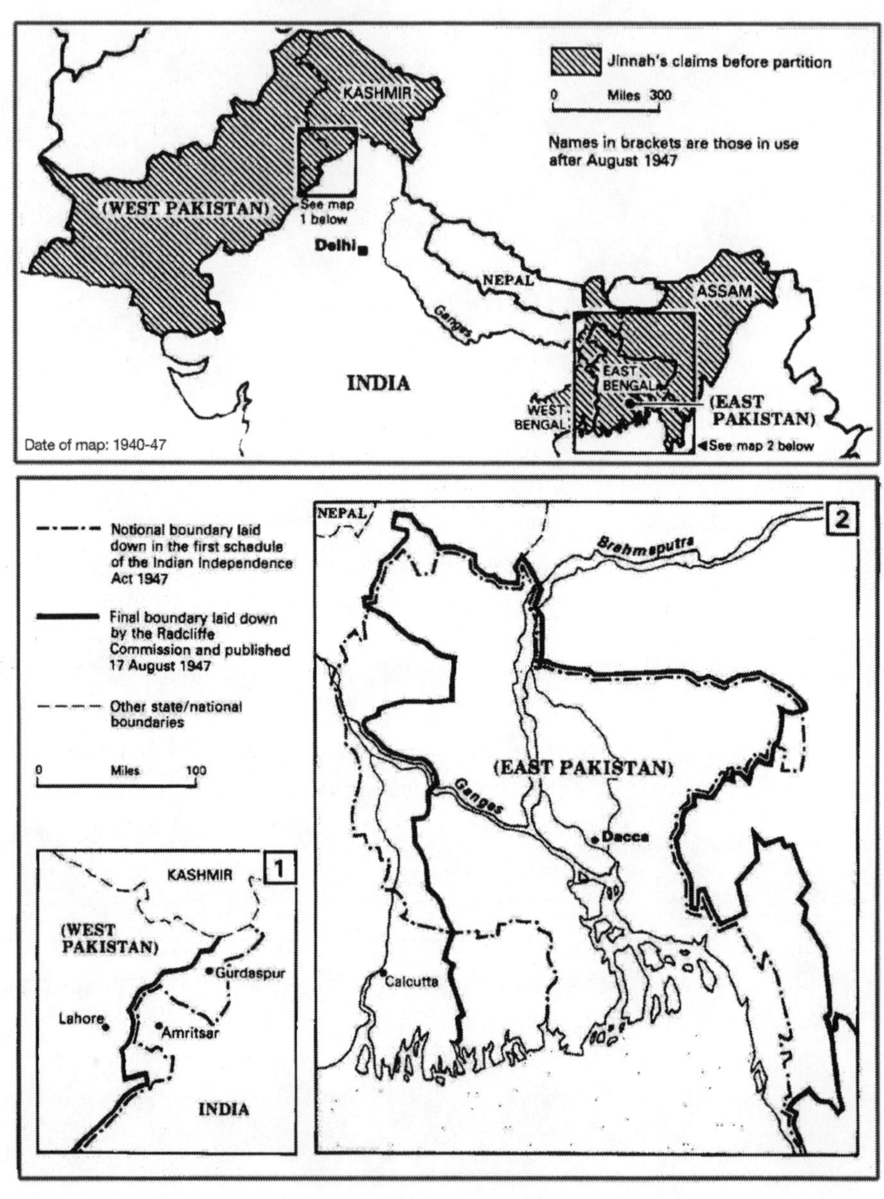

Boundary-lines of Pakistan and India
Before and after Radcliffe award

INTRODUCTION

Daydreaming was part of my growing up, but today I wonder if the invasion by the high-tech gadgetry leaves our youth enough time for such a luxury. I spent many hours sitting on a cliff overlooking the River Tawi in Jammu, visualizing my life. Environs, political and family, have a lot to do with one's fantasies, and during my early childhood, World War II shaped my dreams. One day I was a general leading my imaginary soldiers against the forces of evil, and the next I was a pilot diving somewhere to accomplish a mission. After the conclusion of the war, each day saw large gatherings of people demanding freedom as the focus shifted to the struggle for the independence of India. It was easy to get caught up in the emotional tide of the moment, not knowing what lay ahead. After abandoning my imaginary army and diving planes, I became part of the movement and marched through the streets alongside those who supported the creation of Pakistan. As the day for independence drew closer, the deadly sectarian conflicts spread like wildfire throughout India. My father became concerned about the future for the Muslims in the State of Jammu and Kashmir when the Hindu maharajah of the state intensified the crackdown on the Muslims, although they were in the majority. I began to seek means of escaping a life that had been burdened by frequent curfews, confining us to our homes. My father's admiration of the United States of America led me to imagine about life in such a place. I was fourteen years old when a newspaper article transformed my passing curiosity into a lifelong dream. This is the story of my journey in the pursuit of that dream, and the people I met and the lessons I learned along the way.

The Asian societies are patriarchal, and in a typical family the father is the head of the household and all matters are deferred to him. My family was the exception, where both of my parents were the co-chairpersons, making it difficult to manipulate one against the wishes of the other. If, for example, my father did not agree with my mother's decision in the matter of my discipline, he would not remand it arbitrarily. Instead, in privacy, he would convince my mother to withdraw her edict. My sisters were provided the same opportunities as my brothers and I, and my older sister was the first woman from the State of Jammu and Kashmir to receive an admission into a medical college. The religions throughout the world preach respect for the elders, but the Asian cultures take that to heart and have a deep-rooted tradition of revering their seniors. Besides the parents, one addresses his or her older brothers and sisters by a traditional family honorific before their names. Following are the titles with names of the older members of my family that I have used in the story:

Mother——————*Bayjee*
Father ——————*Abbajee*
Older brother————*Bhaijee Manzoor or Bhaijee*
Older sisters————*Apa Anwari* and *Apa Asghari* or *Apajee*

Jee is an expression of endearment and is used with the titles as shown above.

Many events influenced my thoughts and plans during the pursuit of my dream over a period of three decades. Therefore I have made no attempts, whether historically necessary or not, to correct what I experienced, as my thoughts at the time were influenced by my personal interpretations of the events. However, many historians since have corroborated my recollections of how the boundaries of Pakistan were determined by the order of the late Lord Mountbatten in 1947. The partition of India caused the largest migration of humanity and exposed the human propensity for both compassion and extreme cruelty towards its own. The plights of the refugees are narrated from my own experience.

I have used real names of those who permitted me to do so and those who I failed to locate received fictitious names representing real persons.

The Author

1

During the month of July in the city of Annapolis, Maryland, it can be balmy as the still, warm air, laden with moisture, hangs over the Chesapeake Bay, and frequently the invading, cool breeze from the Atlantic Ocean causes stormy winds and heavy downpours accompanied with lightning. It was such a storm that caused our classes at the sailing school to be cut short, and all the trainees retreated to their hotels or homes. My wife and I were two of the students who were forced to spend the afternoon in the confines of our hotel. Storms have always fascinated me, and the explosive sound of a lightning bolt brought me to the balcony of our room overlooking the bay. As I surveyed the horizon, my gaze was stopped short by a large Stars and Stripes riding the westerly wind so strong that it made the banner appear as if it were suspended in midair. I always become emotional when the flag of my adopted country is raised or the national anthem is sung. The flutter demonstrated its will to stay flying against the heavy rain, rekindling memories of my own determination and the journey that spanned a period of over three decades in the pursuit of my own dream.

ഗ്ഗ

It began in Jammu, one of the major cities in the State of Jammu and Kashmir, presently under the occupation of India. The first fifteen years of my life were spent in that hilly city of temples with its narrow cobblestone alleys, weaving through rows of homes and stores, connecting plazas, and gardens. One day in 1946, I came upon a newspaper article about how one could immigrate to the United States. Its description of the lives of a few of the Indian immigrants and what they had accomplished in their new homeland left a lasting impression. It led me to fantasize about a life away from the city, where prejudice was practiced as a rule. I carried the article in my pocket and waited for an opportune time to discuss the matter with my parents. The financial implications of the impending wedding of my older sister, *Apa Anwari*, and the college expenses for my other sister, *Apa Asghari*, had to be considered. By no means could my family be considered wealthy, though we lived very comfortably in a large house with domestic help. It was a few months before I decided to approach my father, knowing that he would take time to consider the matter, as opposed to my mother, who would make a quick decision.

Muslims are required to perform five prayer rituals a day. Unlike the other four, the evening prayer differs in that the faithful, in order to have time to discuss matters of communal concerns, are required to congregate ahead of the ritual that begins immediately after the *Muezzin*, the one who summons for prayers, finishes his call. I was the *Muezzin* for the day, and I timed the passing of the newspaper article to *Abbajee* so that when he was busy reading, I would be climbing the stairs to the top of the minaret to my station for the *Azan*, the prayer call. My heart was pounding with excitement when I sang out "*Allah hu Akbar...* "As I began my descent after the *Azan*, each step offered mixed feelings of excitement and depression in anticipation of my father's reaction. The people were lining up for the commencement of the prayers when I stepped off the last step and found my father looking at me with a suppressed smile, his way of telling me that my idea had merit.

After the conclusion of the ritual, I approached my father and called out, "*Abbajee?*"

Before I could finish my question, he said, "I was wondering who had cut out that article. I wanted to show it to *Asghari* and you."

Unlike the majority of Muslim homes of the time, males and females enjoyed equal standing in our family, and I felt that *Apa Asghari* would jump at the opportunity to immigrate. I was preparing to present my case when he continued, "My idea is for one of you to open the way so the rest of the family could follow. I know you are more adventurous, and from what I know about the United States, you as a male would have better opportunities. If you want to be the one to do it, you have my support."

I could not believe my ears, and as he held me in an embrace, my eyes swelled with tears of happiness. He cautioned me not to mention it to anybody until he had a chance to discuss it with my mother. Both of us felt that she may have reservations.

A few days had passed before *Abbajee, Bayjee, Apa Asghari,* and I had a discussion about my planned immigration to the United States of America. Everybody applauded me for my decision, although *Bayjee* looked concerned. After the excitement subsided, I was puzzled about why my parents did not convince me to remain at home in the view of the fact that the new country, after independence, would offer many opportunities. Although *Abbajee* was straining not to show it, I could detect that he was very concerned with the unfolding political scenario, while I was too excited about America. With my father's assistance, I wrote a letter to the American consulate in Lahore and a few weeks later completed the required application that registered my name in the long list of those who intended to immigrate. Upon the receipt of my quota number, I began to read anything that I could find about life in the United States of America, where I hoped to begin my college education. The only dark cloud that hung above to dampen my plans was the confusion over the impending independence of India.

I had always wanted to be an entrepreneur ever since a gentleman spoke at one of the student assemblies about the benefits of being a businessman while demonstrating how simple, everyday products could be produced. Following his directions, I had begun selling white shoe polish under the brand name of Sunrise Shoe Polish, and *Abbajee* assisted me in designing and printing a three-color label. I could see myself as the top manager of a business employing many people and could visualize myself addressing large assemblies of people, using my skills that I had acquired as a member of my school's debating team. Ever since I watched John Wayne in *Flying Tigers*, I had wanted to fly, and I could see myself flying my own plane while imagining my family in a beautiful home with a backyard and cars in the driveway, just like the ones shown in the movies.

By the middle of 1946, the process for the independence of India was fast becoming a reality. Earlier, an agreement had been reached between the British Cabinet Mission, the Congress Party, and the Muslim League for the creation of an all-India federation of three autonomous ethnic regions, but that excitement lasted for only a few months. Jawaharlal Nehru, who became the first prime minister of India upon assuming presidency of the Congress Party, annulled all previous agreements and opted for the partition of India, music to the ears of Lord Mountbatten, the new viceroy of India, who had orders to expeditiously extract the United Kingdom out of the subcontinent regardless of the future consequences.

"Divide and rule" had been the mainstay of the British colonial strategy. The majorities of the inhabitants in the Valley of Kashmir were and still are Muslims. The ruler of the Valley of Kashmir was a Muslim, while a Hindu prince ruled over an area known as District of Jammu having a Hindu majority. When the British colonized India, they deposed the Muslim prince of Kashmir and combined the two areas into one State of Jammu and Kashmir under the Hindu prince, whose policies toward Muslims were extremely repressive. Throughout my life in the city of Jammu, I witnessed ruthless suppression of any free speech, especially if it came from the Muslim inhabitants. The police, bearing bamboo sticks called *lathis,* would charge into any gathering of Muslims that was deemed to be a demonstration, regardless of the number of people involved. Living under frequent curfews had become a way of life, and I had become apt at dodging the patrolling troops. The atmosphere was always tense, with infrequent comic interludes. At one occasion, people running in front of an out-of-control cow prompted a forty-eight-hour curfew. But one event that left a deep scar took place in the beginning of the fall just after I had turned eleven.

In the middle of each October, the State government offices moved south from the city of Srinagar to the city of Jammu, and it was customary for the upper level government officials to join in a motorcade that traveled over the major streets of the city. I joined a crowd of people lined on the side of a street anticipating the arrival of the motorcade, and as the leading car occupied by the maharajah's appointed chief minister approached, a wave of excitement seemed to pass over the gathering. Suddenly one of the Muslim leaders in the crowd stepped in the middle of the road and raised his hand, holding a petition. Having failed to present their grievances through the proper channels, this offered the only means to the Muslim political parties to accomplish their objective. Instead of slowing the motorcade, the chief minister ordered his driver to speed up, aiming for the lone man standing in the street. The crowd gasped when someone pointed to the man being dragged under the car, and it had already traveled a few hundred feet before the crowd, breaking through the barricades, surrounded the car and forced it to stop. The still body of the severely injured man was exposed as the car was pushed back by the combined effort of the gathered people. The spokesman of the chief minister demanded that the man be turned over to the police who were accompanying the motorcade, but the crowd refused to comply, as they felt that the man needed immediate medical assistance. The arguments became intense and the police began shooting in the air, and as the crowds dispersed, the police took custody of the seriously hurt man. The motorcade, under the protection of the police on motorcycles, fled the scene, leaving behind a couple of policemen to guard the injured man, as if he was capable of an escape. Hiding behind the corner of a building, I watched the disfigured body lying in the middle of the street, his clothes saturated with blood, while each breath was becoming a greater struggle. I wanted to run, but my inner conflict between the desire to assist the man and the fear of detection by the sentries rendered my feet frozen to the ground where I stood.

My eyes flooded with uncontrolled tears, as the incident had triggered an emotion of anger in me that had been building up over the years of helplessness in the face of the prejudices exhibited by the Hindu teachers and students at the school. Helplessness and frustration were overwhelming, as I felt an urge to run into the policemen, and if I had known how to use a weapon and one had been available, I probably would have used it against them. My thoughts were interrupted by the arrival of a truck bearing a few more uniformed men, and one of the new arrivals comforted the injured man and, with the help of the others, placed him in the back of the truck. An eerie stillness descended on the street as the final act.

Before I could leave my hiding place, I heard a loudspeaker announcing the usual implementation of a forty-eight-hour curfew. After playing hide and seek with the patrolling troops, I stepped into the arms of my worried family. The incident left me in a deep depression, and it took months and a transfer to another school before I returned to my old self again. Later I learned that the man, once healed, received a prison sentence of five years for interfering with an official event.

In June of 1947, Lord Mountbatten announced the decision to partition India, and on July 19, 1947 Indian Independence Act was passed defining the borders of Pakistan but less than a month later arbitrary boundary lines were drawn (see map). Mixed feelings of excitement and fear permeated the population at large leading to sectarian rioting that escalated to murders and property destruction. With the anticipated creation of Pakistan, Muslims could not wait for the day when they would shed the mantle of the prejudicial dominance of predominantly Hindu India. With *Bhai Manzoor* and *Apa Anwari* married and gone, my remaining family consisted of my parents; Masood, my younger brother; and *Apa Asghari,* who was home from college for the summer.

Pakistan became a reality on August 14, 1947.

Apa Asghari and I built a lighted box declaring "Pakistan Zindabad," meaning "Long Live Pakistan," and placed it at a corner of the roof of our home, the highest point in the neighborhood. There were festivities and celebrations throughout the city, although one could sense a tension between Muslims and Hindus. A noticeable change came over the attitudes of my Hindu friends, as they avoided eye contact and pretended to be busy for any after-school activities. A cloud of anticipated trouble hung over all the celebrations when it became known that the final borders granted India a strategic area adjoining the Jammu District. *Abbajee's* enthusiasm further dampened when a letter from *Bhaijee Manzoor,* the then resident medical officer in a village overlooking the new India, informed us that he had witnessed many young Hindus crossing from India into the district. This begged the question; why were Hindus crossing from India into a territory where the majority was Muslims? This news, compounded with the intentional delay by the maharajah in announcing his decision about the state's affiliation, led the Muslim community to believe that the maharajah was conspiring with India. One of my uncles was a colonel in the state's army, and during his latest visit he informed us that the young Hindus entering the Jammu District were in reality Indian paramilitary personnel. Because of this news and the concern for the safety of *Apa Asghari,* who at nineteen would be vulnerable in the event hostilities broke out, my parents came to a decision that split up our family. It was planned that I would accompany my sister and Masood to Daska, a small village in Pakistan approximately ten miles from the Indian border where my maternal grandparents lived. *Bayjee,* in the absence of any communication from the Department of Education, expected to resume her duties as headmistress of a teacher training school as scheduled, and she decided to remain in Jammu. We were to return in a few months when the situation had stabilized, or my parents would follow in the event the conditions deteriorated. I was reluctant to leave my newly established enterprise, Sunrise Shoe Polish Company, as a few bottles had been sold and a few dozen were on consignment. *Abbajee* assured me that he would keep in contact with my customers during my few months' absence. But fate had a different scenario in store for our family.

2

In an environment of political chaos, rumors have a way of exaggerating the events that shape the outcome. News was rampant that train travel had become dangerous because Hindu gangs were attacking the cars that carried Muslims to Pakistan and Muslims were retaliating. As a precaution, *Apa Asghari*, Masood, and I took a bus to Daska, although we had taken that trip many times by train before. It was a few days before my fifteenth birthday, and I still remember my father's parting words: "No matter what happens, do not give up your dream. Do not let detours and obstacles cause you to despair. They are there to prepare you for what lies in the future, and only faith and focus will lead you to your rewards."

As we took our seats on the bus, I was overcome by a feeling of emptiness and wanted the cloud of sadness to go away, but it stayed there like an immovable rock. I could control an unstoppable urge to cry only by reminding myself that a display of such emotion would betray my confidence. The bus was crowded, and there were people sitting even on top of the roof of the vehicle, and it appeared as if everyone was leaving Jammu. I saw *Abbajee* waving to us as the bus rounded the corner and began to accelerate, and as the distance between us increased, he turned and began to walk away with drooping shoulders and hands in his coat pocket. That was the last time I saw him.

In order to avoid attention as a young woman, it was decided that *Apa Asghari* would wear a *burqa,* a tentlike garment that covers a woman's body from head to toe with a net in front of the eyes, a custom inherited from the pagan tribes. My apprehensions faded when I discovered that the majority of the passengers were women with children, making it easy for the three of us to blend with others on the bus. Some passengers sat there gazing at the floor, while others whispered as if they had inside information, and then somebody mentioned that the Indian Army was controlling the border between Jammu and Sialkot, Pakistan, and that the buses were being stopped for inspection. Praying that it was just a rumor, but in the event it was true, the obvious question that came to my mind was, what were they looking for? There had been unconfirmed reports of soldiers raping young female travelers, raising my level of concern, but *Apa Asghari* read my mind and grasped my hand in a gesture of reassurance. I asked, "What will we do?"

She answered, imitating our mother's voice, "Do not worry."

Then she instructed Masood to pretend that she was our mother and that he should address her as *Bayjee* during the rest of the journey, thus easing my mind. The sadness of leaving our home was overwhelming every fiber in my body, and yet I wished for the bus to speed up and cross the border. I was shaken out of my thoughts with a jerk as the bus came to a stop, followed by a deafening silence as the chatter of the passengers died in anticipation. This was an unscheduled stop that alarmed everyone aboard, and I was momentarily paralyzed with fear. Then the tension subsided when the driver announced that he was only picking up a passenger. Finally, the bus crossed the border without any army interference, although one could see a group of patrolling soldiers. At the urging of the fellow travelers, the bus stopped, and some who got out kissed the ground and then shouted, "Pakistan Zindabad." Others began to offer prayers, and somebody began distributing sweets brought for the occasion. The activities held no excitement for me, and we preferred to remain in the bus in order to contemplate the possible loss of our parents and our home, and the possibility of life as refugees.

It was noon by the time we reached Sialkot, where disheartening news awaited us when the driver declared that due to the rapidly changing conditions, he would not drive into the village of Daska on his way to the city of Gujranwala. Instead, we had the option to take a *Tonga,* a two-wheeled horse cart, to travel the remaining fifteen miles from Sialkot or find our own transport for the remaining two-and-a-half miles to the village from the junction of the bypass where he would drop us off. We wanted to save our money, not knowing what the future held, so we decided to continue on the bus. The rest of the journey was uneventful and quiet, and we arrived at the junction point one hour after leaving Sialkot.

It was late afternoon when we stepped off the bus next to a wide-open field that I had walked across as a shortcut many times during my earlier visits. We waited a short time for a passing bus or a *Tonga,* and, in the absence of any and due to impending darkness, we decided to proceed on foot. We had walked only a short distance when a whiff of foul smell made me realize that it was a mistake, and I hoped and prayed that it was just a dead animal. Instead, my scanning eyes focused on a pair of lifeless feet, and one more step revealed a body of a man hidden behind a bush. It appeared that he had been severely beaten to death. *Apa Asghari* must have seen the body at the same time, and, with her tacit approval and against Masood's protests, I covered his eyes and nose with my left hand while carrying a suitcase in the right. This was the second time I was witnessing how one human being could inflict such cruelty upon another, and it saddened me. The rest of the two miles, not a word was spoken as I prayed that we be spared any further such encounters. The sun was preparing to call it a day when we entered the outskirts of the village, and the sky had begun to darken when we arrived at our grandparents' home.

After a good night's sleep, *Apa Asghari* and I got together with my Uncle Nazir to find a way to inform our parents of our safe arrival, and although he was the local physician with political clout, there was nothing he could do to accomplish this. In the meantime, the rumor mill was churning out conflicting information about the situation in Kashmir, none of which was very encouraging. According to the radio news, some of the state's army units had captured remote areas and declared independence, and a military conflict ensued when the maharajah, with the aid of the Indian Army, retaliated. We had no other choice but to accept the situation and pray for the safety of our family, but we had a nagging concern for the safety of *Bhai Manzoor*, who was living in a village where the Hindus outnumbered Muslims by five to one. Luckily his wife and children were spending the summer with his sister-in-law in the city of Srinagar, and *Apa Anwari* and her two children were also there with her in-laws. We presumed that they would be safe among a mostly Muslim population and hoped that our family would be together soon, either in Jammu or in Daska. Confusing news and loss of contact with my parents had begun to take its toll, and *Apa Asghari* must have sensed my anxiety when she reminded me of our father's parting words about having faith. From then on, each time bad news overwhelmed me, I would find strength in *Abbajee's* words and acknowledge the present situation as one of the detours he had mentioned, and would begin to get busy with the problems at hand.

Mass migration was taking place across the border from the District of Gurdaspur, which had been arbitrarily awarded to India in spite of heavy Muslim majorities. The demarcation was done under the orders of Lord Mountbatten, and later it became known as the Radcliffe Award, after the name of the junior officer who actually drew the boundary line on the map (see map). Locally in the village, Hindus, for fear of retaliation, were fleeing to India, and the Muslims were moving inland because of rumors that India may attempt to annex the village. Governmental agencies had become dysfunctional, as many of the bureaucrats were leaving their posts, even closing the schools. To make matters worse, refugees from

India began to flood into the village looking for food and shelter, their numbers increasing with each passing day. Uncle Nazir, with the help of area businessmen, organized a way station in the local school building where *Apa Asghari,* along with our uncle's daughters, began to take care of the female arrivals. My cousin Mahmood and my younger Uncle Saleem, with the authority of the local police, began to collect bedding and other needed articles from the homes of those Hindus who had fled. We stockpiled all the collected articles in a part of the local high school and laid out cots for the incoming refugees. Some people volunteered to act as scouts, riding their bicycles, watching the border to count the number of arriving men, women, and children. My job was to gather this information and pass it on to the appropriate facilitators, who then prepared the food and other amenities for the arriving refugees. I also was responsible for cataloging and storing all the articles matching with the addresses from where the collections were made. It had been over a month since I had bid farewell to my parents in Jammu, but for the moment my volunteering was keeping me too busy from continually thinking about them and my brother.

One afternoon while we were at the Refugee Center, the new name for the school, my uncle's servant came running while loudly uttering something that I could not understand because the words became jumbled due to his excitement. He had brought the news of my mother's arrival. *Apa Asghari* and I dropped whatever we were doing and ran home to see *Bayjee,* who informed us that *Abbajee* would follow in a week after securing the house. She further informed us that the areas of the state controlled by the state's army had declared independence and that fighting was in progress in the north. She took the opportunity to accompany one of the neighbors, who had decided to go to her daughter in Sialkot. When they arrived at the border, the soldiers would not let the bus leave but allowed some of the older women and men to walk across to Pakistan, where *Tongas* were available for transportation to Sialkot, and then a bus brought her to Daska. She had seen military convoys traveling the main roads in the District of Jammu.

The excitement of seeing my mother was overshadowed by my concern for the still-missing members of my family, and there was nothing we could do except pray and wait. In the meantime, the Refugee Center proved to be a blessing in disguise to help me pass the time.

3

The center became very busy during the month of October. The number of people arriving increased tenfold as the word spread that Daska had the best reception center, attracting refugees not only from the nearest border villages, but also from miles away. Soon my uncle became concerned when some of the incoming older people began to display injuries as if they had been beaten, and I noticed that most of the young girls were tagging far behind their families. When questioned, *Apa Asghari*, who was coordinating the care of the women, informed me that the soldiers had seriously hurt these girls, and later in the evening, at dinner, Uncle Saleem related some of the stories that were making the rounds among the refugees. The Hindu nationalists, with the aid of paramilitary personnel, were forcing Muslims from their homes and then transporting them to the Pakistan border. They would arrive in the proximity of the border late in the evening, where they were held in an improvised camp. Military vehicles would surround their camp with their darkened headlights pointing to the center, and in the middle of the night, when everyone was fast asleep, the headlights would be turned on and the soldiers would grab young girls who had been targeted earlier. Whoever interfered was beaten while the abducted girls were carried away into the trucks.

The behavior of the injured girls was demonstrably at odds with the rest of the families, who were overjoyed to be in their new country. Some of the girls were as young as thirteen and did not wear *Burqas,* while their fixed gazes and uncaring attitudes betrayed their deep feelings of rejection and depression. Girls were and to some extent still are considered a burden to their families in that part of the world, and the prevailing customs required considerable dowry to marry off a daughter. It would be dishonorable for a husband to take a bride that had been damaged (raped). Rasheeda, at nineteen, was one of the raped girls who had discarded her *Burqa,* probably in response to having been disowned by her family. She had the typical fixed gaze, and her big, beautiful, brown eyes had lost their shine, as if brushed over by the paint of fear and uncertainty. *Apa Asghari,* being the same age, had befriended her and discovered that she was scheduled to be married in a few months, but the groom's family had cancelled the wedding immediately after the incident. The lines on her pale face, presently devoid of any expression, betrayed her earlier smiles anticipating her married life, before she became "damaged." Marriage was the most important event in the life of a girl, but Rasheeda's dreams were shattered by one evening of cruel and indiscriminate action on the part of another human being. The perpetrator probably did not hesitate even for a second to think of the consequences of his action that was motivated purely by hate. The plight of these girls magnified the hopelessness of my own situation, and my plans to immigrate to the United States now seemed beyond reach. Reports from Jammu and Kashmir were not encouraging, and the odds against my ever reuniting with my father and brother were mounting each day.

By early November, colleges began to open their doors, and *Apa Asghari,* with one more year to complete her college degree in teaching at the Women's College in Lahore, decided to resume her studies. Uncle Saleem volunteered to escort her to Lahore and, upon his return, informed me that he had secured my admission to Murray College in Sialkot. I did not want to leave, as my mind was filled with all sorts of negative feelings and I did not desire to face strangers. My emotions were on a roller coaster—up with good news and down with discouraging information. *Bayjee,* having been a teacher, felt that resumption of a college education would be therapeutic. There were still a few weeks before my departure, and the fast-moving events of the last few months had made rational thinking virtually impossible. In the absence of *Abbajee* and my brother, the responsibility of the family would fall on my shoulders as the eldest living son—an overwhelming responsibility for a boy of fifteen. As my dreams and plans for the future appeared to be crumbling, I could hear my father's voice repeating his mantra, "When faced with an adversity, faith in Allah and a prayer will provide what is needed." This thought led me to believe that going to college was another detour that I had to take, and with great reluctance I began the preparation for my move to the hostel of Murray College in Sialkot.

The day before my departure for Sialkot, my brother showed up without any prior notice. It was a joyous moment, and we could not contain our tears of happiness while my grandfather pulled out his prayer rug and offered thanks for his grandson's safe return. *Bhai Manzoor* was wearing an ill-fitting military uniform and looked very tired and had lost quite a bit of weight. His return removed a big burden off my shoulder with the thought that our family would be well taken care of in the event that we could not resume our lives in Jammu. I delayed my departure for a day so I could be with him and hear about his story of escape.

He had traveled many miles under an assumed Hindu name across the areas that had become India. His ordeal began when one of his Hindu patients made a "friendly" suggestion that it was time for him to disappear before something awful happened and offered a plan setting a time for the "escape." Suspecting the motives behind the offer, *Bhai Manzoor* slipped out of the village under the cover of darkness a few days earlier than the appointed time and rode out of the village disguised as a farmhand on the back of a donkey. Being the medical officer of the village, he had the use of a donkey—doctor on a donkey making house calls. He took only his personal belongings and, with his knowledge of the local Hindi dialect, passed as a poor peasant traveling to be with his sister in a distant village. When he encountered a gang of Hindus staring at him in a threatening manner, he made sure to avoid any further contacts, as he feared that next time he might not be so lucky. Many Hindu gangs would force their prospective male victims to drop their pants to ascertain their religious orientation, Muslims being circumcised. He got rid of the donkey and began to travel by buses and *Tongas* to reach Amritsar, the city he knew well from his college days there. He discovered that there was a Muslim refugee camp on the outskirts of the city that was managed by the Pakistani Army under a reciprocal agreement with India. One evening he slipped into the camp, where his medical services were direly needed, and a few weeks later, when the Indian government permitted a few trucks to cross the border, he made his escape to Lahore, Pakistan, and then by bus to Daska. It appeared that my prayers had been answered, and I hoped that the same would be true with *Abbajee.*

Two days later, I left for Sialkot. *Bhai Manzoor,* deciding not to return to Jammu District even if he could, purchased a small pharmacy in Gujranwala, fifteen miles north of Daska, and converted it into a medical practice. The government of Pakistan had begun to take the abandoned homes of those who had fled the country and allot them to the incoming refugees. In the culture of the time, many generations lived together and, as a result, the homes were built to accommodate multiple families. Our family was allotted the second story of a very large house. A side door provided access to the staircase that led to the entrance to our floor, passing by a door that provided access to the mezzanine. There was a large atrium-like opening to the roof, covered with a weight-bearing iron grate to allow daylight into the first floor. Two families occupied the first floor, and another lived in the mezzanine, all related. The building was within walking distance of *Bhai Manzoor›s* practice.

Murray College was a coed private teaching institution, the campus of which, with its wide-open, manicured lawns, volleyball courts, and cricket field, was very impressive. Three students and I shared a large room on the second floor with four beds and four desks. The volleyball and badminton courts were situated on the left of the staircase from my dormitory. I, the only one in the family with any athletic inclinations, joined the cricket team because I had played it in my high school years. Unlike the schools and colleges in the United States, sports were never a part of the school activities, and a teacher would volunteer his time to be the coach of a team made up of willing players. I enjoyed participating in these sports, as the exercise alleviated mental anguish, but when it came to studying, I could not concentrate. Uncle Saleem had given me his old bicycle that allowed me to get around the city, and once in a while, when the dorm food became unbearable, I would take a ride to the city to enjoy a sizeable portion of shish kebabs, my soul food. It was during one of these trips that I ran into Ahmed, an old acquaintance of my brother.

Ahmed informed me that he had crossed the border about a week ago and that the Jammu police personnel were "encouraging" Muslims to leave the city. All businesses owned by Muslims had been closed, and buses were bringing Muslim refugees to the border, where they could cross into Pakistan. He had seen *Abbajee* a few weeks before he boarded one of those buses. According to him, four of my father's friends were staying at our home, and the Indian Army was patrolling the Muslim areas of the city in a threatening manner. *Abbajee* had given him a letter that he had mailed to Daska a few days earlier. In order to intercept the letter, I took the next available bus to Daska, hoping to carry it personally to Gujranwala and avoid further delay by the disrupted postal service. The letter and I arrived in Daska almost at the same time, and although I wanted to know the contents, it would have to wait till I got to Gujranwala, where we all sat with anticipation as *Bayjee* opened it with her shaking hands and began to read it aloud. Always the optimist, *Abbajee* attempted to paint an encouraging picture, but the message could not hide his feeling of hopelessness, as he mentioned that the Muslim areas were under siege and that they did not know how long they could hold out. His friends were on the wanted list, and the only reason they could surmise was that they were Muslim officials in the service of the state. Although *Abbajee* had retired many years ago, he was probably on the list because one of the officials was *Bhai Manzoor›s* brother-in-law. All of them had resolved to stay in the house and fight if necessary, as he ominously declared, "We will take some of them with us." *Bayjee* struggled to suppress her emotions as she continued to read the letter. He had messages for each one of my siblings, and his message to me was to keep pursuing my dreams and have faith in Allah. We all sat in a daze as his words sank in and we realized that he was saying his farewells to the family. No matter how hard I tried to think positively, I could not shake the nagging feeling that we would not see him again. Masood was too young to understand, and *Bhai Manzoor* could only make some consoling statements. The only person not present was *Apa Asghari,* who was at her college in Lahore, so *Bayjee* decided to inform her when she came home for a weekend, which she did frequently.

The letter conveyed a sense of finality to the fact that we would never return to Jammu, and it saddened me to realize that I would never see the mountains and the river again. I would miss the Residency Road, with its big houses and large backyards; Urdu Bazaar, where the delicious aroma of shish kebabs filled the air and the sound of music emanated from the dance houses; Mundar Bazaar, bustling with people moving in and out of the fancy stores and street vendors serving my favorite finger food; the produce market, where I accompanied my father many times to buy mangos and pears; the parade ground, where the military bands held concerts each month: the Tilab Park, with its beautiful gardens and open lawns where Eid festivals were held. I would never walk on the streets and alleys where, as a child during the war years, I had raced with other boys pretending to be leading military convoys. Most of all I would miss the family picnics down by the river Tawi and my favorite cliff that rose over one hundred feet above the river bed, where I sat many hours in solitude, day dreaming.

I was shaken out of these thoughts by a reminder that it was time to leave for Sialkot. *Bayjee,* hiding her own feelings, insisted that my mental state would improve once I got busy with my studies, although the college routine presented a challenge in my state of depression.

4

It was late Sunday afternoon when, with great reluctance, I arrived at my hostel not knowing what fate had befallen my father. Jammu was only twenty-five miles away, and I could sneak across the border and find out the truth about *Abbajee.* The idea began to take hold, as I felt confident that I could dodge the military patrols, having done that during the curfews, and that I knew the city better than the outsiders who were holding it hostage. In the hope that he could provide some more details about the situation in Jammu, I began my search for Ahmed, which took over three weeks. He advised me that his information would not be accurate any longer, as conditions were changing daily, and I probably could get firsthand information from the refugees who were trickling over the border each day. When I arrived at the point of crossing, I found ten to twelve persons and three *Tongas* standing in the middle of the road that I had traveled by bus only a few months ago. There was a temporarily erected barricade approximately two hundred yards away, manned by two sentries, and a nearby tent that probably provided shelter for the other soldiers. The people were there, just as I was, hoping to see their loved ones walk across the barrier.

A few minutes passed when I saw the shimmering image of what resembled a military truck fast approaching the fence, where it stopped to discharge a few civilians. A wave of anticipation spread over those, including me, who had been waiting, and some who attempted to run towards the opening were reminded by others to stay behind the posted signs for the no-man's land. The mood became somber as only two of the persons were rewarded for their wait when they recognized an approaching family member. One person informed me that Jammu was almost cleared of its Muslim population, and if I thought of going there I would be taking my life into my own hands. Each morning I rode my bike to the border in the hope of getting some information, but most of the people crossing could not offer anything useful. Except for my mother and brother, who were concerned, the neglect of my studies did not matter much to me. Each time as I witnessed someone reuniting with his or her family, a great sense of loss would permeate my body, and I hoped that one day I would also be rewarded.

It was during the latter part of the month of December 1947 that I saw a familiar face approaching the border. Kareem, who was the cook at the home of one of our family friends, had a blanket wrapped around his torn clothes. His face had thinned and his hairs were unkempt, and he began to cry as soon as he laid his eyes on me. While sobbing, he repeated over and over, "I am sorry. I am so sorry..." He was becoming hysterical as I tried to console him, and when he recovered his composure, I heard the devastating news.

Abbajee, along with his friends, had been killed.

These few words hit me like a tsunami, and I stood still for what seemed like an eternity. Uncontrolled tears ran down my face, and sobs followed one after the other as my body shook with a burst of anger that had erupted like a volcano, followed by a realization that his last letter had foretold this day. This news was nothing more than a confirmation, and *Abbajee* had already bid us farewell. In reality, he had predicted the time and manner of his death to the month four years earlier.

In 1943, *Abbajee* had been stricken by typhoid fever, and the complications kept him bedridden for over six months. It was a difficult period for our family, and each one of us took turns in caring for him around the clock. Unlike today, there were no tests available that could diagnose with precision what ailed him. Contrary to the advice of the specialists, *Bhai Manzoor* refused to give up and sustained *Abbajee's* body functions by intravenously giving him large doses of vitamin C and glucose in the hope that his own body would speed up the recovery. He had to use very large syringes, as IVs were not available at that time. Using all the family influence, my brother had managed to get temporarily assigned to Jammu as part of the state's efforts to combat the spread of cholera. This way he could continue his treatment of our father. One Wednesday with great effort, *Abbajee* whispered to *Bhai Manzoor* that he wanted to discontinue the treatments, but in response to the family's pleas, he agreed to the postponement till Friday—an unusual request, but his wishes had to be honored. I still remember that Friday when he called all of us together and announced that his life had been extended by four years. The injections were resumed and his recovery was nothing less than a miracle.

Six months in bed had taken its toll on his muscles, and he needed assistance for sitting up and walking. He needed exercise, and for many months, each day after school, he would put his hands on my shoulders for support while we walked and I enjoyed listening to his philosophies about life and learned the teachings of Islam and his understanding of the Quran's message. *Abbajee* had told me that praying five times a day does not make a good Muslim, but good deeds do, and that the Quran directs Muslims to build a just and compassionate society by taking care of the poor and the indigents. Our discussions laid the foundations for my belief system and became the moral compass that would guide me throughout my life. Explaining the events of that Friday, he told me that he had an out-of-body experience where he saw a group of robed persons standing around his bed engaged in an animated discussion while frequently pointing to his body. Then an elderly man, having a semblance to his grandfather, looked at him and announced the extension of four years and explained to *Abbajee* that he would not like the end but not to worry, all would be well with the family.

Kareem›s nudge stopped the replay of the events of four years before. I gave him some money that he needed to travel to the village where some of his relatives lived. My head bowed in despair as I rode my bicycle in the direction of the city and wished that I could sit at the edge of my favorite cliff overseeing the river Tawi where I received my inspirations, but that lay in the opposite direction, where I could not go. One tends to remember the happier days when one suffers from emotional pain. As I pedaled slowly for almost two hours, I remembered one year when we were housebound in Srinagar because of heavy snow and *Abbajee,* using old newspapers, crafted a papier-mâché *Tonga* complete with a horse. I also recalled the many instances when he interceded on my behalf when *Bayjee,* the strict disciplinarian with high expectations, wanted to punish me for even minor infractions. When I began to question the imam's religious teachings in the mosque, he encouraged my inquisitiveness instead of scolding me like the imam attempted to do. I would miss *Abbajee*'s constantly encouraging words. By the time I reached my dormitory, I felt an overwhelming desire to be with my family.

I arrived home in Gujranwala unexpectedly late that evening, just in time for dinner, and related Kareem›s story that he and four other people, including *Abbajee* and *Bhai Manzoor's* brother-in-law, were taken from our house to a military camp in the outskirts of the city. Kareem was separated from the rest and kept in a room overseeing the compound, and each day he saw soldiers escorting *Abbajee* and his companions, one by one, to an office and then taken back. It went on for over a week, and then one day all four of them were lined up against the wall and shot. My father was reciting the Quran just before he collapsed to the ground. One morning Kareem just walked out of the camp and swam across the canal to join other people who were traveling to the border. Decades later, the assassination was confirmed by the son of one of the victims, who went to Jammu and brought back pictures of the wall with bullet holes and that of the mass grave where our loved ones were buried. In the absence of a body, there could be no funeral and no proper closure. Uncle Saleem, who was the family counselor tending to our psychological needs, stayed with us after most of the relatives had left. His attempts at lightening the pain could not comfort me because the manner in which my father died intensified my anger, which would become my constant companion for many years. *Abbajee* was the only one who shared in my dream and kept me focused, and now, with him gone, I had nobody that understood the intensity of my desire to live in the United States. At the moment my plans were overshadowed by an acute need to avenge his murder. I could not shake this feeling, and for many years would spend my waking hours playing various scenarios in my mind to exact revenge for his death.

As normalcy, whatever that was, returned to the house, *Apa Asghari* departed for college in Lahore. After that, *Bayjee* spoke little, and her demeanor changed from the take-charge professional that she was, to a sad person who had lost her independence. Laughter had taken a holiday from our home. *Bhai Manzoor,* in order to establish his practice, traveled throughout the countryside making house calls, with his mode of transportation upgraded from a donkey to a bicycle. He started early in the morning and returned late in the evening. While the established doctors with rich patients did very well, a new man on the scene had to survive by attending to those who could not always afford to pay cash, and many times he would bring home a chicken or vegetables as payment in exchange for his services. I felt uncomfortable with the thought that he had to carry the burden of taking care of his brothers and sister while his own family was hundreds of miles away in enemy territory. In the absence of usual family interaction, it seemed that a heavy fog of sadness surrounded our new home, and I felt that my place was beside my brother, assisting him in his burden of caring for the family and a need to be among familiar faces during the time of our loss. Against *Bayjee's* wishes to stay in Sialkot, I completed my transfer to Islamia College in Gujranwala.

Unlike the campus at Murray College, with its wide-open spaces, Islamia College in Gujranwala was a cluster of classrooms in a large brick building. It did nothing to overcome my depression and anger. At another time and under different circumstances, I probably would have enjoyed my life at Murray College, but the traumatic events of the past months had rendered the situation anything but normal. It seemed that the future had moved far away, and the flame of my dream was now only a flicker. *Abbajee›s* death had brought forth an overwhelming emotion of rage, and a strong desire to avenge his death consumed all my waking hours. At the same time, I felt duty bound to assist *Bhai Manzoor* in taking care of the family. This was the state of my mind when I began my life at our new home.

There were free public hospitals that offered inpatient and outpatient services, but they were overcrowded and understaffed. The peasants in the villages who did not receive adequate attention at the public hospitals and rich farmers and businessmen needing personal attention preferred private doctors. At that time medicines did not come in the form of pills, and a prescription had to be compounded using elixirs of various roots and plants. Unlike the present-day doctor's office with nurses and administrators, the only help that was affordable had been a person who could compound a prescription. In order to save money, *Bhai Manzoor* also performed the duties of a *compounder*, but I began to assist him in mixing the medicines after my classes, as I was not motivated to pursue studies. I was attending college only to please *Bayjee*. In order to be alone to think, each day after dinner, rain or shine, I began to take long walks along the Grand Trunk Road, the main north-south highway. That time was spent to figure out ways to punish those who were responsible for *Abbajee's* death, and many times I considered joining the volunteer resistance groups in the Indian-occupied areas of Kashmir. That idea had to be abandoned when it became known that I had to provide my own weapon. Joining the Pakistani Army became my next best hope.

In the meantime, I was taking on more of the duties at the clinic. One day at midnight we heard an insistent knock, and the visitor at the door introduced himself as one of the assistants of the local bus transportation company owner, known as the *Wrestler*. It seemed that he needed a doctor who could give his boss a series of injections precisely four hours apart because his regular doctor was indisposed due to an accident. The search brought the stranger to our door, and *Bhai Manzoor* was more than willing to oblige. He stayed at the home of the *Wrestler* during the nights and gradually gained his new patient's trust. Not having seen any improvement, the patient had asked for a second opinion and agreed to a new treatment suggested by *Bhai Manzoor*. The practice turned a corner when the *Wrestler's* condition improved rapidly and the word spread throughout the wealthy circles of the city. It became apparent that healing people was in the family genes, because besides mixing drugs, I had begun to give intravenous injections and once pulled a tooth and also sutured a serious wound. Medical licensing was lax and there were many quacks practicing the art. I, at least, had qualified supervision.

5

It was early in the year of 1948 when a United Nations mandated ceasefire between India and Pakistan had taken hold in Kashmir. It was followed by a resolution by the World Body requiring all fighting forces to withdraw and to hold a plebiscite under the auspices of the United Nations to determine the future affiliation of the state. It also required all the refugees to be repatriated before the referendum could be held. At that time, these developments kindled a little hope that we might return to our homes, but it was short lived, as India, knowing that the vote would be against it, was successful in maneuvering to delay the event while adding more troops instead of removing them. We began to adapt to our life in the new home as the financial situation improved, and I even detected a faint smile on *Bayjee's* face. *Apa Asghari* was taking her final examinations, but one day after her exams ended, we received a telegram from her college informing us that she had fallen ill and would need help with her travel home. I took a bus to Lahore and was shocked to see her thinned, pale face. It appeared that she had been hiding her condition in order to complete her exams. Since her childhood she had suffered from a type of recurring malaria that attacked every fifteen days, and she had thought that her illness was related to her condition and did not let it interfere with her studies. The forty-mile train journey from Lahore to Gujranwala was very exhausting for her, and immediately after arrival, she became bedridden.

A few weeks passed and when her fever did not break, the blood tests revealed that she not only had malaria but also suffered from typhoid. Like clockwork, every third day malaria attacks would begin with shivers so severe that her teeth would chatter, typical of the disease. In order to control her shakes, we had to cover her with many layers of blankets, and once the fever had risen to 105 degrees, the trembling would stop. The blankets had to be replaced with ice-cold sheets to prevent the fever from rising higher. Uncle Nazir and my grandparents came from Daska to stay and help. Everybody heaved a sigh of relief when, after about a month, her fever suddenly broke, but the ordeal had left her so weak that she needed assistance to sit up or turn on her side. Our happiness lasted only for one evening, because the following morning *Bayjee* found her in distress and gasping for breath. By the time Uncle Nazir and *Bhaijee Manzoor* reached the bed, her vital signs were deteriorating rapidly, and she was unable to speak. Each time they tried to inject saline intravenously, it failed because her blood had begun to coagulate. By 10 a.m., my dearest sister gasped as life escaped her body, and while her struggle ended, ours began. It was surmised that because of her weakened state, she probably inhaled some of the vomit, causing pneumonia. My brother kept repeating, "I am sorry. I did not know what else to do. I am sorry."

All my relatives arrived in preparation for the funeral, as in the Muslim culture the dead have to be buried within twenty-four hours. It was a very sad day for all our family, and the verses of Quran, professionally recited as a tradition, were supposed to calm the bereaved, but our loss was too overwhelming. After burial, the silence in our house was deafening, all of us wiping our silent tears that kept flowing like nonstop fountains. I could not understand why a beautiful, intelligent, young woman like *Apa Asghari,* with a great future, had to die. Most of my youth had been spent playing with her, and I would miss our duets with her improvised lyrics and her contagious laugh. She was closest to my age and was the big sister I could depend on taking my side. After *Abbajee's* death less than half a year earlier, her loss was too much to bear, and small things would trigger a deep emotion of anger, leading to crying fits when I would take refuge in the corner of a room or on the rooftop, isolating myself from the rest of the family. Her death intensified the sense of all the losses my family and I had suffered during the recent past.

The grieving process lasts for forty days, at which time the survivors are supposed to resume their normal lives, whatever that was. I could not understand how *Bayjee* was coping with the losses, as the children are supposed to survive the parents. Her face took on an expression of total resignation, and her eyes without the usual shine betrayed her apparently calm demeanor. *Bhai Manzoor,* quieter than his usual self, got busy with his practice, and once again sadness became my companion. I was in a state of mind that today would be called deep depression, and my long walks became more intense as I struggled with scary and conflicting thoughts. One day I would plan to end my life, and another day I would contemplate joining the resistance forces in Kashmir.

One evening, when I made my left turn on the Grand Trunk Road, an elderly man taking long strides caught up and began to walk with me. I was in no mood to speak with a stranger, but it seemed that he was intent on engaging me in a conversation.

"My name is Akbar Khan. What is yours?" he said.

"Maqbool," I answered curtly with the hope that he would get the message that I wanted to be left alone.

"I have seen you a few times going by here," he continued. "Do you walk here every day?"

"Yes," I retorted to discourage further interaction.

"I do not know if you remember me. I am a patient of Dr. Manzoor. Are you his brother?"

"Yes."

"It seems that something is bothering you," he said.

"Is it that visible?" I asked.

"I am the headmaster of the Iqbal High School, and observing students is part of my job."

I began to pick up my pace in order to get away from him, but he kept up with some effort. Finally, he said, "I believe you need to talk, and when you decide to do so, I am available. You could stop by anytime after school hours and we could have tea." Then he began to fall back. I was relieved to see him turn around and walk in the opposite direction.

I began to reflect on this meeting during the rest of my walk. At home, all of us were internalizing our grief, and as a family we never openly discussed the loss of our home, *Abbajee*, and now *Apa Asghari*. Friends and relatives assisted the family through a prescribed collective grieving ritual, but it did not cure what was hurting me. I was unable to concentrate on my studies while feeling sorry for myself, had no plans for the future, and was prepared to give up my dream of immigrating to the United States. I could not hear *Abbajee's* encouraging words that could do wonders in restoring my self-confidence. By the time I returned from the walk, I had decided to accept Mr. Khan's invitation.

Four days elapsed before I could muster enough courage to approach Mr. Khan's house. He escorted me to his living area and ordered his housekeeper to prepare tea for two. I was expecting that he would persuade me to pay attention to my studies or I would amount to nothing, as *Bayjee* had been reminding me very frequently. It appeared that he was aware of my predicament, because we sat there in silence for few minutes that seemed like an eternity. Finally he broke the silence.

"How are you feeling today?"

"The usual. I miss *Abbajee* and *Apa Asghari*, our home in Jammu, and my school friends," I said, surprising myself.

"I can understand. I lost my brother and all our belongings as we fled from New Delhi. Those were hard times."

"Was there a burial for your brother?"

"Yes," he answered.

"*Abbajee* had no funeral, and there was no burial." I was fighting to hold my tears.

"It must be very hard. But we have choices. We can wallow in the past, believing that our plans or dreams might have come true if only the unexpected events had not occurred. But that would be a conjecture and not the reality. The prudent course would be to accept the fact that we cannot change the past and that the present always offers opportunities to refocus on our dreams. Life offers detours as tests of our resolve, and as long as we keep our eyes on our dreams, the detours can be considered as learning tools." It sounded like what *Abbajee* would have said.

Mr. Khan gave me his copy of *How Not to Worry*, by Dale Carnegie, before my departure. I made use of his open invitation and visited him often, as his words were always soothing and encouraging without criticism. He understood my lack of interest in my studies. *Bayjee*, on the other hand, would constantly criticize me for not pursuing my studies seriously, as she had high expectations and constantly reminded me that without studies I would amount to nothing. The loaned book became my survival guide, and I read it many times. Each time my anger receded a notch. After some time Mr. Khan's words began to sink in and life began to take on a new meaning, although college work still eluded me. Instead, work at the clinic felt more satisfying, and over time I began to fill the role of a practitioner's assistance by gaining more skills. I considered this to be a temporary situation and expected to resume my studies as soon as we returned to Jammu in accordance with the U.N. mandate.

6

By the spring of 1949, it was becoming clear that our return home would not happen any time soon, and the news pointed to the fact that India had agreed to the U.N. resolutions in order to secure the end of the hostilities and had no desire to follow through with the plebiscite, knowing full well that the result would not be what it desired. We had not heard from *Apa Anwari* and *Bhabijee, Bhai Manzoor's* wife, since our departure from Jammu, and all attempts to contact them bore no fruit. I could notice that *Bhaijee* was getting impatient for the company of his family. Feeling confident that his practice could sustain us in his few weeks' absence, he began to make plans for his travel to Srinagar. He had found that the camp at Amritsar was scheduled to be closed in the fall. So by late summer, he had completed his plans to travel to the camp after having trained me in the care of his patients. I made a list of their needs and, in order to gain their trust, began to take care of them under his supervision. He arranged for one of his doctor friends to keep an eye on the practice, and the arrangement worked out well, as Dr. Ashraf was very gracious to allow me to fill the prescriptions of the new patients, thereby sharing the revenue.

It was expected that *Bhai Manzoor* would be gone for no more than ten days and return with his and *Apa Anwari's* family.

His trip was timed to coincide with the departure of the seasonal residents from their summer retreats in Srinagar, so a family traveling with children would not draw suspicions. The plan was risky for him and worrisome for me, as I did not feel confident to take on the responsibility of the family in the event he failed to return. With the assistance of his contacts, *Bhai Manzoor* hitched a ride on one of the military vehicles traveling to the camp, impersonating an army soldier, and once there, under the cover of the night, he left the camp and took a train to New Delhi, where he boarded a flight to Srinagar. By bribing the reservation clerk, he made the arrangements so the families could travel with him on his return trip.

Two days after that, he, along with *Bhabijee, Apa Anwari,* and four children, boarded the flight to New Delhi. They had adopted Hindu names, and the children were taught to address the elders by Hindi titles, which are different than the ones common among the Muslims. The flight was short and passed quickly without any incident, but during the train trip from New Delhi to Amritsar, there were close calls when the children became tired and tended to forget the instructions. They had to be constantly reminded to use proper words. In Amritsar, they hired a *Tonga* to get to a street near the camp, and when they arrived in the vicinity of the camp in the evening as planned, the children, aged one to three years, were restless and crying after a whole day of travel. That made it necessary to cut the trip short and get the children into the camp instead of walking back half a mile from the destined street. When the *Tonga* driver made a remark questioning the motive for stopping close to the refugee camp, *Bhai Manzoor* became uncomfortable and mentioned the incident to the officer at the camp.

Their departure to Pakistan was scheduled for the following evening after a day's rest, but in the early morning the camp received a surprise visit by an Indian Army officer accompanied by two soldiers for an unscheduled census taking. It was suspected that the *Tonga* driver might have shared his suspicions with the local officials. The major in charge of the camp, while keeping the visitors waiting, quickly managed to dispatch a truck carrying *Bhai Manzoor* and the families to Pakistan. The soldier driving the vehicle knew only that he was transporting Captain Qurashi and the cargo of boxes to Pakistan as the camp was being dismantled. Hidden behind the boxes were the other members of my family. The Indian officer probably did not believe the explanation given by the major about the sudden departure of a vehicle, because the truck was stopped on the Indian side of the border for a search. After ordering the driver to be ready for a quick departure, *Bhai Manzoor* politely told the Indian officer that the agreement between the two governments had allowed free passage without inspection and that the truck would not be submitted for search. There were tense moments while the Indian officer contemplated his decision and *Apa Anwari* and *Bhabijee* held their hands on the mouths of the children to keep them quiet. Everyone was praying and hoping that the officer would not call the bluff. After a wait that appeared to last forever, the officer relented and waved them on after signing some papers.

When a *Tonga* occupied with very familiar faces pulled up in front of the clinic, I heaved a sigh of relief and thanked Allah for the return of the remaining members of our family. The other reason for my happiness was that I could hand over the responsibility of the clinic to *Bhai Manzoor*. While he was away, it was very stressful for me at the age of seventeen to pretend to be a doctor; Allah probably was bored by my numerous prayers as I constantly worried about the prescriptions that I compounded. No wonder, then, that I was overjoyed to see everybody and felt as if a very heavy load had suddenly disappeared from my shoulders. But the joy of the reunion did not heal the deep wounds left by the loss of my father and sister that hung there like a cloud.

We closed the clinic for the day. Our family, what remained of it, was finally together again, and tears of joy were flowing freely all around. As *Bhai Manzoor* related his story of the border encounter, a deafening silence fell when the seriousness of the fact that they almost did not make it hit home. *Bhai Manzoor* sat in a corner by himself, reflecting on his recent adventure, knowing full well that a different decision by the Indian Army officer could have had a very disastrous outcome. He was facing the typical letdown after an emotional high.

I had always been very close to *Bhai Manzoor* and his family, and although there was a difference of fourteen years between us brothers, we had a special bond. As was customary, I named his first-born son, Shaukat, and, in accordance with the Islamic tradition, he heard my voice whispering the *Azan,* the prayer call, in his ear right after his birth. I had accompanied the family on their vacations and spent my eighth grade living with them. As a child, I used to walk four to five miles to the train station when my brother or sisters came home from college because I missed them while they were away. When he was doing his internship at the local hospital, I frequently visited him after school and accompanied him on his rounds of the patients, after which he would help me with my homework. He taught me how to multiply fractions and opened up the wonders of mathematics for me.

With nieces and nephews around, life began to offer a different perspective, and in the face of new challenges my anger and desire for revenge began to recede. Although the college studies still eluded me, the institution itself offered an environment where I could discover some of my hidden traits. While growing up in Jammu, I could recite and mimic, word for word, the speeches of the movie characters such as Alexander the Great, Emperor Akbar, and others. When I was in second grade, the headmaster of the school assisted me in overcoming my stage fright, and since then I had always felt at home speaking to an audience. One of the professors in charge of the intercollegiate debating team asked me to fill in for one of the debaters who had fallen ill, offering me a perfect opportunity to practice the art of public speaking. I had to research the war in Korea and challenge the opponents of the conflict, and that led to my interest in world affairs. I also began to participate in the annual college variety show, where I became one of the featured singers, and when the first elections were held for the Provincial Assembly of Punjab, I gladly accepted an invitation to deliver the message of the Muslim League candidate, riding a *Tonga* equipped with loudspeakers. This experience would come in handy in later years when I would be called upon to moderate a debate between the Republican and Democratic candidates for the Congress of the United States. The grade level I received at the completion of a two-year college did not fare well in getting admission to the only engineering institute in the country, where the curriculum was heavily weighted to train civil engineers who would be hired by the Public Works Department to manage construction projects. Mechanical engineering was my passion, and I had no interest in building roads or dams. The textile industry was the only large-scale private enterprise that was hiring anything that came close to a mechanical engineer. A nonengineering degree would have provided me an entry into a public administration position, but I had too much of an enterprising spirit to succumb to a confining career in the employment of the government, notwithstanding the prestige that it provided in that part of the world. The other reason was that the flame of my dream had begun to flicker again.

Apa Anwari opted to move to Lahore to complete further medical courses that would allow her to join the public health service, and *Bhai Manzoor*, in order to expand his practice, acquired a building across from his office and, after the renovation had been completed, he installed an x-ray machine. This was very timely in the face of rapidly spreading tuberculosis. The chest x-rays were in demand, and in order to develop the film, we converted a closet over the bathroom in the house into a dark room. I quickly learned to operate the machine and spent many hours in that room developing films, providing me with some isolation for self-analysis and planning. It became very hectic when other doctors began to refer their patients to us instead of sending them to the local public hospital, where there was a long wait. During this time I contacted the U.S. consulate in Lahore to inform them about my whereabouts and refer them to my quota number. After many inquiries, I was informed that there could be a wait of five to seven years before my quota number would arrive, and invoking my refugee status to speed up the process was to no avail. The U.S. consulate informed me that Kashmiris were not classified as refugees because of the pending U.N. resolutions. *Abbajee* used to remind us, "You may desire to get to your goals in a hurry, but the timing belongs with Allah, and the delays may have reasons. You will have smooth sailing if you can merge your timing with God's." To me it meant that I should have faith and go with the flow. What else could I do? This practice would stand me in good stead in my life, and it was not long after that I had to call upon God's favors again.

It happened when *Bhai Manzoor* began to experience a lack of energy and one morning was not able to get out of the bed. He asked me to mind the clinic for the day. When his condition did not improve, Dr. Ashraf, our family friend, paid a house visit and determined that my brother had contracted jaundice, as his skin had turned yellow and the urine had dark brown coloration. Once again I was called upon to impersonate my brother as a doctor, but this time for many months. Lucky for us, the pharmaceutical company provided him with the medications he needed, and Uncle Nazir from Daska arrived with his microscope and began to check the red blood count. As months passed, the patients at the clinic began to address me as "doctor," and some even complimented me for doing a better job than my brother of diagnosing their conditions. I was fortunate enough not to get a patient with some real serious problem and was feeling at home in the environment of a clinic. My problem patient was at home, as doctors make difficult patients. There was nothing to do but pray and hope that his body cleansed itself while the medicines did their job.

The mood at home was gloomy and not much was spoken among the members of the family. *Bayjee* spent her time on the prayer rug while *Bhabijee* was taking care of my nephew and niece. I could not pay too much attention to Masood, as most of my time was taken up by the clinic and I had to present a face of confidence, being the acting head of the household. But it was very hard, as I was only eighteen years old, bearing this heavy responsibility. One day when I came home for lunch, I found my patient in a very depressed mood.

"What is wrong?" I asked.

He showed me his fingernails and said, "See the nails? They are turning blue. That is a precursor of death." He continued, "I think you should ask Dr. Ashraf to take me to the Mayo Hospital in Lahore."

Dr. Ameer-ud-Din was his professor at the medical college that he attended. I ran to Dr. Ashraf's office and related what had transpired, and he promised to be at our house within a half hour. While I got *Bhai Manzoor* ready for the forty-mile trip to Lahore, he began to give me instructions in case he did not make it. He said, "In the event I do not make it, please take care of the family. Make sure Shaukat (my nephew) completes his education. You should be able to sell the x-ray machine for good money that will help you keep going for a while and..."

I had stopped listening to him, as tears were running down my cheeks. I assured him that he was not dying and that he should not even talk like that because he was scaring everybody. Before he could continue his very disturbing rambling, Dr. Ashraf arrived with his car, and while I occupied the seat on the passenger side, my brother lay down on the back seat. The silence afforded me the time to ponder the situation, over which I had no control. In such predicaments I always tried to remember *Abbajee's* advice: "Have faith and let Allah carry the burden." Following every prayer, I always felt a surge of confidence and a strong feeling that all would be well. My thoughts were interrupted when the car stopped in front of the doctor's office. Dr. Ameer-ud-Din ordered a quick blood count, the only test available at the time. The other diagnostic tools consisted of observing the color of the tongue and the eyes, blood pressure, the use of a stethoscope to listen to lungs and heart, and pressing around the abdomen for telltale signs of distress. The doctor ordered *Bhaijee Manzoor* to stick his tongue out and then pull it back in, and once the exercise was completed, Dr. Din, while looking at me, addressed my brother with a raised voice: "Don't scare your family. Come back when you cannot get your tongue back in."

To lighten the mood while driving back, I commented, "Now I know why the patients at the clinic are saying that I am a better diagnostician than you are."

With a broad smile he replied, "You are not going to push me out that easy. Remember, I have a piece of paper to prove that I am the doctor."

I said, "Then behave like one."

He alarmed us with his statements of imminent death a few more times during the following months, and each time I asked him to do the tongue exercise, and then I would scold him for not being sensitive to the family's feelings. Circumstances had forced this role upon me, and although I attempted to accept the responsibility with confidence, there were times I wished to be just a teenager. But in the moments of solitude, my façade would break down and tears would flow freely. This role was taxing and I had difficulty sleeping at night. Many times *Bayjee* had to wake me up in the middle of the night because I was mumbling in my sleep, and I spent many hours on the rooftop looking at the star-filled nights in the hope that Allah was listening to my prayers. At the end of the third month, my prayers were answered when *Bhaijee's* blood count showed improvement and the yellow color began its retreat. It would be another two months before he could step into his clinic again. I heaved a sigh of relief to see him sitting in his chair. I could become a teenager again.

Looking at the list of patients whom he treated during a period of two weeks prior to his sickness, we came upon a possible event that could have caused the jaundice. A man was brought into the clinic complaining of sudden pain in his leg as if he had been shot. When asked what he was doing when he first experienced the pain, he replied that he was walking by an ironsmith's shop. As a usual practice, ironsmiths hammered their hot irons into shapes in the open by the side of a street. A mark on the patient's leg raised the suspicion that a sliver of steel might have entered his leg, and in order to confirm this, *Bhaijee,* by the use of an x-ray screen, observed that a sliver of metal was traveling in the vein of the leg. Fearing that it could lodge into the man's heart, he proceeded to remove the splinter, and it took three incisions and over half an hour working from behind the x-ray screen to successfully remove the piece of metal. Dr. Ashraf and *Bhai Manzoor*, after consulting others, arrived at the conclusion that the cause for his sickness had been exposure to radiation. After that we became more conscious of the safety requirements around the x-ray machine.

Slowly life returned to normal, and suddenly I was without the stress that came with playing the role of a doctor at the clinic and managing a paranoiac patient at home. I managed to reasonably maintain the income level and enjoyed the responsibility and the experience even though there were difficult moments. During the last six months I had had little time to think about myself, and now, in the absence of stress, the feeling of emptiness returned, and my yearning for America intensified. Home and clinic began to appear inhospitable, and although the family was very appreciative, I could not overcome my restlessness. In the absence of any alternative, I got busy at the clinic and resumed my long, therapeutic walks.

I had just returned from picking up the usual shipment of x-ray films from the train station when I observed *Bhai Manzoor* and Dr. Ashraf in an intense discussion. When they waved me to join them, I discovered that they were studying the surgical procedure to correct a hernia. Anatomy and other medical books lay open on the desk, and before I could ask what the meeting was about, *Bhai Manzoor* said, "Abdul Ghani, the farmer, has been suffering from a hernia for some time now, but the condition has to be corrected and he does not want to go to Lahore. It is his desire that it be done here by us."

I had assisted him before when he performed small surgeries, but till that day, the most difficult operation he had done was removing stones from the bladder. I asked, "What facilities are you going to use for this procedure?"

He had already begun to prepare the upstairs room for this purpose, but what startled me was when they informed me that I was selected to be the anesthesiologist. I had dispensed chloroform, the anesthesia of choice at the time, for very short periods of time in the past. This operation would take a longer time, and I was given a quick training in determining the relationship between the blood pressure, heartbeat, and the chloroform-dispensing rate.

Mr. Ghani arrived early in the morning with a big smile on his face, demonstrating his full confidence in our capabilities. Trust is the glue that binds the societies in the Asian countries, and it exists naturally among the family members and extends to clans and tribes. Once a stranger has earned it, he or she is treated just as a member of the clan, and *Bhai Manzoor* had gained Mr. Ghani's trust. We had been accepted in his family, and nothing could convince him to have his surgery done by anybody other than Dr. Qurashi. So the patient was directed to lie down on the "operating table" and, after offering a prayer, the doctors gave me the signal to begin the anesthesia. I placed the chloroform mask on the patient's nose and mouth and asked him to count backward from ninety-nine. As he began the count, I poured a predetermined amount of the chemical into the mask and heard Ghani's voice counting, "Ninety-five, ninety-four, ninety-three, ninety-two, ninety-one…ninety…eighty-nine." When he stopped the count, I called his name aloud with no answer. Dr. Ashraf checked his eyes and asked me to check the blood pressure and the pulse, and after I announced the readings, *Bhai Manzoor* made his incision. The rip was extensive and required temporarily removing the testicles from their sacks. I continue to call out the numbers after each check of the vital signs throughout the procedure. As a foresight, *Bhaijee* had marked the pertinent pages in the anatomy book, which came handy when the doctors discovered that the muscles attached to the testicles somehow got twisted during the removal and I had to open the pertinent pages for the doctors to see in a picture how it was supposed to be. Everyone breathed a sigh of relief after the final sutures had been tied and the patient's family members were instructed how to attend to his needs. Dr. Ashraf and *Bhai Manzoor,* alternately, stayed at the clinic for the first few nights after the surgery, and the patient's brother remained at the clinic till he was ready to go home. He began to walk after a week and, on the tenth day, felt strong enough to go home. The operation was a success. Just to make sure that the job was done properly, it was decided to get Mr. Ghani checked by a surgeon in Lahore, where the patient was given a clean bill of health. For many years after that, baskets of fruits and vegetables would arrive for us like clockwork.

I had been fully immersed in the events of the last few months, but now the feeling of restlessness had returned again. I had the urge to move on, but the big question was where.

7

Pakistan became the recipient of aid from the United States under the Southeast Asia Treaty Organization (SEATO) to build its armed forces at the height of the cold war, and the air force began to recruit for its cadet program, which included advanced training in the United States after graduation from the Pakistan Air Force Academy. I traveled to an Air Force recruiting office in Lahore, where I was informed that I was qualified to apply. After successfully completing the first two interviews and the aptitude test, I was required to attend a four-day leadership camp, where I joined up with nineteen other candidates. We were ushered into an auditorium, where a voice told us to take seats, and as soon as everybody settled down, one of the uniformed men standing on the platform stepped forward and announced, "I am Captain Asif Ali Khan, in charge of this field test. These officers will observe your performance during the next few days and evaluate your physical, mental, and leadership abilities."

After each one of us introduced ourselves, the captain initiated a discussion about the political situation in the world at large. The topics ranged from the Korean War to communism and capitalism.

It became clear that the moderator was keenly observing the political leaning of the candidates, and I found that I felt at home in such a forum. The following day we were divided into four groups, and the members of each company received written copies of their objective. Our assignment was to move four crates of varying sizes across a terrain resembling that of a thick jungle presenting many obstacles that included, among others, a fast-flowing stream without a bridge, a field of poisonous plants, a thicket of tall trees, and a high wall with sharp broken glass pieces embedded on the top. An observer was lurking in the shadows at all times. I was a skinny person and shy in close encounters with strangers, the probable reason that the other four candidates ignored me. I quietly observed as each of them offered his plan and began discussions without waiting for my ideas. The debate became heated as each one wanted to impose his solution on the others. When they got tired of their arguments, I said that we were wasting time and offered a plan of action that included some elements of each of their ideas, and from that time on everyone looked to me for answers. My newfound strength proliferated a strong feeling of self-confidence. After successfully completing our project, we were required to critique our performance while the observer watched.

At the end of the fourth day, we were informed that the results of the tests would be mailed out after two weeks and those who were successful would receive instructions for the next phase in the selection process. The waiting was agonizing. There were moments when I could see myself soaring between the clouds, and other times it was an effort to escape the claws of deep anxiety. I had to constantly remind myself of Dale Carnegie's message that the future was beyond our control and, therefore, worrying about it resulted in a stressful life. I could understand *Bayjee's* motives in her attempts to persuade me to give up my idea of joining the air force because she could not face the loss of one more member of the family. Her fears were further reinforced by a recent crash of a cadet on a training flight. The much-awaited letter arrived three weeks after I had returned. I was hesitant to open it because it could carry the unpleasant news of my failing the test at the camp. Instead I was directed to report for a medical examination at the

Pakistan Air Force base in Lahore. *Bhai Manzoor*, having served as medical recruiting officer during World War II, found nothing of concern after he completed my physical examination.

I reported to the medical building, where I met some of the others who had successfully completed the camp. We all stood in a line as one of the doctors examined our ears, eyes, and nose, and my heart sank when I, along with three others, was ordered to step forward. The doctor informed us that we had a buildup of wax in our ears, and we were to report back in two days after getting the ears cleaned. When the examination resumed, the most embarrassing occasion was when we were ordered to disrobe and bend down for the rectal examination. Just before inserting his finger, the doctor questioned one of the examinees about whether he smoked, and the man asked, "Why? Is smoke coming out of there?"

We all burst out laughing, lightening the atmosphere, although the doctor was not amused, probably lacking any sense of humor. After the examination I returned home to wait again for my final notification. When I left the facility, I was not sure about my chances because one of the physicians repeatedly listened to my heart with his stethoscope and appeared to show some concern. There were also the comments about my being underweight, as I weighed only 116 pounds at the age of nineteen. My fears were confirmed when I received a letter from the PAF that informed me that although I had scored high in all the tests, I had failed to satisfy the medical requirements necessary to maintain the safety standards. *Bhai Manzoor* called the doctor and found that I suffered from a very slight condition of arrhythmia. I was devastated, not because of failing the test, but because my path to independence was blocked once more, and clouds of despondency had once again engulfed my hopes and dreams. As in the past, Dale Carnegie's *How Not to Worry* offered some solace and means to lift my spirits. Once more, long walks provided the opportunity for self-analysis, and after a few weeks I began to look at the air force experience in a positive light. The process had given me a great insight into my leadership qualities.

Longing to gain my independence, I went to Lahore, where Uncle Saleem was a student at the medical college and allowed me to sneak into his room at the college dormitory to spend the night. I never understood why he was studying medicine, because what he really desired was to be a screenwriter and a director, and he had written very interesting dramas. We always enjoyed each other's company, and while we both had the talent to sing, he knew how to play a harmonium, a wind instrument. One evening we ended up singing a few songs that provided some entertainment to the other students, and after that, nobody complained about my presence at the dormitory. I had been searching the local newspaper for some kind of job, although I was at a loss about the kind of work that would suit me.

One morning I saw an announcement about an open audition for future singers for Radio Pakistan, which broadcast live performances by the artist, unlike radios in the United States, where discs of prerecorded popular music were played. Coaxing by Uncle Saleem and his friends led me to the offices of the radio station, where, after filling out an application, I was led to the audition room, rectangular in shape, with padded walls for soundproofing. Five musicians with various instruments sat on the floor of a stage that occupied a quarter of the room, and a microphone stood in the middle of the room. There were other candidates in the audition room, allowing me the opportunity to learn the process by watching those who were ahead of me. A lunch break was announced after the fourth singer had finished his performance, and I was second in line when we returned. Although I was comfortable with rendering a song of my favorite singer of the time, I was extremely nervous about doing so in the company of an ensemble of musicians. While waiting for my turn, I was singing my selection repeatedly in my head and was somewhat encouraged by the demeanor of the audition director, who wore a broad smile when he called my name.

"Have you ever performed accompanied by an orchestra?" he asked.

"No."

He explained that I would sing one line of the song unaccompanied by the musicians to allow them to know my key. I had no idea what he was talking about and did not know that I had a key, but I followed his instructions. When the master musician heard my voice, he told the director that I did not have to sing, and as I was ready to leave, I heard the director saying, "We are looking for a new voice, and he thinks you possess it and that training would take care of the rest. He does not need to hear you perform." In order to experience the accompaniment of an orchestra, I asked whether I could sing anyway, and when I ended my performance, everybody clapped. The director handed me a copy of a contract and told me to bring it back by the following Monday and that the training would start in two weeks.

As I stepped out of the radio station building, I was already feeling like a celebrity. At that time, a singer became famous not only by performing for the radio, but also by providing the singing voice for movie actors who did the lip-synching on the screens, and I could easily see myself in that role. My head was still in the clouds when I shared my excitement with my uncle by relating what took place at the studios. The following day, my dream of a movie career came to a sudden end when I saw Uncle Saleem*'s* discouraged look. He had read the contract and explained its contents. I would have to train, at my own expense, for a period of eight weeks, made necessary because there was no music language and each composition had to be memorized by rehearsing it repeatedly. There was no guarantee that after that I would have a job, as the contract stipulated that after the training, my performance would be broadcast twice a week for a period of six weeks, and each time I would be paid a paltry sum of 50 rupees. Following that, if and only if the public gave positive feedback, the contract would take effect, and it would be for three years. *Bayjee* opposed it vehemently, because she informed me that it was beneath the standards of a descendant of maharajas and religious scholars to sing in public; the performing artists had not gained celebrity status among the public at large at that time. Her strong opposition preempted my plan to request a loan in order to begin my singing career, because I felt strongly that the public would have loved my singing; the neighborhood did. This opportunity could have been a ticket to my independence, but I did not want to burden *Bayjee's* already heavy heart. She had suffered enough, and this would have added to her already defeatist attitude. My goal was the United States of America, where a Pakistani singing artist would have difficulty earning a living, and in the event that my quota number for the United States came up, it would have been difficult to walk away from a contract. I did not return to the radio station.

With no other alternative, once again I resumed my duties at the clinic and wondered what Allah had in store for me. That answer presented itself a month later when one of the patients, who used to be an auto mechanic in Jammu, made an appealing proposal to *Bhai Manzoor*. The government had begun to dispose of the old cars that were left behind by the people who had fled to India. He led us to a storage yard where old cars were crammed together like sardines. In this confusion of steel shapes, he pointed to a 1931 soft-top Ford, the canvas of which was in shreds, exposing here and there parts of the foldable steel structure that had made the car a convertible. Wires were hanging out of the holes where once the headlights had been, and the radiator had a few dents. The seat covers had met the same fate as the canvas roof, and the springs were poking their heads through the decayed covering as if to take a peek at the world around. The price was 50 rupees and he estimated that it would cost another 600 rupees, including labor, parts, and 50 rupees as payment to an assistant. I volunteered to assist, as mechanical stuff came natural to me, and the money provided the added motivation.

We fixed the tires, towed the car to a rented garage, and cleaned it from end to end while Hameed, the mechanic, explained how the engine, transmission, the drive shaft, differential, wheel hubs, and other components worked. At a glance, the engine looked like an iron block, but a closer look brought into focus other attachments, such as spark plugs, distributor, carburetor, exhaust pipes, etc. I learned the functions of the flywheel and how the differential worked. When compared to the engine compartments of modern cars, the engine of this Ford was lost under the hood. We took apart each and every part of the drive train from the engine to the rear axles. I learned the names and the function of each part while reassembling them after a thorough cleaning. Unlike the specialized tools required to service an automobile of the present day, all we needed to rebuild the Ford was a set of wrenches, a pair of pliers, and a screwdriver. Instead of the high-tension cables connecting the distributor to the spark plugs, this car had thick copper strips doing the same job. After three weeks of work that I enjoyed thoroughly, the drive train was fully assembled, although the seats, the roof, the headlights, and some other nonessential items still had to be found and installed. The battery was in poor operating condition and could hold charge for only a short period of time, and a replacement was not readily available. The battery had been charged at a shop, and the technician had warned us about its condition. The generator could continue running the engine once it had been started, so I was told. When we pushed the starter button, located on the floor, the engine was reluctant to rotate.

Hameed said, "I was afraid of that. There are two ways we can get this machine going. One is to crank the engine by hand, and the other is to push the car, and when it picks up speed, shifting the gear will turn the engine. Let us try to crank it, and if that does not work, then we will get some help to push it."

He added that if we had to push start it, he hoped that the clutch worked. What confidence! Being up in age, he could not do it, so I, following his instructions, attempted to crank the engine by hand. The first few attempts failed because I failed to complete the rotation, as the engine would reverse halfway through and the crank handle would smash into my wrist. Each time that happened, Hameed confirmed that the engine had an excellent compression, although that failed to ease the throbs in my wrist. Finally I was successful against the engine and managed to rotate it a full circle, enabling it to come alive. It was an exhilarating moment to hear the fruits of many weeks of labor. The pain of the swollen wrist vanished as we got fully absorbed in listening to the rhythmic sound of the engine. It was the first time in many years that I felt a spark of real happiness, the last time being when I saw *Abbajee's* approving smile in support of my quest to immigrate to the United States. We threw a blanket over the torn seats and jumped in the car, and Hameed, the only driver, pushed the clutch and shifted the gear, propelling the car forward. The excitement lasted for only a short time, as the engine died after having driven just a few miles. Hameed took a long-stemmed screwdriver and touched the terminals of the battery, producing a very weak spark, and then reasoned that the generator was not working because it could have supplied the needed power to the plugs once the engine was turning. The generator had to be rewired, taking a week, and when installed, it worked properly, although I still had to crank the engine. What Hameed taught me would come handy in future adventures with the Ford and other dilapidated cars that *Bhai Manzoor* tended to purchase.

Very few people owned cars in the city of Gujranwala, and the few that were on the road were made in Britain, with names like Austin, Morris, Hillman, or Vauxhall. Dr. Manzoor's Ford became well known in the city not only because it was American, but also because it needed a manual push or cranking to start. Each night, the car was parked in a narrow alley in front of the house, and it needed a push to get going. Every morning the neighborhood children waited in excitement to get the chance to push "Doctor Sahib's" car. It took more than six months to acquire the proper battery and all the other missing parts before the Ford was restored to a functioning automobile. Windshield wipers operated by using the suction created by the engine, and the speed of the wipers depended upon how fast the engine was running. In the absence of hydraulics, power assistance for brakes and steering was non-existent, and the mechanical braking required leg power and steering needed arm muscles. Working on the car occupied my attention and kept me from thinking about anything else, and I discovered that it came naturally to me to solve mechanical problems. This experience sowed the seeds for my romance with automobiles, and a car repair garage began to come into focus as a viable business in the United States after my immigration. I had seen such car garages in U.S. movies. My duties now included driving the car and its maintenance, besides being a compounder and an x-ray technician.

8

One day an invitation arrived from the local deputy commissioner (DC), the chief administrator of the city. *Bhai Manzoor* felt elated because a stranger did not get invited to the DC residence. He felt that probably it had to do with some medical problem, and all eyes were upon him when he returned from his meeting with the DC. It seemed that the Ford, the only American car in the town, had caught the DC's eye, and he offered 1,200 rupees, but it was finally sold for 1,500 rupees. I was sad to see it go, as I had grown very fond of it. Within a few months, *Bhai Manzoor* came into the possession of another car as a payment of a loan. It was a green Morris Minor, built in 1934, and when I looked at it, I could not help but exclaim, "Why did you buy this piece of junk?" It had a body made of wood, and the doors could not be closed properly, as the material had shrunk due to dryness and neglect. The steering wheel had a play of at least a quarter of a rotation before it could turn the wheels. Still, that little Morris became my partner for a few exciting adventures.

The family decided to take a twenty-five-mile trip from Gujranwala to Ban Bajwa, an agricultural village where my paternal uncle's son lived. Four adults and three children crammed into the car that was built to carry only four persons. We had one spare tire, one spare tube, an assortment of repair kits, and a hand pump. As they did not have tubeless tires at the time, standard tools included a set of tire irons, used to remove the tubes. We had planned to leave at 9:00 a.m. and have a leisurely lunch in Daska at my uncle's house before proceeding to the village, but the journey could only begin after 11:00 a.m. because of the sudden appearance of a patient needing critical attention. The travel to Daska was uneventful, and the lunch lasted longer than expected as Uncle Nazir got deeply immersed in the merits of the prime minister's visit to the United States of America. Although we attempted to leave a few times, convention dictated that we remain till my uncle, being the oldest, indicated to do so. It was 3:30 p.m. before we embarked on the next leg of our journey, expecting to reach Ban around 5:00 p.m., just in time for dinner. The expectations were just that, expectations.

A few miles out of Daska, the pavement disappeared, replaced by a heavily traveled dirt road. The vehicles that traversed that road were not cars, but *Tongas* and bullock carts and, when loaded, their thin wheels would dig deep into the surface, creating grooves and high ridges, hardened by alternating rain and dryness across the entire width. The zigzag of the ruts resembled the surface of a large tire when laid out flat, presenting our little overloaded chariot with a few challenges. The ridges were like deep ruts, and once the wheels got caught between them it was difficult to change the direction of travel, because the vehicle freewheeled during the time it took to overcome the steering wheel play. It was amusing to watch *Bhaijee* attempting to steer the car, which always went in the opposite direction to where it was intended to go. Lacking the directional control, the car could not be driven more than ten miles per hour. The darkness was descending fast and the headlights were no help because at the time they were used more to declare the presence of the vehicle than to illuminate the road. In order to get a better view, I secured myself on top of the roof and directed my brother to the areas of the "road" that exhibited the least amount of ridges. I swayed side to side like a branch of a tree on a windy day as the car teetered left and right. The plan worked, and we began to make some headway.

Bhaijee stopped the car with a jerk, almost throwing me off the roof, and screamed, "Now what? I am having a tough time steering the car." Climbing down from the roof, I commented, "I hope that the steering wheel is not broken." As he looked at me with an apprehensive stare, I began to investigate the cause of the problem. The left front wheel was flat. Whoever sold the car to my brother forgot to include the jack, a tool that could not be purchased as auto parts stores were nonexistent at the time in that part of the world. However, I was prepared for the challenge and had brought along a few bricks and a short length of two-inch-by-six-inch wood. In front of the flat tire, I built a ramp high enough to allow the mounting of a fully inflated wheel. Then the car, with the rear wheel drive, was driven till the defective wheel reached the top of the incline making enough room under the chassis to improvise a jack, which I did by stacking the remaining bricks. The car fell only about a quarter of an inch on top of the makeshift lift once the ramp was dismantled by forcing out the piece of wood. Mounting the good wheel presented no problem. In order to dislodge the car from the lift, all we had to do was to drive the car forward. It took just over half an hour to complete the repairs, and after retrieving my "tools," we were back on our way, looking forward to a nice meal.

I could savor that thought for only a short time when the car hit a bump and had to be stopped once again. This time it was the rear right tire that had gone flat, and before it could be replaced, I had to fix the tube in the old tire. Using the tire irons, I removed the tube, and a cursory inspection of the inside of the tire did not reveal the cause of the problem until I inflated the tube. Then I could see the leak without the use of the soap and water solution that was also included in my ditty bag. The location of the tear identified itself by producing a whistling sound as the air escaped from under an older repair patch. That was easy to fix, but it took some time to inflate the tire as *Bhai Manzoor* and I took turns at the old pump, wasting another hour before resuming our journey. It seemed that the tires had conspired to protest against the weight (overweight in this case) they were required to carry, because before we reached our destination, all four tubes had to be repaired. It was midnight before I found a bed to rest my aching body.

The following day after lunch, we embarked on our return trip and decided to take the paved road through the city of Sialkot, even though the distance would be longer. I was glad that I had picked up some more tube repair patches while in the city, because ten miles from Gujranwala, the rear left tire blew up with a loud noise. It was 11:00 p.m. and I had run out of repairing materials after the ninth patch. We were preparing to spend the night by the side of the road when we saw the dark shape of an approaching *Tonga,* whose driver was on his way home to the nearby village. After much haggling, he accepted 25 rupees to transport my family and a tire to Gujranwala while I stayed with the car. By then my muscles were crying out for relief, and to ease the pain, I lay down on the back seat, thinking about my garage in the United States of America. It was not long before the body succumbed to its own analgesics and fell into a deep slumber. Around noon the following day, I saw a shadow appearing in the distance, its outline shimmering in the rising heat of the day. As it drew closer, it looked like an upside-down spire with a wide base, and only when it was a few hundred feet away did I recognize the approaching figure. It was my friend Hanif, who cut a comic figure riding a bike while balancing the wheel on his head.

"I see you have started a new business," I commented laughingly.

Without answering, he threw the tire on the side of the road and jumped into the nearby canal, where I joined him, and it felt great to be in the cold water. Tied to the handle bar of the bike was a bag with some food that provided for a nice picnic. He said, "I should have taken a *Tonga,* but they wanted too much money, so I decided to use my bike. I will never do that again."

After changing the wheel, we took another dip in the canal, tied the bicycle on top of the roof using the rope that Hanif had the sense to bring along, and headed home. It was 3:00 in the afternoon when I pulled the car in front of the clinic and thanked God for a safe return. On reflection, it was a tiresome yet hilarious adventure.

The drive on the dirt road while overloaded did not fare well with the old car, as the fine dirt accumulated under the carbon contacts in the generator, resulting in reduced power output. During the troubleshooting process, I discovered that the British cars had odd electrical systems, with the positive of the battery grounded instead of the negative, as in the case of the Ford. It was one problem after another, and once the power problem was repaired, the hydraulic brakes failed. During the few months while waiting for the replacement parts, the mechanical emergency hand brake was the only means to stop the car. After the repairs, on the way back from the shop, I approached an intersection manned by a policeman. He signaled me to stop as he was about to change the direction of the traffic. To my surprise, when I pushed the pedal, nothing happened, and the car kept going. In a panic, I began to down shift the gears, and as the vehicle slowed down, I steered it to the left to avoid the vehicles coming from the right. The traffic flows in the opposite direction from that in the United States. The expression on the face of the policeman changed from a smile to disbelief to fear and finally to anger as he saw a car out of control heading directly at him. Eventually the car came to a stop, and I stepped out from behind the wheel, apologizing as he approached, shouting furiously, "You could have caused an accident with your maneuver. Are you stupid?"

But as soon as our eyes met and he recognized me, his attitude became very courteous and instead of counting the number of violations, I heard him say, "Doctor Sahib! I am sorry I did not recognize you with all the traffic. Is there something wrong with the car? How can I help you?"

Because I was the brother of a doctor, everybody addressed me with the title of "doctor," just as in Jammu I was addressed as *Maulvi Sahib,* the title of my father. I thanked the policeman for his offer, restarted the car, and headed towards home. I was not prepared for what lay ahead.

In the absence of pasteurization, the dairy stores boiled the milk in large cauldrons, over one meter in diameter, placed on an open brick fireplaces located at the outer edges of the stores. Two blocks from the clinic, such a vendor was preparing to light the fire under the vessel, one third of which extended into the street. Nearing the location, my attempt to steer the car to the right bore no fruit as the car continued on its path to left. Next the car stopped with a crashing sound, and the front was awash with milk. The cauldron, three-quarters full of fresh milk, had overturned when the car smashed into it, and I found the owner of the store standing there with his hands up in the air displaying an expression of dismay and disbelief. Luckily no one was hurt, but we had to compensate the store owner for the damages, and that was when *Bhai Manzoor* decided that a dealer in Lahore should perform proper repairs.

In preparation for the drive to Lahore, I removed the doors because they could not stay closed any longer. Hanif and another friend accompanied me so that after dropping off the car at the dealership, we could take in an afternoon movie before returning to Gujranwala. But it was not to be, as it took us nine hours to travel forty miles because I had to improvise to overcome a multitude of mechanical problems. It was midnight when we were stopped at the outskirts of the city by the road patrol. The police officer, wearing a sergeant's stripes, looked at me with an astonished expression and asked, "What is this?" I decided to humor him and replied, "It was a car when I started the trip." He did not think it was funny. While ordering me to show him my license and car registration, he retorted, "I thought a car comes with doors and lights that shine at night." I had never attempted to get a driver's license. Ignoring my pleadings, he cited me with a number of violations and ordered me to appear before a magistrate in three days to answer the charges. We managed to get to my aunt's house and delivered the car to the dealer the following morning, after which my friends returned to Gujranwala while I stayed behind to face the judge.

9

At the appointed time I arrived at the address mentioned in my citation and was told to stand on the right side of a large room with a large desk on an elevated platform. I had never been in a court before and had no idea what to do. I felt intimidated when my eyes met those of the policeman who had cited me. The magistrate entered through a door behind the dais, and as he took a quick glance at the types of offenders he would be trying, his gazing stopped when he saw me. Immediately after that, excusing himself, he retreated to his private chambers. That confused all those present, but a few minutes later his bailiff approached me and asked me to follow him. I was puzzled but did what was told and found myself facing the magistrate in his private office. He looked at me with a big smile.

"As-Saalam-Alaaikum," I said.

"Wa-Alaaikum-Saalam," he responded, and then added, "I am glad to see you. How is Manzoor?"

Listening to his voice, I suddenly remembered that he was a junior magistrate in Gujranwala a few years ago.

"He is fine, but my presence here is due to driving violations. You know the kind of cars *Bhai Manzoor* owns, and I was driving his Morris to Lahore for repairs..."

Before I could finish, he rang for his bailiff and asked him to look for the citation against Maqbool Qurashi while we continued our chat. A few minutes later, the bailiff returned and stated that no such citation was found. Following Mr. Shahbaz out of his private office into the court room, I searched for the officer who was responsible for my presence there, but he was nowhere to be found. As I began my departure by shaking Mr. Khan's hand, he said, "Give my regards to Manzoor."

"Thank you, Shahbaz Sahib," I said and exited the courtroom.

This experience left me with a bad taste of my new country's justice system, but I was relieved to get off without any punishment. The agency declared the car irreparable, and it had to be junked. A 1942 Ford followed the Morris. The car had style, with a big V8 engine, but the problem was the location of its distributor. It was at the lowest point in the front of the engine, behind the radiator, and every time the vehicle was driven through a puddle of water, the distributor would get wet, thus stopping the car. It had become automatic for me to jump out of the car, open the hood, reach down, remove the cap and the rotor, and, after drying all the parts, reassemble them. I kept a towel for that very purpose.

While I enjoyed repairing cars, I could not see spending my life doing that in Pakistan without any compensation. Something inside me was stirring, and I was becoming restless and needed a change in my situation. Five years had passed since we left Jammu, and my life had been in limbo ever since. The practice at the clinic had grown so that *Bhai Manzoor* had to hire another person to help him. The feeling for a change had never been as strong.

Apa Anwari, after receiving her certification in advanced medicine, accepted a position as a resident medical officer at Sutlej Textile Mills in the city of Okara. Uncle Saleem assisted her in the move. He was the kind of person who could understand the feelings of his family members and somehow was always there whenever he was needed. He had a special way to communicate with the young and was always there when I required his advice. One day after his return from Okara, he invited me for a shish kebab dinner, where I asked him, "How does *Apa* like her new job at the mill?"

"It is a nice place, and she has spacious quarters, and children can go to school right there within the mill compound," he answered. After a pause he addressed me by the nickname he had given me. "*Shahjee,* tell me truthfully how you are doing." *Shahjee* meant "Big Honcho."

"OK. But I would like to do something better, to be on my own," I replied.

"I think it will be a good idea if you spend some time with your sister in Okara and see the mill. There could be some opportunities there," he suggested.

I was ready to try anything, so two weeks later I boarded a train to Okara and took a *Tonga* to the mills, arriving there at midafternoon. There was a large, secured entrance to the factory, and the guards had been informed by *Apa Anwari* about my arrival. One of them escorted me to her house and explained what was being done in each of the buildings that we passed along the way. The enormity of the mill's compound amazed me. Uncle Saleem had informed me that the mill provided residences for the management and supervisory personnel, which numbered more than one thousand, and the self-sustaining colony was set apart from the main factory. Multistory apartment buildings in the rear were where the foremen and their families lived. The rows of townhomes were for the supervisory staff, while the managers were given large houses with courtyards and porches. *Apa Anwari* had a large house, which she shared with her assistant, who happened to be the sister of a college classmate. Unlike Gujranwala, where the streets had open wastewater channels, here the sewer drains were buried and the streets were clean. The running water, instead of hand pump, made it easier to have a shower. I prayed that I could get some work there.

In the evening when we all gathered for dinner, *Apa Anwari* informed me that she had arranged an interview for me with

Mr. Parr, who was the manager of the spinning department at the mill and would entertain the idea of offering me an unpaid apprenticeship. Having worked without a paycheck for years, here at least I had an opportunity that could lead to a paying position. The following morning I walked to the office of Mr. W. Arthur Parr, a tall Englishman with reddish hair and a pale complexion. He asked me to take a seat. Thanks to *Bayjee*, I had learned to hold a conversation in English, but I had difficulty understanding his dialect.

"Your sister is a good doctor. I had a terrible stomach problem and she took care of it," he said.

"The medical profession comes naturally in our family. We have many doctors," I said.

"How come you did not pursue that field?"

"I am more inclined to repair machines than humans," I answered.

"That is good, because we have many types of machines here, and the first order in learning the trade is to understand their workings. You know that you will not be paid during the training, but you will get priority when a suitable position becomes available." "I understand. I am a quick study," I commented.

"Good," he said while getting up from his chair. "Let me show you around and then introduce you to our head mechanic."

As I followed him through a wide door, I could not contain my excitement. The vastness of the factory floor was overwhelming, and there were machines lined up as far as the eye could see. We entered the spinning floor, where cotton was transformed from bales into yarns of various thicknesses, and then continued the tour into the very noisy weaving floor, where the yarn was transformed into various styles of cloth. When we returned to his office, a gray-haired gentleman was waiting in the lobby. His name was Haider Ali, the master mechanic in charge of the maintenance of the spinning floor. His expression displayed his annoyance at having been summoned from his work with little notice, and he appeared disturbed when Mr. Parr, in his broken Punjabi, informed him of who I was and that I would be part of his crew for some time. I had hoped that the sponsorship of the boss would make my apprenticeship a pleasant experience, but I was mistaken. It did not take long before it became clear that I was an unwelcome addition to his crew. If Mr. Parr had discussed my position with Ali before our meeting, he would not have felt so threatened—a lesson I would practice in the future. For a few months I had to tag along with Ali, who behaved as if I did not exist, and my questions went unanswered. He was an enigma. Eager to learn, I had no choice but to stand back and figure out the workings of each of the machines on my own, by observation.

I felt confident that I could help Ali lighten his load, but he had created an impregnable shell around himself and was always suspicious of me. Unlike Hameed, the car mechanic, Ali did not appear to be very bright and was very reluctant to share technical information. There were no institutions in Pakistan where one could receive training in spinning room maintenance, or any other trade, for that matter, so I could understand Ali's concerns. With little formal education, he had learned his skills over many years of hit-and-miss techniques, and now, up in age and concerned about his job security, he was not about to give away his painfully acquired knowledge to a young apprentice who was not his choice to begin with. I refrained from complaining to Mr. Parr about Ali's behavior, because that would have been counterproductive, so I decided to find a way to make him understand that I was not after his job. Two of his assistants were always present whenever I was close by, and my attempts to engage in small talk met with discouraging responses. It was a while before an opportunity arrived that would change our relationship.

One of Ali's assistants, named Sharif, was working on one of the large machines that was used to break up the clumps of compressed cotton bales. Under the belly of the machine was a large, removable pan that collected dust and other particles as the compressed cotton fibers were loosened up, and in order to dispose of the waste, the pan had to be removed. Sharif, ignoring the safety requirement, attempted to remove the pan without stopping the machine, and in the process his index finger got caught between the two moving parts. I happen to passing by when I heard a cry for help and, after a quick survey of the situation, proceeded to stop the machine. After slowly removing his hand from under the pan, I wrapped my handkerchief around his finger and, with the help of another worker, took him to the dispensary. His arm would have been crushed if the machine had not been stopped in time. *Apa Anwari* looked at his severely mangled finger and declared that it had to be amputated, as the bones were crushed beyond repair. Shortly afterwards, Ali arrived with a concerned expression because he had heard that Sharif would lose his arm, just as another worker had done many years earlier in a similar accident. As Ali realized that it was my quick action that prevented Sharif from the same fate, he began to display a more conciliatory attitude, and from then on, I became a member of his inner circle, allowing me to assist him in major overhauls of the machines.

Ali's knowledge, limited only to the maintenance of the machines, could not satisfy my inquiries about the workings of a spinning mill, leading me to enroll in a home study course in cotton spinning offered by the International Correspondence Schools from Scranton, Pennsylvania. Mr. Parr agreed to supervise my tests while frequently reminding me that I should not corrupt my spellings with the Yankee English. The textbooks were written in the United States of America, and therefore many words, such as "color" and "fiber," were spelled differently than in the King's English. It took me three months to complete the course, and I hoped that this would lead me to a paying employment at the mill, but Mr. Parr was noncommittal. He pointed out that he did not want to place me in a dead-end job as I had managerial talents, and that I should have patience. It had been a year since I had begun my apprenticeship, and by that time I was very confident of my ability to handle a responsible position. Finding none at the mill, I solicited Mr. Parr's guidance. After a few days, he invited *Apa Anwari* and me for a breakfast meeting at his house in order to discuss my future course of action.

We arrived at his residence at 8:00 in the morning, and his cook had prepared a typical English breakfast. The meeting began with small talk, and he jokingly mentioned that *Apa Anwari's* visit to his home for a meal would probably give the management people something to gossip about, which gave us a good laugh. I was tense and getting impatient when finally, addressing *Apa Anwari,* he said, "The textile industry will be seeing a great growth in the coming years, and there will be demand for middle- to upper-management personnel. Your brother possesses the managerial and technical talent to fill that need, and I recommend that he get a certificate from a recognized two-year technical college in England."

"Do I have the proper qualifications to gain admission to such an institution?" I asked.

"The manufacturers of textile machinery in England are given sponsorship rights for a certain number of admissions to colleges. There is a way to arrange a sponsorship for you. You will have to bear the expenses," he explained.

Before I could say anything, *Apa Anwari* said, "How soon do we need to begin the process so he could join the classes this year?"

"This is January, and classes begin in September. If you agree, I will contact a company in England, and Maqbool can write a letter to their representatives in Karachi. This should get the ball rolling."

Looking at me, he said, "You will probably have to go to Karachi for an interview."

Apa Anwari thanked him for his interest in me and told him that we would need a few days to have a family meeting. On the way home, she told me, "You can depend on my partial contribution; let's see what others can do."

The following day I boarded a bus to Gujranwala to consult Uncle Saleem, who happened to be there and could plead my case to the others. After listening to what had transpired in Okara, he began the discussion with others at the evening dinner by saying, "The Englishman at the mill feels that Maqbool has great possibilities and has volunteered to recommend him for admission to a college in England to further his education in textile engineering." Then he asked me to explain the rest, and before *Bhai Manzoor* could inquire, I told him that Mr. Parr felt that I would need £30 per month for living expenses for a period of two years. One could have heard a pin drop in the ensuing silence, which seemed to last an eternity. Finally, I said, "*Apa Anwari* is willing to contribute, and I can also ask Uncle Nazir." If anybody in the family had money, it was he. I left for Daska, as *Bhaijee* wanted to think about it for a few days.

Uncle Nazir was well off, but he never shared his good fortune with his relations; even his prized ruby red oranges that he grew in his large backyard never found their way to any relative's table except once. That happened when Uncle Saleem and I picked all his crop of oranges while he was away in Lahore for a few days and distributed the fruit to the rest of the family. Otherwise, we were only allowed to eat a few of the fruits while visiting him but could not take any with us. During the time when we closely worked together taking care of incoming refugees, I had felt a special bond had grown between us, and during my visits he had demonstrated that by always showing interest in my life. We had enjoyed many animated political discussions, and this would be a test to determine if my feelings were reciprocated. When I informed him about the reason of my visit, he put his hand on my shoulder and said, "You can count on me."

I hugged him with tears of happiness and it appeared that my plan to go to England might become a reality.

My half-hour bus ride to Gujranwala was filled with emotions, as I felt this to be a very positive step towards the ultimate goal—the United States of America. *Bhaijee Manzoor*, too, had good news for me, and with these assurances of assistance, I traveled back to Okara and requested Mr. Parr to proceed with his recommendations. On January 6, 1954, I mailed a letter, written with his assistance, to Mr. Crawther, requesting a sponsorship by the Textile Engineers of Pakistan Ltd. in Karachi, the agents of Platt Brothers, Ltd., of Oldham. A prompt reply informed me that the last day for the receipt of the admission applications was February 1, but if his company agreed to sponsor me to a college, the date was not important and therefore there was no hurry and that Mr. Parr would be informed about the date for the interview when somebody from the Platt Brothers visited Karachi. Waiting, no matter the reason and no matter how long, requires discipline and a reservoir of patience, as minutes become hours and hours extend to days and it feels like an eternity. That is what I had to do, and the mixed emotions of excitement, fear, and anticipation were having a field day. My walks from one area of the mill to another always made a detour by Mr. Parr's office. At the end of the day, I would rush home to see if there was some news in the mail.

On Tuesday, February 9, when I was about to exit the building, Mr. Parr approached me and said, "You better get ready to travel to Karachi tomorrow to meet with Mr. Walwyn for an interview, as he is here only during this week." I had just gotten used to the art of waiting and now had to come to grips with a time squeeze, never having experienced this kind of stress before. The thoughts of failure that had begun to creep into my mind could not be assuaged by Mr. Parr's assurances, so whenever I found myself in this kind of situation, I reminded myself what *Abbajee* had told me so often: "The final outcome belongs with *Allah*; our job is to continue our efforts and look at the failures as training for what lies ahead."

This mantra helped to calm my nerves so I could focus on the tasks that needed to be completed before I could receive that much-coveted acceptance letter from a college.

10

I had never been in Karachi before. Pakistan Airlines was in its infancy and not affordable, leaving the railway as the only available mode of transportation between Karachi and the northern cities of Pakistan. Although the ticketing clerk at Okara cautioned me that the train to Karachi would be very crowded, I did not pay too much attention to his statement at the time, as I was used to traveling in crowded trains. His warning hit home when the train's arrival was announced and a flood of humanity broke through the gates to occupy every available space on the platform. Some were there to see off the departing passengers and some to receive the arriving ones, and I quickly worked my way to the edge of the platform. When the train approached, I saw some people sitting on the roof of the train, while others were hanging onto the sidebars of the doorsteps, as shown in newspaper pictures. The instant the train stopped, there was a mad rush towards the doors of the cars, and the passengers who were hanging on the sidebars made a push to gain the seats vacated by those who were trying to get off. I had a small piece of luggage containing toiletries, a shirt, my only jacket, and a pair of pants, carefully folded. As soon as I noticed that no one was hanging on one of the sidebars, I jumped on a step and put my right arm around the bar while holding on to my luggage with my left hand. I stayed away from the actual opening of the door to avoid being crushed and resolved to remain in this position at least till the next stop that was about two hours away. It was around midnight when we arrived at the next large city, Multan, and, lucky for me, the passengers leaving the train far exceeded the number that boarded it, providing me with a seat on a bench in between five other comfortably seated passengers. The bench was made for six persons, and before dawn there was enough space for me to lie down, although only for a short period of time.

The train arrived at Karachi station in the morning, and I took a *Tonga* taxi to the office of one of my relations, named Afzal. His office was not open yet, so I parked myself in front of the door, and at 9:30 a.m., somebody opened the door. I was allowed in, and when I informed him that I was waiting for Afzal Sahib, he offered me a cup of tea and some English biscuits. Uncle Afzal was surprised to see me and told me that he would have been happy to pick me up at the train station if he had known of my arrival. I explained the reason for my unannounced appearance, and when I asked where I could quickly shave and shower, he pointed me to the fully equipped bathroom that was available in the office. A delicious takeout breakfast was waiting as I stepped out of the shower, and, while eating, I asked his guidance for my interview. He frequently traveled overseas as part of his job as sales director for an exporter of marble and onyx. He invited me to stay for the night after my interview, which I declined, although I knew that my aunt would never forgive him if I left without seeing her.

My mind was too occupied to notice the passing scenery of the city while riding in Uncle Afzal's car to the office of the Textile Engineers, Ltd., that was located near the Karachi harbor, the only port of entry. At that time Karachi was the capital of the country, and the number of cars plying the wide boulevards was overwhelming. The four-wheel horse-drawn carriages, called Victorias, were something I had only seen in pictures before, and I called them the rich man's *Tongas*. As we approached the harbor, I could not avoid watching several ships docked at the piers, some discharging their cargo, while the others loaded bales of cotton as more waited in line for the availability of a berth. The high level of energy that permeated the air added to my nervous excitement as we began to look for the intended address after we entered the West Wharf Road. Finally our search paid off when, pointing to the Sheraz House, I exclaimed, "There it is." I declined Uncle Afzal's offer to wait for me, as I did not want to create a wrong impression, and told him that after the meeting I would take a taxi back to his office.

It was 11:00 a.m. when I attempted to open a wide door in the front of the building, and my heart sank when I realized that the door was locked. Panicked, I had just begun a frantic search for some other office when one of the signs next to a row of three doors caught my eye. I found the Textile Engineers of Pakistan, Ltd., appearing under the third-floor listing. There was a set of stairs behind the door that had number three painted above it. Once on top, I found a clerk seated behind a desk at the opposite end of the hallway and said, "My name is Maqbool Qurashi, and I am here to see Mr. Walwyn."

"I am Saeed. Let me see if he is in," he replied in Urdu, the local language.

"I hope so; I have come all the way from Okara," I said in Urdu as he was leaving his chair.

He returned shortly and informed me that Mr. Walwyn had just stepped out and was expected to return any moment. He pointed to one of the two empty chairs for me to sit and offered tea, which I accepted. It is not polite to decline when invited for tea, which is the social drink in Asian cultures and is offered to visitors at all times of the day. I was too tense to engage in small talk and had almost finished my cup of tea when I heard somebody stepping onto the landing from the staircase. Saeed looked up and, addressing the approaching gentleman, said, "Mr. Walwyn, this is Mr. Maqbool Qurashi, from Okara, sir."

Mr. Walwyn looked at me and stated, "Hello, give me few minutes and I will call you."

Mr. Walwyn wore the countenance of a kind man in his late forties, with light brown hair, taller than I, and an inviting demeanor.

I was already feeling comfortable about the pending interview. Fifteen minutes had passed when Saeed answered the phone at his desk and, after hanging it up, told me to go through the door on the right to the second office on the left. Mr. Walwyn appeared relaxed as he extended his hand, which I shook nervously.

"Maqbool Qurashi. Am I pronouncing it right?" He inquired while pointing to the chair across from his desk for me to take a seat.

"Yes sir. Thank you for making time to see me. Mr. Parr told me that you..."

"How is the old chap Arthur? Is he behaving himself?" he inquired before I could finish my sentence.

"He is in good health, sir," I said, feeling at ease with the knowledge that perhaps Mr. Parr and Mr. Walwyn were friends.

"Tell me about yourself."

I summarized my life story in as few words as I could.

"Where did you learn to speak English?"

I replied, "I was taught by my mother, who was a teacher. She made sure that I could read and write English. I read many of Kipling's books and short stories. But the speaking skills came by interacting with Mr. Parr."

"You will do fine in England." As an afterthought he added, "How did you end up in Okara?"

I explained to him about *Apa Anwari* and said, "I love to work with machines and am a quick learner."

He explained, "If all goes well, you should hear from a college by the middle of April. That should give you enough time to get all the paperwork completed for your travel to Great Britain by the middle of August."

"Do you anticipate any problem with the admission process?"

"I do not see any if the company accepts my recommendations and there is still time to nominate our candidates for admission. But as we say in England, there is many a slip between a cup and the lips." He stood up, signaling that the interview was over.

I got up from my chair and said, "Thank you very much, sir. I appreciate your time." I shook his hand with newly gained confidence.

I heard him say, "Good luck," as I headed to the door.

❧

It was 1:00 p.m. when I thanked Saeed and stepped out on the street with high spirits and excitedly looking forward to a bright future. I found a *Tonga* a few hundred yards from the office and enjoyed the ride back to Uncle Afzal's office. The surroundings, which I had ignored before, were reflecting my improved attitude. The unique features of Karachi, previously hidden behind my nervous veil, were coming into sharp focus, teaching me that one's mental state has a lot to do with one's life. Uncle Afzal was waiting for me with anticipation, and after I recounted what had transpired at the interview, we both arrived at the same conclusion—that Mr. Walwyn wanted to make sure that I had the proper demeanor to attend a learning institution in England. I wished I could share my excitement with my family, but the telephone service in private homes was nonexistent. Even the businesses had to qualify to own a telephone, and a long-distance call through the post office would take at least four or five hours to complete. A telegram was the alternative, but I decided against it.

❧

There was a wait for six hours before the departure of the train to Okara, and Uncle Afzal decided to drive me to Clifton Beach to watch the sunset before going home for dinner. The approaching twilight made the sun appear like a huge orange ball falling into the sea. Nature celebrated this event by brush painting the horizon in shades of reds, oranges, grays, and purples in their vivid brilliancy, while the high clouds filled in the gaps to complete the artwork. The reflection of this artistry in the Arabian Sea left me in awe. The display began to melt into its reflection as the sun prepared to call it a night. While this drama was concluding in the west, the manmade wonder of the city lights began to unfold to the east. I had never had such an experience before, and the idea that I might witness more wonders like this beyond the horizon added to my already overwhelming excitement. I was deep in such thoughts when we arrived at his house, and my aunt showered me with kisses and complimented me for my looks. I had never understood why aunts, whether closely or remotely related, always displayed great emotions at such meetings. She inquired about each of the members of my family and had a thousand questions, but my thoughts were immersed in my future plans, making my answers short or just grunts. I was treated to a great meal, which was shared with his two young children, and then it was time to leave. I apologized for being absent minded, but they understood my mental state. It was 9:30 p.m. when Uncle Afzal dropped me off at the train station.

The trip back to Okara was uneventful, and, Karachi being the originating point for northbound trains, there were ample seats available, allowing me to lie down on one of the benches and take a nap for about two hours. By the time I reached Okara, the compartment was crowded enough that I had to push my way out of the car, and it was close to 8:00 a.m. when I arrived at the mill and walked directly to my sister's office and announced, "I am going to England." She looked up with a quizzical expression on her face, and I told her what had transpired and that it would be the middle of April before I knew for certain. The next stop was Mr. Parr's office to convey Mr. Walwyn's best wishes. He explained that the company always followed Mr. Walwyn's recommendations, and he felt that I had made a good impression on his friend. I took a quick trip to Gujranwala and Daska to bring the good news to *Bayjee, Bhaijee,* and Uncle Nazir. For the next two months I stayed at the mill while waiting for news from some college in the United Kingdom, and it was difficult to concentrate on my work. I kept myself busy writing a paper titled "Prospects of Pakistan's Cotton Textile Industry," which was nominated for the award of the Feroz Medal by the Pakistan Textile Association.

It was April 20 when I opened a package from the Technical College in Bolton in the County of Lancashire, United Kingdom.

The letter informed me that I had been accepted to attend the textile engineering course and that the orientation was scheduled at 10:00 a.m. on Friday, September 10, with classes to begin on September 13, 1954. Also included in the package was a blue book titled *How to Live in Great Britain* and a list of rooming houses that were approved by the college. *Apa Anwari* agreed that I should proceed to Gujranwala, where it might be convenient for me to gather my traveling documents. I bid my farewell to Okara and began my adventure through the bureaucratic maze of the Government of Pakistan.

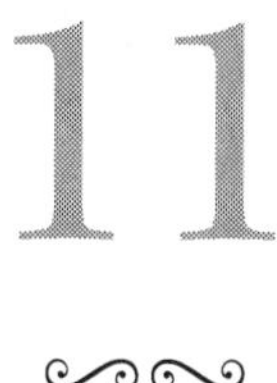

Uncle Afzal had recommended that I should contact a travel agent to tie down a departure date. Thomas Cook, the travel agency, informed me that a freighter of the Lloyd Steamship Company was departing Karachi for Liverpool, United Kingdom, on August 12, 1954, allowing me sufficient time to get to Bolton and find suitable living quarters. In order to secure a confirmed passage, I needed to have all the documents no later than July 25. Although I could have reserved my lodging in advance by selecting from the list that was provided by the college, it could not be done without the exchange permit required to remit the deposit. It became clear that nothing could be done without a passport. That became an adventure in its own right.

During the colonial days, the object of the bureaucratic procedures was to constantly remind the populace that they were subjects of the British Empire. Pakistan had existed for just over six years at the time, and the government officials were still in the colonial mind-set and felt that their job was to direct the lives of the inhabitants. The deputy commissioner (DC), an appointed official as in the past, was still the chief executive of the city. I had to petition his office to forward my request for a passport to the responsible office. The head clerk asked me to put the request in writing, with prescribed stamps, explaining why I should be *granted* a passport. I was appalled at his use of the word "*granted,*" but managed to control my outrage. The following day I presented him with my written petition, complete with a certified copy of the acceptance letter from the college. He, dismissing my pleas for expediency because of time constraints, placed it in a basket and told me to come back in a week. *Bhai Manzoor* commented on my dejected expression when I entered his office at the clinic and assured me that he would find somebody who could influence Mr. Sajid, the head clerk.

Two days had passed when Charley, the new assistant at the clinic, told me that my brother wanted to see me as soon as possible. As I entered his office, he pointed to his visitor and said to me, "You know Akbar Sahib. He has been asking about you."

After proper salutations, I said, "I am trying to get my passport so I could go to England for studies, but I am having trouble expediting it."

"Did you send your petition to the DC's office?" Akbar Sahib asked.

"I personally took it to Sajid, but he told me to come back next week. That will be Monday," I answered

"Sajid? He is my nephew. He wants everyone to recognize his new authority. He has to be handled gently," he explained.

"What do you suggest I do?" I asked.

He thought for a while and then said, "Get to Sajid's office around 10:00 a.m. tomorrow and I will stop there, as if by chance, and then see what develops."

"I do not know how to thank you."

"Do not count your chickens yet. He is not a very amenable person," he remarked as he left the clinic.

My roller coaster of hope began its climb again.

I arrived at Sajid's office at the appointed time. His assistant told me that there was a visitor with Sajid Sahib and that I should wait in the lobby till his visitor had left. I sat in an empty chair, and when the clock on the wall struck 10:30, I felt that probably I had missed Akbar Sahib. I began to formulate a strategy to drop Akbar's name if he did not show and was deep in thought when the door to Sajid's office opened and, to my surprise, Akbar Sahib appeared, followed by Sajid, who had accompanied his uncle to the door. Before Sajid could turn back, Akbar Sahib extended his hand towards me saying, "Hello, Maqbool. How are you? How is Doctor Sahib?"

Then, turning to Sajid, he continued, "Sajid, meet Maqbool. He is the brother of my very good friend Dr. Manzoor. He just got admission to a college in England."

Sajid, in deference to his uncle, reluctantly shook my hand while Akbar Sahib was departing through the door.

I followed Sajid into his office and sat down in the reluctantly offered chair. He began to riffle through a stack of papers in search of my petition, which he read quickly and, after scrutinizing the copy of the letter from the college, asked me how I managed to get the admission. When I told him what had transpired till then, his expression became friendly as he handed me a printed form. It was the application for a passport, for which I had to sign in a register to acknowledge its receipt. He explained that I needed to get clearances from each of the police departments of the cities where I had lived during the past five years. I thanked him, and as I stood up to leave, he said, "Did Uncle Akbar arrange for you to be here?" Without waiting for my answer, he continued, "He does that to me all the time, but I do not mind. This way I can spend some time with him. He has always been good to me."

"I have an uncle just like him. He is the family listening post," I commented while exiting his office. My spirits were high once again.

Next stop was the District Police Office at Gujranwala, where I had to deliver a written request for a clearance certificate to the desk sergeant. Knowing that I was the brother of Dr. Qurashi, he assured me that he would have the document within a few days. Okara Police Office, on the other hand, presented a challenge. First I had to produce evidence that I had resided in the city during 1953 and part of 1954. A letter from the mill was satisfactory to the desk clerk, who asked me to come back in a week. But when I returned after one week, the certificate was not ready. I was prepared to give a lecture about the responsibility of a government in a free country when I realized that it was not his fault. I clenched my fist in my pocket and agreed to come back. Two weeks had passed when I picked up the letter from the police department in Okara stating that there was no record of my having been arrested for any crime without mentioning any dates. He could have easily looked up my name among the list of offenders and saved time.

Back in Gujranwala, the completed application package was delivered to Sajid's office on July 1, 1954. It contained the properly filled-out form; police certificates from Okara and Gujranwala; an affidavit of support duly signed by *Bhaijee Manzoor* and certified by an attorney; the acceptance letter from the college; and two frontal pictures. Sajid informed me that I should expect the passport in twenty to twenty-five days. The travel agency, in reply to my letter, informed me that my name would stay on the passenger list unless I failed to acquire the necessary documents by the first of August. I proceeded to get vaccinations against cholera and smallpox as required, and now had time to read the blue booklet that was sent by the college.

The booklet contained a host of information about public transportation, lodging, health, and other citizen services. There was an enlightening chapter about lodging such as rooming houses and bed-and-breakfast facilities. But the chapter titled "How to Behave in the British Isles" loudly broadcast the colonial mind-set. Maybe the following instructions were necessary for some of my countrymen who had no education, but personally I felt insulted:

Do not enter a British home without invitation.

Do not stay past a mealtime, unless asked to do so.

Do not approach an English person unless formally introduced.

Do not hug your relatives or friends in public.

Always use a fork in the left hand

And so on.

The book gave me a fairly good idea about the thought process of the people who had ruled part of my world for many centuries. I was about to live among the former masters who had left only seven years ago when Pakistan had become an equal with the other countries of the world. A nagging question in the back of my mind was, what kind of interaction should I expect while in England?

*

The postal service was still as efficient as it was during the British Raj. The passport was issued on July 19, 1954, and delivered to me in Gujranwala on Wednesday, two days later. It was an important moment of my life when I opened the package to retrieve a green booklet, four inches by six inches and one-quarter of an inch thick. My name appeared at the top and the passport number at the bottom of the cover. As I held the little booklet in my hands, my body experienced an avalanche of conflicting emotions, and a wave of confidence permeated my senses when I read the first paragraph inside the front cover. It said, "These are to request and require in the name of the Governor General of Pakistan all those whom it may concern to allow the bearer to pass freely without let or hindrance and to afford him every assistance and protection of which he may stand in need." This was my ticket to adventure, and perhaps to fulfilling my dream. The countries that I was allowed to enter were listed on page 4 and included the United Kingdom, France, Italy, Belgium, Holland, Lebanon, Jordan, Iraq, and Egypt. I was gently flipping through the pages when the last page caught my eye. It had columns requiring official entries whenever the rupees were exchanged for British pounds, and I was suddenly reminded that I still had to get an exchange permit from the State Bank of Pakistan.

The next stop was the State Bank of Pakistan exchange office in Lahore, where it took half a day standing in a line before being escorted to an office. The man who sat behind a desk was meticulously attired in a dark suit, wearing an expression that had no message, and he appeared to be a by-the-book professional. I broke the ice by announcing, "My name is Maqbool Qurashi, and I have been accepted to study at the Technical College, Bolton, in the United Kingdom, and I need an exchange permit." He reached into a drawer while raising his eyes to look at me without moving his head, and I saw his hand move effortlessly when he handed me a form and asked me to follow the instructions and come back with the supporting documents. Disregarding my pleas, he pointed to the door. He never changed his expression during our short interaction, and I was sure that when he spoke those few words, his lips did not move. The following day when I returned with the completed documents, he asked me to sit down on the chair across his desk while he looked over the papers. He opened my passport to the last page and stamped it twice after writing something and then explained, "You are not qualified for the basic travel quota. There is a special quota of £25 for students, and after that you are allowed to receive an exchange of £30 per month as long as you are studying there." He returned my passport and wished me good luck, and when I thanked him, he cracked an acknowledging smile, making me rethink about him, as it appeared that behind that poker face countenance there was a real human after all. It was the third of August, and I had nine days before departure.

My luggage consisted of an old jacket and a pair of trousers that previously belonged to *Bhaijee Manzoor* but was altered to my size, a plaid sweater knitted by *Apa Anwari*, and three shirts that were tailored for me before the partition of India in preparation for college. I was getting impatient, and the thoughts of being far away from my family saddened me. *Bayjee* did not share my excitement and wore a sad expression; her actions were that of a submissive audience, and that worried me. The tickets arrived on the eighth of August, assuring my departure, so I began my travels to various relatives to bid them farewell. When I boarded a train for Karachi on the evening of August 11, 1954, my relatives and many of my friends came to the train station, each one placing a real flower garland around my neck, a custom for a departing or arriving person. There were so many garlands around my neck that I had to take some off in order to be able to speak. As the time of departure approached, I thanked everyone and, with tears in my eyes, I held my mother in my embrace for a long time. I stayed at the window looking back at my family as their faces melted into the background. Departures are saddening affairs, especially for those who stay behind, because the mind of the traveler becomes occupied with anticipation. As the train sped towards Lahore, the hypnotic noise of the wheel bumps lulled me into sleep.

I was awakened by a screeching noise of braking wheels rubbing on the tracks as the train came to a stop at Lahore Junction, where the tactical challenge to navigate through a multitude of people rushing in various directions, provided a distraction from the sadness that pervaded me. As the train to Karachi originated in Lahore, I had enough time to select a comfortable seat where I might get to nap during my journey of nineteen hours. The train departed on time at 5:00 p.m., and an hour later I ate my favorite ground meat *prathas*, fried flat bread stuffed with cooked ground beef, which *Bayjee* had prepared for my journey. My mind wandered to the times in the past when I had enjoyed similar meals as a child, and it saddened me to think that I would not taste my favorite food for some time. It was not long before I nodded off to the dream world. Each time the train slowed down to make its stops at various towns, the screeching of the brakes would wake me up. We arrived at Karachi Cantonment station at 2:00 p.m. and had two hours to get to the pier before boarding the ship. After passing through customs, I checked my luggage at the entrance to the ship and entered a large holding room, where the ship steward welcomed the passengers and explained the ship's routine. SS *Cilicia*, a Lloyd Steamship freighter, carried only thirty passengers. The immigration service representatives began their documentation inspection and stamping the passports. It seemed that there had to be stamping of documents when dealing with government bureaucrats, and as the inspector waved me towards the lobby of the ship, a fleeting moment of deep sadness invaded my thoughts but was quickly replaced by a sense of happy anticipation that lifted my spirits. I was prepared to face the challenges of a future that looked very promising.

12

My cabin companion was a Pakistani named Sadiq Butt, who was also heading to Bolton College. Later we met Aziz Ahmed, another Pakistani, and Ramesh, an Indian, who were also destined to the same college. The four of us began to hang out together throughout the voyage and became close friends by the time we reached Liverpool. There were approximately twenty-five passengers of different nationalities, including some other Pakistanis and Indian students bound for various learning institutions. The entertainment consisted of Indian, American, and British movies, shown at the discretion of somebody in the management, and one could play games such as Monopoly, Snakes and Ladders, or the Carom board. There was table tennis that I enjoyed while others occupied themselves with playing cards. A fair amount of my time was spent watching the waves, walking around the deck, wondering what the future held.

The SS *Cilicia* was scheduled to call on Port Suez and Port Said in Egypt; Naples, Italy; and then on to Liverpool, United Kingdom. One morning it was announced that we had entered the Red Sea and that there would be an unscheduled stop at Port Sudan in order to take on some cargo. Immediately after breakfast, I rushed outside to witness the crossing of the Red Sea, and the deep blue color of the water surprised me. Somehow I had expected it to be murky green because of its high salinity; instead, the clarity of the water made it appear like a large bowl of blue gelatin, complete with wiggles caused by the slow-moving undercurrents. It was midmorning when the ship docked at the Port Sudan, where the passengers were allowed to disembark for a few hours and see the sights.

After receiving our transit passes, Butt, Aziz, Ramesh, and I stepped off the staircase onto the concrete surface of the dock. It was a welcome escape from the hypnotic clanging of the engine and the swishing sound of the propellers. I had always been curious about other cultures, and this offered me the first opportunity to interact with someone on another continent. The air temperature was 104°F, humid, with a very light breeze, and we spent most of the time walking the street near the harbor. I stopped at a produce store and greeted the storekeeper, *"As-salaam Alaaikum."*

"Wa-Alaaikum-As-Salaam," he responded, the usual greetings of Muslims.

He probably had more knowledge than I had of people from other parts of the world. He immediately asked, "Bakistan?" There is no P in the Arabic alphabet. I could only nod, although I wished to expand our conversation to other subjects, but my knowledge of the Arabic language was restricted to reading the Quran without understanding its meaning. We managed to negotiate to purchase a very large mango. There were over forty varieties of mangoes in the Indo-Pakistan subcontinent, but the size of this mango amazed me. It was as large as an oversized cantaloupe. The street was lined with ethnic restaurants, serving sailors from various countries, and stores catering to the tourist trade.

A man carrying a camera inquired if we wanted to be photographed, promising that the photos would be ready by the departure time and he would deliver them at the entrance to the ship, to which we agreed. We were now a group of six, and each of us paid him in exchange for a card that listed his address. As he shifted our positions around to compose a balanced picture, I placed my mango on a large leaf on the pavement while a few spectators gathered around. It took five or ten minutes before the picture shooting ended, at the conclusion of which I reached for my mango and presto! It was gone. My expression of loss and anger brought laughter from the gallery as an older gentleman explained in broken English that I should be wary of thieves and pickpockets. He warned that these scoundrels prey on unsuspecting tourists, prompting me to look for the photographer, who had evaporated into thin air. We suspected that he had rushed off to develop the film. A horde of enterprising individuals followed us everywhere, attempting to sell an assortment of articles. We waited at the bottom of the stairs for the photos till the last blast of the horn, but there was no sign of the photographer. He and the mango thief were probably sharing their spoils and teaching me a lesson not to part with my money till after I had received the goods.

The stop at Suez was short, mostly to drop off those who desired to take a bus tour through the Pyramids at Giza and Cairo and join up with the ship at Port Said. I would have liked to join the tour, but the lack of funds preempted that desire. We joined up with a convoy of other ships heading north through the canal. As most of its length the canal could only handle one-way traffic, our convoy was instructed to anchor in the holding area of the Great Bitter Lake in order to allow the southbound ships to pass. The temperatures during the late August can rise to 104°F, and the dry, light breeze from the eastern desert, gathering moisture, added to our discomfort. We languished there for four hours in the late afternoon with high humidity. The morning found us docked at Port Said, where we had almost half a day to see the sights. The head steward, also called a purser, advised me that this was a good place to buy a raincoat, as I would need one the moment we arrived in Liverpool. He also informed me that I should not pay more than £2 for a lined London Fog coat.

Butt, Aziz, and I treated ourselves to a lunch of shish kebabs, although they were nothing like the ones in Gujranwala. The restaurant owner, named Hasaani, upon learning that we were from Pakistan, offered us Turkish coffee. I had never before tasted coffee, any kind of coffee. This was black, molasseslike, thick liquid served in tiny cups, and it tasted very bitter. I was humbled by Mr. Hasaani's hospitality and could not refuse the offering; I finished the drink with great difficulty, but as soon as I placed the empty cup on its saucer, it was immediately replenished. I forgot the rule that, if one did not want a refill, one should leave a small amount in the dish or the cup. I added three spoons of sugar and drank some more of the "coffee" before departing. The next task was to purchase a coat, and Hasaani had recommended a friend's store. But before getting there, I visited two other shops, just to be sure about the prices. Each of the stores had racks full of clothes of all sizes and styles, which was something new to me as ready-made clothes had not made their debut in Pakistan. We had to get our clothes made by a tailor. Each of the stores quoted a price that ranged between £3 and £4. Hasaani's friend had the best price, but still higher than what I was willing to pay. I decided to buy just a shirt and forego the purchase of the coat.

I had seen pictures of Sarhan Mosque with its tall minarets, and now I had the opportunity to visit it. The interior walls of the mosque were decorated traditionally with the verses from the Quran in Arabic, created with arranging tiny mosaic tiles. The brilliancy of the colors and the arrangements created a solemn environment. Calmness that I had never experienced before overtook me as I stood in the middle of the main prayer hall. Worries seemed to have been brushed away, replaced by happy thoughts and a high level of confidence. I was lost in my thoughts when I heard someone reminding me that it was time to head for the ship. We passed by the clothing stores that I had visited earlier, and Mr. Hasaani's friend, standing in the doorway of his store, wished me good luck. As I approached the docks, I saw a man carrying a coat on his arm hurrying towards me and then handing me the coat as he said, "The boss says you can have this for one pound and twelve shillings." It was the same coat that I had tried on at the store earlier. This experience was quite different from the one in Sudan.

Four days later we docked at Naples, Italy, where as soon as we set foot on the ground, crowds of vendors began to surround us. Unlike their counterparts in Egypt, these entrepreneurs were more aggressive, peddling everything from expensive watches to fountain pens (the ballpoint variety had not been invented yet) to all kinds of jewelry guaranteed by the sellers to be genuine. These purveyors were persistent and followed us throughout our stay in Naples. The cobblestone streets reminded me of the pathways of Jammu, and the plazas with their fountains and statues offered a paradise for the camera buffs. There was much more to see, but time constraints prevented us from venturing into this beautiful city.

Two days out at sea, the Muslim passengers refused to eat the dessert of the day. Someone had spread a rumor that the dish contained pork products. The head steward requested me to accompany him to meet the captain, who assured me that the food had no pork products and that the management was cognizant of the sensibilities of the Muslims with respect to pork. Mentioning that half of his crewmembers were Muslims from Indonesia, he asked me, as a favor, to convey this to the passengers. I managed to convince the nine men that the captain had guaranteed me that the dessert was pork free, thus ending the protest. A few days away from Liverpool, I suffered from a terrible stomachache, confining me to my cabin. The ship's doctor gave me a medicine that provided some relief.

It was the morning of August 31 when the announcement on the public address system outlined the procedure for disembarkation. I quickly packed my luggage and rushed to the top deck to view the approaching city. The skyline appeared like an outline of a mesa, darkened by the lighter sky in the background; the smoke chimneys protruded above the rooftops, resembling a series of fence posts without the fencing. Sparsely spread in between all that were taller and wider chimneys belching thick smoke, and as the ship neared the dock, the shape of the streets and the houses came into clearer focus. Once the ship was secured, the passengers were ushered into a lobby, where the immigration officials began to inspect the documents. Pakistanis, being citizens of a member state of the British Commonwealth, did not require a visa, thereby obviating the need for an entry stamp. The sky was overcast, and when I stepped off the ship, the light cold drizzle gave me the shivers. The head steward was correct in his advice that I would need the rain coat.

The four of us took a taxi to the railway station, but halfway there I screamed at the driver to take me to a doctor. The stomachache had come back with a vengeance. After a quick examination, the doctor, at an outpatient facility of a local hospital, gave me a bottle containing three doses of a liquid prescription, the kind I used to compound when I impersonated a doctor back at home. It eased the pain, allowing us to continue our journey. We took our seats in a railway car bound for Manchester, where a change of train to Bolton would be required. Although I still had stomach discomfort, we were a happy group commenting about our observations of the land that was new to us. We were speaking in Punjabi. In pre-partition India, most of us had seen an Englishman only from a distance, but here we were among the Britons, who were not the ruling bureaucrats, but average, working-class people, and they were looking at us. One Englishman stood out from among the rest because of his very reddish complexion. One of my companions, discretely pointing to him, commented in Punjabi, "Look at his face; it looks like a monkey's bottom, and he probably was a big boss in India."

The gentleman wore a pleasant smile and did not seem to react to our comments. Most of the passengers displayed friendly smiles, but there were some who were not comfortable in the company of foreigners. As the train approached Manchester, the gentleman with the ruddy face stood up and said in clear Punjabi, "This monkey bids you farewell. You better get off here and change trains. Have a pleasant stay in England." Now it was our turn for red faces, and I, feeling very small, wanted to hide somewhere.

We changed the train and at the same time looked around for the gentleman who was the target of our ridicule. Thank God that he was not on the train to Bolton, because I would not have been able to face him. It was a short ride, but my stomach began to act up again, and by the time we got off the train, I was doubling up with pain. I deposited my luggage in the Left Luggage, a luggage storage facility, and took a taxi directly to the local hospital, where the doctor at the Royal Infirmary decided that I should be admitted for observation. I was given a bed in a ward for twenty patients, ten on each side. The attending physician was a Pakistani named Munir Qureshi, no relation. He ruled out appendicitis and the medicine began to ease my pain, and by the second day I felt back to normal. I wanted to leave the hospital; instead they transferred me to a convalescent hall. That day Mr. and Mrs. Jenkins visited me. He was the principal of the Bolton Community College and thought that I probably was feeling lonely and could use a visitor. He informed me that a room had been reserved for me at a boarding house. He added that some of my friends were also staying there and that I would have a place to go to when discharged from the hospital. I was touched by this act and could not thank him enough. The following day I was discharged.

Transportation to the Broome Street boarding house was provided by the courtesy of the British National Health Services. Along the way I picked up my luggage from the railway station, and as soon as I entered the house, a very heavyset landlady pulled me towards her and gave me a hug, which was not in accordance with the blue book. I was sure that she was speaking English, though I had difficulty recognizing some of the words: "Welcome, luv, yo por dear, we had heard yo was sick. Doun't worry, luv, I'm gona take gud care of ya." I could not understand why she was calling me a loaf.

I was led to my second-story room and was shown the one bathroom down the hall that served four residents. In the absence of any central heating, the fireplace was equipped with some kind of heating system that I had not seen before. Mrs. Riley, the landlady, explained that it was a gas heater and that in order to light it I had to deposit shilling coins in a slot, forgetting to inform me that on a cold day its hunger for coins was insatiable. Sadiq had left a note informing me that he and Ramesh had traveled to London and I could join him at the listed address if I so desired. I decided to take him up on his offer. I felt well enough to travel, and the orientation was not till Friday, September 10. So I decided to take the night train to London. It was Sunday morning when the train began its slow approach to Victoria Station, where the number of train tracks, scattered over more than two lengths of a football field, amazed me. It seemed that many rail lines had not been used for a long time as evidenced by the thick layers of rust. It reminded me that Britain was a world power once and had all the resources of the empire to build extensive network of infrastructures, including railroads, for the convenience of its population. I also understood where the resources of the colonized lands had been spent and why there were overcrowded trains in my country. My thinking was interrupted as the train came to a jerky stop, and, after stepping out of the station, I began to search for the entrance to the Underground, the London subway, also called the Tube. A map on the wall depicted in color all the underground trains, their routes and stops. I took a train to Paddington station and began the search for the street address that I had been given by Sadiq. As I was searching for the house number, a handwritten sign on one of the houses startled me. Under the word vacancy, it read, "No Indians and Dogs Allowed." A wave of anger overtook me, but I managed to ward it off by thinking that some people had not caught up to the reality that India was no longer a British colony.

After meeting up with my friends, we spent the short time we had visiting London Bridge, London Tower, and the British Museum. We walked to Piccadilly Circus, Trafalgar Square, and Buckingham Palace. I had heard about moving stairs, and now I was riding them to various train levels. All these mechanical conveniences intrigued me. As I looked at Westminster, I wondered how this island nation had managed to build an empire where the sun never set. I wanted to see more, but September 10 was approaching fast, and we had no choice but to get back to Bolton.

13

At 9:00 a.m., the orientation began promptly for the nineteen students who came from Greece to Brazil and the lands in between. The only female was one of the four English students. The Syrian and Lebanese came from families that owned factories. The Syrian had his piano shipped from his home, and the movers had to take out a window in his rented apartment in order to deliver it. From the very beginning, the Englishmen made it clear by their attitude that they would not have anything to do with the rest of the class. Mavis, on the other hand, was congenial and outgoing. Unlike colleges in the States where students have to run from one classroom to the other, in Pakistan and now in Bolton, our class was assigned a permanent room. The instructors visited the room to deliver their lectures, and each day we occupied the assigned seat, leaving only when work was required in the laboratories. Sadiq took the seat on my left while Ramesh sat on my right.

At the boarding house, Mrs. Riley gave us a warning about inviting girls into the house and told us to wear a dressing gown even at night when going to the bathroom, the excessive use of which was not allowed. One morning she asked if any of us had a stomach problem because someone was going to the bathroom too many times. There was a squeaky floor plank just in front of the bathroom, and she could hear the noise from her room below. We had to give her at least one day's notice when we desired to take a bath. The hot water tank was installed in the chimney, and in order to heat the water, the fireplace had to be lit. Lucky for me, I found a public bathhouse near the college where ten pennies got me a fresh towel, a bar of soap, and the use of a bathroom fully equipped with a tub and a shower.

Daily breakfast consisted of toast, fried tomatoes, a boiled egg, a cup of tea, and some pastry. There was a cafeteria at the campus that served a hearty lunch and high tea in the late afternoon. Tea, as coffee is in the United States of America, was the brew of choice and accompanied every meal. "High tea" is a misnomer because it really is an early evening dinner. Our high tea consisted of slices of meat, potatoes, and vegetables, all boiled and very bland, and to give it some taste I used to load it up with ground black pepper. By eight in the evening, hunger pangs would force us to walk to Bradshaw Gate for a sandwich, straining our budgets.

Sadiq and I were not happy with this arrangement and began to entertain the idea of moving to some other location. That decision came easy one day when, while at the market, I saw Mrs. Riley purchasing a large quantity of sliced horse meat and later found the wrapping in her trash bin. This knowledge led us to seek other abodes, and one week later we moved to two rooms at a boarding house that was owned by a Hungarian widow. Although it was some distance away from the college, her Hungarian goulash was worth a "tupence haypanee" (two and a half pence) bus ride to the college. When the owner began to impose her religious views, we moved to the corner house on Russell Street that became my home for the rest of my stay in Bolton. The rent was reasonable for a furnished room with linen service and the use of kitchen and the bathroom. There was a fireplace in the room that burned coal. The landlady, living in the adjoining house with her husband and their three-year-old daughter, suggested that I get the required permit from the city to buy the coal. Two days later I found my pile of it in the shared rear courtyard.

The weather in England was something that I had never encountered before. During the fall and the winter, overcast skies poured down fine mist that was frequently accentuated by snow and sleet. Rain showers and the sun played hide and seek during the spring, and the summer season saw clear skies and warm temperatures interrupted by the occasional downpour. I wore my raincoat and a hat almost all the time and carried an umbrella whenever thick clouds portended rain. The umbrella came in handy when Sadiq and I had to wait for two hours in pouring rain in order to see *Hollywood or Bust* at the Ritz Cinema. During the first winter, when the rain turned to snow, Sadiq, Aziz, and Ramesh could not contain their excitement, as they had not seen snow before. A thin layer of ice coated the streets, and it was comical when the three of them slipped while crossing the street and fell like dominoes. I had learned how to handle the white stuff while living in Srinagar, where I used to chase *Apa Asghari* through two feet of it.

The buildings were covered with a thick layer of black coating, probably the ash spewing out from the chimneys of the textile factories that used coal to produce steam. One winter month the city was engulfed in a thick fog, and the coal ash added to the misery. The visibility was reduced to no more than a foot, and people were ordered to stay indoors while the factories were closed. If one had to go out, it was recommended to take a flash light in order to avoid a collision. My handkerchief would have black soot on it each time I blew my nose. After suffering for three days, a heavy downpour was a welcome relief.

My first attempt at making a coal fire ended up in a disaster when the smoke, instead of going up the chimney, began to blow back into the room. Instead of alleviating the problem, pouring a little water on the burning newspapers only added to the chaos. Although opening the windows offered a more convenient escape for the smoke, the smell lingered long after the room had cleared. I learned that I should have opened the damper, and that for the coal to catch fire, it was necessary to create a draft up the chimney. To accomplish this, I had to hold a lit newspaper high in the fireplace and as close to the chimney as possible. After a few unsuccessful attempts, I finally heard the swooshing sound of the air rushing up the chimney and saw the color of the coal turning from black to orange red. Warmth began to radiate as the flames engulfed the pile of the coal in the fireplace. But the warmth confined itself only in the close proximity of the fireplace, as the chimney began to suck the cold air from the crevices around the ill-fitted door and the windows. As a result, the front of the body felt warm while the back shivered with cold, requiring a blanket. Whenever Sadiq and I went out for the evening, I would forego the fire-making ritual and, as was customary, used a hot water bottle to warm the bed. It was said that the French use sex while the English use the hot water bottle to warm their beds, and I was in England.

The classes started in earnest on September 13, 1954. We wore suits or slacks and jackets with ties in class, and the teachers addressed us by our last names. I had to get used to being called "Qurashi" instead of "Doctor Sahib" or "Maulvi Sahib." It also took some time before I grasped the Lancashire dialect and idiom and "cheerio" or "ta ta, luv" became part of my vernacular.

Frequently, I attended the local Foreign Students Association meetings. Each month the college authorities held an alcohol-free dance party in the activities center. Sadiq had an outgoing disposition and had no problem hopping around with a girl pretending to be dancing. I could not do this. It was difficult for me to approach an unacquainted girl, and not knowing how to dance did not help much. I wanted to be able to dance since I had watched Fred Astaire and Ginger Roger in the movies, so I decided to take a few lessons at the local dance school.

While dancing required an effort on my part, the college work came easy for me. I was receiving high grades without too much effort and frequently exchanged the top of the class position with one of the English students, who displayed a high level of anxiety when the instructors gave out the test scores. He would argue with the instructor whenever I bettered him in a test, which was quite often. He got the last laugh, though, when he graduated on top of the class, which was not a big deal for me.

Many times I accompanied Sadiq to a local dance hall called Palais de Dance (Dancing Palace). Always well attended, it was the gathering place for young people. It was a very large hall with balconies where soft drinks, coffee, and pastry were served. For the cost of a few shillings, one could enjoy dancing to the music of an orchestra playing real instruments. Tables and chairs were set up around an expansive dance floor where one could sit while sipping soft drinks. Wednesdays were set aside for American dances such as swing or jiving, while on Saturdays the orchestras played only English and Latin ballroom dance music, attracting large crowds. It was in the spring of 1955 when Sadiq and I decided to spend the evening at the local Palais de Dance. Sadiq was roaming the floor for a possible date and, while sitting at a table by myself, I was scanning the people at other tables. Suddenly my gaze froze on a face that became visible for a split second through the shifting human shapes. It seemed like someone had opened a window. That instant a voice within me declared, “That is the one.” By the time I could muster enough courage to approach the table, no one was there. I went back to the Palais two or three times to look for her without success. In the meantime I got busy preparing for the end-of-the-semester exams.

Many of the students scattered to spend their summer vacations away from Bolton, but my finances restricted me to day trips to Blackpool or Southport. In order to make some extra money to support my hobby of photography, I got a night job at an ice cream factory that made ice cream sandwiches, a slice of ice cream between two wafers. My shift began at 10:00 p.m. and ended at 8:00 a.m. the following morning. The process began with the cutting of a large block of ice cream into the sandwich-sized strips. Next two wafers were slapped on each side of the strip, followed by the wrapping of the single sandwich that was transported to my station. My job was transferring a stack of six sandwiches from the belt on my left to the machine on my right for six-pack wrapping. One evening the failure of the cutting machine created chaos in the subsequent workstations, and one block of ice cream after another invaded my station with a vengeance. I had to jump off my stool as the blocks of ice cream tumbled off the belt onto the floor. A pile of four or five blocks lay on the floor before the machine could be stopped, and I had to step out of the building to get some fresh air in order to avoid getting sick because of the concentrated smell of vanilla. After that incident, I could not bring myself to return to the factory, nor could I eat the ice cream for many years to come.

One Friday during late July, Sadiq asked, "What are you doing tomorrow?"

"Not much. Do you have something in mind?"

"I want to go to Southport with this girl I met, but she does not want to leave her friend alone. We need you to join us to make a foursome."

"I hope she is not some fat girl who cannot get a date, but no matter, I will go with you. I have nothing else to do," I said.

Friday night I went to the bathhouse to shower, and I shaved on the following morning before accompanying Sadiq to the bus stop at 9:00 a.m. As we turned left on New Chorley Road to go to the meeting place, I saw two girls waiting there. As we approached them, I felt a twinge—one of the girls was the very one whose face I had seen at the Palais. I prayed that she would be my date and not that of Sadiq. He looked at the other girl and said, "This is Brunhilde."

As I extended my hand, he told her, "He is Qurashi."

All this time the pounding in my chest was reaching a crescendo while my eyes were fixed on the face of the first girl. Finally, while looking at me, Brunhilde said, "Meet Reinhild, your date," adding, "Thanks for coming at such a short notice."

Recovering from my paralyzed state, I managed to ask if they were from Germany. Both of them answered, "Ja."

I said something like, "I always wanted to learn more about Germany."

"India has always fascinated me," Reinhild said. The bus had arrived and we boarded the double-decker, climbing to the upper level where we took our seats. This was the same route that I took every morning to college, and the Trinity Street Station was across from the stop. We arrived just in time for the 9:45 train to Southport.

It was a warm and sunny day, and fifty minutes later we walked from the Southport Railway Station to the Promenade and the amusement area on the beach. We strolled around the beach in our bare feet and had a tasty lunch of fish and chips at a local restaurant. Later we rode on a roller coaster and other contraptions created to give the riders an adrenaline rush. The roller coasters of the time were simple compared to the ones at present that scale dizzying heights and have inverted loops. Finally, we ended up at the tea-cup carousal where the cups, with seats, whipped around as the platform under them traveled in a circle. Sadiq and Brunhilde occupied one cup and Reinhild and I jumped into another. Half of the cup was covered by a canopy, and I felt that the setting was perfect for me to take a chance in getting closer to Reinhild. My feeling was misguided, as I was reminded that we hardly knew each other. We passed the rest of the day engaged in small talk, and back in Bolton in the evening, Sadiq and I walked them to the entrance of the nurses' living quarters. I did manage to get the phone number where I could reach her.

I discovered that Reinhild and her friend were nurses in training at the Royal Infirmary that was not far from where we lived, and they were living at the dormitories provided by the hospital. A few days after our Southport trip, I rang the number from one of the red public phone booths. Not recognizing the person who answered the phone, I asked if I could talk to Nurse Rümenap, her maiden name, without success. When more of my phone calls went unanswered, I persuaded Sadiq to arrange for another double date. The following day he informed me she had agreed to join us for a movie. I was so happy to see Reinhild again, not knowing if she reciprocated my feelings. Lucky for me, we had to wait in line for over an hour to get in the cinema playing *Doctor in the House*, a comedy. That allowed us to exchange our life histories.

"Where do you live in Germany?" I asked.

"Near Göttingen in a village called Sattenhausen," she replied.

"Have you lived there all the time?" I asked.

"We came there as refugees from an area that used to be in the eastern part of Germany," she explained and asked, "Where do you live in Pakistan?"

I explained to her how my family ended up in Gujranwala. She said, "My father was also killed during the war in 1944 in

Normandy. At the time we lived in Liegnitz, and when Germany was divided after the conclusion of the war, it was given to Poland." Then she recounted the circumstances that brought her family to Sattenhausen.

The airport at Liegnitz had been converted into an air base where Stuka bombers were stationed to serve the Eastern Front. Her father was employed there before joining the war effort. She was two months shy of ten in January 1945 when airport officials advised her mother that as the surviving family of a former employee, they could get space on the train leaving the city for the western part of the country. Her sick mother, older sister, Renate, younger brother, Reinhart, and she, along with a caretaker friend, boarded the last train that was leaving the city. It was bitter cold with a few feet of snow on the ground. Their destination was Göttingen, where her mother's father lived. The train's forward progress was continually interrupted, as the only available locomotive had to alternate between moving the cars with civilians and the cars loaded with the disassembled planes which had to be delivered to the West. Nobody was prepared to spend five days on a trip that in normal circumstances would have taken only half a day. There was no food or water, and one day when the train was stopped, a few women walked to a nearby farm for help. In exchange for contributions from the passengers, the farmers gave them a hurriedly made mixture of flour and hot water in large milk cans. Luckily, her mother had picked up a jar of cherries that she had preserved, and it came in handy to enhance the taste of the flour mixture by adding the contents of the jar into the "soup." Her grandfather, having remarried, was not as generous as my grandparents were. As a consequence, they ended up at the high school in Göttingen that her mother had attended. It had been converted into a receiving station for the refugees, who were mostly women and children, as the men had gone to the war front. The authorities would load up a few families on a truck and drive to the farmland, where they would locate a farm that could house one or two families. Her family ended up at the Müller farm in Sattenhausen, a village about sixteen kilometers from the city of Göttingen. They were given two rooms above the laundry and, because of her mother's sickness, all the children had to work in the fields in exchange for food. Later in their teens, Reinhild and her siblings began to receive monetary compensation.

My trials after losing our home and father in Jammu paled when compared to her hardships. I never experienced hunger as her family did during their ordeal. This exchange brought us closer, and we began to take comfort in each other's company. I was regularly invited as her guest to the nurses' monthly dance party at their recreational facility, known as the Bridgehouse, and she accompanied me at the college dance parties. Many evenings we sat in front of the fire in my room and toasted bread for a snack. The head nurse, known as Head Sister, in charge of the dormitories had strict rules whereby the doors were locked promptly at 10:30 at night followed by a head count. Permission from Head Sister was needed if any nurse desired to stay out past that time. It was a hassle for Reinhild to ask for the key to the front door when one day the four of us went to the movies. Instead of requesting the pass, Reinhild left one of the lounge windows open a crack. I could not understand why all public transportation, including taxis, stopped at 10:30 p.m. while the movies ended at 11:00. That was the time when we returned from the movies that night and we had to sneak through an opening between a brick fence and a hedge of bushes before we could reach the open window, where the ladies needed a lift to reach the ledge. By this time it was becoming clear that Cupid was having a field day.

I was falling in love.

14

During the early month of December, the Liverpool Symphony Orchestra was making an appearance at the Bolton Hippodrome to play Handel's *Messiah.* One of the teachers at the college arranged for our class to attend the recital. With Reinhild sitting next to me, it was a memorable experience that led me to appreciate Western classical music. We began to see each other more frequently, and she would come over during her breaks at the Royal Infirmary whenever I was at my room. Many times Sadiq and Brunhilde would join us for a double date. I was in a joyous state each time I was with Reinhild. On December 16, 1955, Reinhild, Brunhilde, and Renate left for Germany on a three weeks' vacation. I saw the group off at the railway station and walked back to my room with a feeling of emptiness. Although we wrote to each other every day, I had never felt so lonely. It became a game with my friends, who would hold her letter as a hostage in exchange for a promise to help them with their studies. Her letters were reciprocating my feelings. The college had also closed for the Christmas holidays, which made the separation unbearable. In order to divert my attention, I took a job with the local post office delivering parcels. The postman to whom I was assigned was very helpful, and one evening after we had delivered the last package, he invited me to join his family for supper. It was a wonderful experience meeting a working English family.

Once my work with the post office was over, Sadiq and I took a trip to London. It was supposed to ease my blues; instead it only intensified the longing as I watched young couples moving about in the streets of London. By the time we returned to Bolton, it became clear that I needed to take a trip to Germany. By the end of the year I had earned enough money from my job with the postal service to afford the trip. I was bitten by a love bug, and rational thinking was out of the question. In her absence, it felt as if a part of me was missing, leading me to realize that love could be a tormentor. I had to be with Reinhild.

After receiving the transit visa from the Belgian consulate in Manchester, I informed her by a telegram about my arrival in Germany on the seventh of January. I took the night ferry from Dover in England to Antwerp, Belgium, where I boarded a train to Göttingen, arriving there late morning. The telegram missed her in Sattenhausen because Reinhild and Renate had gone to a relative in Göttingen for the night, and by the time her mother attempted to contact them, the sisters were already on the bus back to the village. I was excited in anticipation of a warm embrace as I descended the stairs from the platform. My search for the familiar face among the throngs of people was unsuccessful. An elderly lady approached me and, in broken English, asked if I was Mr. Qurashi. Her words conveyed the message that she was Reinhild's grandmother and that Reinhild would come in the afternoon. Probably thinking that I was a person of means, she assisted me to check into the Bahnhof Hotel to wait till the afternoon. After a long journey, I was hungry and tired, in that order, and with money left over after paying for the trip decided to have lunch at the restaurant. Halfway through it, Reinhild and Renate arrived and, unable to contain my excitement, the hunger and tiredness disappeared and I jumped off my seat and put my arms around her. I did not know how long we had held each other when Renate reminded her that it was time to catch the next bus.

An hour later we arrived in the small farm village. As I was led up a set of steep stairs, I heard an insistent bark of a dog. I was warned that Puck, the dog, did not like strangers and that it had already bitten someone. It was a small two-room apartment. The small room was the parlor, where a nice couch awaited the visitors. Reinhild held Puck back as I entered the room. As soon as she released the chain, Puck came in and put his head on my feet. I felt that it was an encouraging sign that the family pooch had accepted me. I would spend my next five nights in that room. I met *Mutti*, the mother, and Reinhart, the brother, the latter attending high school. The resourcefulness of the family was praiseworthy. Before the children could work in the fields, *Mutti* tutored the farmers' children in exchange for food and also read cards to provide solace to the women who were seeking the whereabouts of their husbands missing in the war. One day we took a bus ride to Göttingen, the city famous for its university, where we were invited to dine with her step-grandmother, Omi. Her specialty was steamed brussels sprouts, and in order to be polite I mentioned that I liked the vegetable, which was a mistake, because as soon as I finished the offering, it was quickly replenished, and to this day I have difficulty eating sprouts.

Reinhild and I, along with Brunhilde and her brother, Dieter, returned to Bolton on January 12. The day I returned to the class, I was summoned to the office of Professor Robinson, the dean, who reprimanded me for skipping the classes and told me that he had received an inquiry from my brother about my whereabouts and suggested that I write to him immediately. I had neglected to correspond with my family, so I wrote a long letter apologizing for my tardiness but did not mention about my affair of the heart. I felt that such news had to be delivered in person. At that time in my culture, love was expected to bloom after a marriage that was usually arranged in order to expand the influences of the family.

On Reinhild's twenty-first birthday, I proposed to her and we got married immediately after the completion of my studies. Many Indians and Pakistanis had married local girls and returned home without them. Although the licensing bureau had a pamphlet warning girls about marrying the foreign students, it did not deter Reinhild because of our love for each other. It was raining cats and dogs on the day we got married in the simplest wedding ceremony conducted by a registrar, which did not matter because of our mutual trust and commitment to each other. I prepared chicken curry and a rice dish for our reception. We anticipated our life together to begin in Pakistan as soon as I got a job. Therefore, she continued to live at the nurses' quarters during rest of her stay in Bolton, although we were together most of the time. Somewhere during that time my wife became pregnant, after which I embarked on my journey back to Pakistan. Although the lack of funds was one of the reasons for her not accompanying me, the other was that it would be easier to explain personally to my family in Pakistan about my marriage to a German Christian girl. So I promised Reinhild that I would send her a ticket as soon as I got a job and had a talk with my family.

On July 27, 1956, with a heavy heart, I boarded the train to Dover. As the train began to move, Reinhild walked next to it and then began to run as the train accelerated. I was concerned about her pregnancy and tried to gesture to her to stop running. Finally she stopped as the end of platform approached, and the image of her standing there as the train rounded the corner is still planted in my brain. On August 30, after receiving her certificate as a graduate nurse, she left for Germany to prepare for her journey to Pakistan.

The vacation season had begun, and the crowds were queuing up everywhere to get to their destinations. There were more passengers than available seats in the ferry from Dover, United Kingdom, to Holland, forcing me to sit on my heavy trunk, stowed in an empty corner, in the hope of getting some sleep during the night crossing. A few minutes later I was awakened as the English Channel, living up to its reputation, battered the boat, which pitched and rolled during most of the journey. After docking at Hook von Holland, I took a train to Köln (Cologne), Germany, where I used the two-hour wait to tour the war-battered cathedral, still displaying its grandeur with its high spires. I had been pulling my heavy trunk on a set of strap-on, two-inch wheels only eight inches apart; the modern luggage with built-in wheels had not been invented yet. The straps were made of jute, which stretched with each pull as I maneuvered the trunk through the crowds at train stations. The bumps, and there were many due to the uneven surfaces, made the trunk slide to the right or to the left, challenging my physical strength. Finally I decided to transfer the responsibility of my luggage to the railroad personnel before boarding the train for Basle, Switzerland. My trunk and I would join up again at the pier in Genoa, Italy. This way I could enjoy the views of the Swiss Alps and Lake Geneva through the windows of the fleeting train.

I arrived at the Genoa train station at noon, and the statue of Columbus greeted me as I stepped out of the building. I hailed a taxi and asked the driver, “Hotelo Porto?”

I had converted a few of the British pounds into Italian liras at the Thomas Cook Agency before leaving England, and as the smallest note was five thousand liras, I had hundreds of them. The taxi ride to the hotel, which was not very far, came to about twelve thousand liras. The driver gave me some aluminum coins in change. The hotel was a three-story stone building, the lobby of which was decorated with heavy tapestry drapes in gold, red, and yellow. My room was small, with a space large enough for a single bed, a wardrobe, and a corner table supporting a basin and a large jug of water, and my key would allow me access to the toilet located down the hallway. After settling down in my room and consuming a pasta dinner, I went for a walk around the city’s cobblestone streets. I’d had a passion for watching movies ever since I saw *King Solomon’s Mines* in the forties. So I ended up in a cinema playing *Robin Hood* with Errol Flynn that I had not seen before. It was dubbed in Italian with English subtitles, and I had to chuckle as soon as Robin Hood opened his mouth and a squeaky voice filled the theater, far removed from Errol Flynn's own voice that I had heard earlier in *Destination Burma.* Watching the movie passed the evening and temporarily eased the pain of separation from Reinhild.

The breakfast was included in the price of the room, and in the morning I was introduced to spaghetti and sauce. Having no experience in eating this Italian staple in the past, each time I attempted to pick up the strands with my fork, they kept slipping away before the fork could reach its destination. A couple seated next to me must have noticed my lack of spaghetti technique. The man, approaching my table, said in a heavy German accent, "It seems that you have not eaten spaghetti before. It is easy if you use the spoon."

He showed me how to rotate my fork in the spoon in order to wrap the strands around the fork. The same could have been accomplished more efficiently by using the God-given fork with flexible prongs called hands. My spaghetti instructor, along with his wife and a three-year-old daughter, were returning to his job in Kabul, Afghanistan, after their vacation. He was a civil engineer and recommended that I take an inexpensive day trip to Santa Margherita Ligure, a fishing village.

I had a whole day to kill, so I took his advice and the hotel concierge directed me to the tour bus. It was a two-hour journey on a narrow, mountainous road having vertical drops of five hundred to eight hundred feet, with no guard rails or stone barriers. That did not deter the bus driver from passing slow-moving cars driven by timid vacationers. I made a comment about the driver's manner of driving, mostly to myself, but in response, one of the passengers from England told me a story that confirmed the recklessness of the drivers of the region. It was a very foggy day when the drivers of two buses were looking at the road ahead by sticking their heads outside the side windows. They were driving in the opposite direction and the visibility was so bad that one could not see the other approaching. Luckily none of the passengers were hurt as the heads of the drivers collided, although I am sure they had headaches for many days. I remembered reading about this in a newspaper in Bolton.

As the bus began its descent towards the town, the deep blue color of the Gulf of Tigulia presented itself in its full brilliance. Soon after, the view expanded to include clusters of homes built in the side of the hills surrounding a crescent-shaped beach. At one end of the beach were marinas, deserted at the time by the fishing boats that had sailed out to sea for the day. Behind the marinas, the fishing nets were hung to dry on tall poles. This village lacked the usual tourist traps, and it had only one general store and a small bistro where I had a delicious lunch without the spaghetti. There was a small church on top of one of the hills, and it was built in such a way that while complete darkness engulfed the interior, the statue of Christ behind the altar was illuminated by a ray of sun piercing through the only skylight. It made a memorable picture, and this little village was an answer to a photographer's prayers. It was a pleasing experience that I would very much have liked to have shared with Reinhild.

On July 30, 1956, I walked from the hotel to the pier to claim my trunk, and although I had paid in advance in Germany for its transportation, the Italian authorities demanded another fourteen thousand liras. I was told that this payment was to cover the expenses to move it from the railway station to the customs at the pier, contrary to the entry on the receipt. But lacking the Italian language skill, I had to acquiesce to their demand before I could board the ship. After clearing customs and immigration, I finally entered the ship that left Genoa late in the afternoon on its way to Karachi. The passengers hailed from many parts of the world; there were Pakistanis, Indians, Germans, and even some Japanese. We sailed by the Island of Corsica late after dinner and arrived at Naples early in the morning of July 31. We had a whole day to ourselves, and the ship's purser advised us that a trip to the ruins of Pompeii should provide great photo opportunities. Our small group followed that advice and boarded a bus for a guided tour.

An hour later we stepped off the bus in front of a gate that led us to the Forum, an open area adjacent to what had been the governmental buildings, typical of the Roman cities of the time. It provided a place for the citizens to worship their deities and also to market their wares. In 79 CE, Vesuvius erupted with a vengeance destroying most of the city of forty thousand inhabitants. The remnants bore witness to its grandeur. There were stone-paved alleys emanating from plazas and squares. Lines of tall columns stood there as if seeking their burden that had been wiped away, yet the ash that choked the human life preserved the frescoes on the walls of the buildings that survived. Amazingly, a brothel was completely intact. The entrance to this house of ill repute opened into a large hall that was lined with small rooms where the women practiced their trade. The preserved paintings on the walls depicted the many ways one could experience the act. The guide stated that "God saved this building in order to remind human beings that these types of activities will bring his wrath."

The explicit sexual artwork in the villas and the bathhouses supported his views. One of the frescos in the entrance to a large villa caught my attention, as the colors looked as fresh as if the artist had just completed his work. Not a single blemish was visible, but it was the subject matter that really shook my senses. Priapus, the Greek god of fertility, in a larger than life portrait was depicted weighing his oversized phallus. It appeared that the inhabitants of this doomed city loved art rich in sexual themes and were engaged in a prosperous lifestyle. The city also had a well-planned infrastructure of streets and a very practical water delivery system. As I boarded the bus to Naples, I attempted to visualize the panic-stricken inhabitants struggling to stay alive in an ash-laden atmosphere without any air. What a terrible way to die. My thoughts were interrupted when the bus had come to a complete stop and I heard one of the passengers calling, "Qurashi! It is time to board the ship."

As I write this, the guide's statement of the time past begs the question, "Should we be worrying about a calamity of perhaps greater proportions, as our culture is being proliferated by sexual abuses and pornography?"

The ship negotiated through the Tyrrhenian Sea around Sicily into the Mediterranean. We crossed the Suez Canal and the Red Sea and, on August 7, 1956, arrived at Port Aden, then a British colony and a free port. Unlike many passengers, I could not afford to purchase any of the beautiful articles available at very attractive prices. My mind was occupied with problems such as finding a job and, toughest of all, informing my family about my married status. My anxiety level climbed exponentially as the ship approached Pakistan. It was August 11; I stepped ashore at the harbor of Karachi exactly two years after my departure. Uncle Afzal was waiting for me outside the customs, and after exchanging pleasantries we began our trip to his home. As I looked out of his car's window, the sight of dusty streets and shabby stores engulfed me with a wave of depression. He was asking many questions, but I did not feel very communicative. Finally he said, "We will talk tomorrow after you have had a night's rest, as you must be tired."

I looked forward to a home-cooked meal after a long time, and my aunt had prepared a nice dinner, during which my responses to Uncle Afzal's many questions were robotic. I could not sleep during the night.

15

I arrived in Gujranwala in the afternoon of August 12. *Bhaijee Manzoor* and Masood were at the railway station waiting for me. It was an emotional reunion as we hugged each other. At home *Bayjee* and *Bhabijee* were waiting with anticipation, and they wanted to see my diploma. I decided to lighten the situation and showed them a certificate I had received when I was placed third in a ballroom dancing contest. I saw my brother's demeanor change from excitement to rage when he stated, "I knew you would not finish your studies. When are you going…"

I interrupted him and snatched the paper from his hands, replacing it with my diploma that declared that I had graduated in second place. My real task was to begin in earnest on Monday. I had never looked for a job before and did not know how to proceed. The people that I knew had found their employment through personal contacts, and we immediately began a search for such a person. In the meantime, I had to stay in Gujranwala. I did send a letter to Mr. Parr at the Sutlej Textile Mills in Okara, in response to which I was informed by the works manager that Mr. Parr had left his position and that presently no suitable position was available.

Being a doctor, *Bhaijee* was allowed to have a phone line at the clinic and at the house. One day while I was at home, the phone rang, and at the other end was my brother asking me to come to his office. When I got there, I was anticipating an introduction to somebody who would assist me in finding a job, but instead, pointing to a patient, he said, "You remember Ali Sahib? He was *your* patient when you practiced here. He will only consult with you."

I shook hands with Mr. Ali and asked him, "Tell me what was wrong with you when I saw you last time."

"I had a very bad stomachache and your medicine cured it. I know you went to England to study and that you are probably more expensive now." I tried to interrupt him, but, pointing to *Bhaijee*, he continued, "This doctor won't let me see you, and I am willing to pay your higher fees."

I replied, "I went to England to study engineering and I have given up medical practice." Pointing to *Bhaijee,* I continued, "But you should be happy to know that everything he knows about medicine, I taught him, and you can trust him without fear." Ali was disappointed, but as he turned to look at my brother, he stated to me, "You were such a good doctor—why did you have to give it up?"

A few days later I got an offer from a textile mill in Jahengira near the city of Peshawar in the North West Frontier Province. The position was in the weaving department as assistant weaving master. Although I would have preferred to work in the yarn-spinning department, I accepted the offer in order to hasten the day of my reunion with Reinhild. It was a small mill, nothing like the one in Okara. But it would serve my needs for now. After a few weeks, I decided to take a weekend and share my secret with my family in Gujranwala.

I was very nervous when I arrived home late on a Friday evening. *Bayjee,* being a mother, immediately noticed my stressed demeanor and asked, "What is the matter?"

I decided that it was time that I broke the news and called all the members of the family to join me. When everybody was seated,

I began, "In England, I met a German girl and we fell in love. I want to let you know that I am married to her and am asking for your acceptance and support so she can come here."

The silence was deafening. It seemed like an eternity before *Bhaijee* looked at *Bayjee* and loudly pronounced, "I knew something was up because of the letters you have been getting from Germany. You could have told us earlier." I affirmed that, and before I could continue, he asked, "Can we get it annulled? We can pay her whatever she wants. You can have your pick here from rich and respectable families."

I was hurt by his statements and became enraged and walked out of the room stating, "I love her and she is pregnant, and there is no way anybody is going to force me to give them up."

I left the house for the railway station to catch the next train to Jahengira that was due in two hours. As I was waiting there, Masood arrived with a message from *Bayjee*. He said, "*Bayjee* wants you to come back so we can work something out." I told him that I was too upset to go back now but I would return next weekend. I showed him Reinhild's picture from my wallet. He looked at me affectionately and said, "I am looking forward to meeting her, and I will explain the situation to *Apa Anwari* and Uncle Saleem." I knew I could count on their support. He stayed with me till my departure.

The news of my married status spread throughout my extended family, and all of them descended on Gujranwala to have a family discussion. By the time I returned the following weekend, it seemed that the family had come to a decision. In the meantime, I had also made up my mind to return to Bolton in the event I did not get any support from the family, but before I could explain my position, *Apa Anwari*, with her typical encouraging smile, said, "It is high time that new blood came into our family. I have heard good things about German girls."

It appeared that *Bhaijee* had been outvoted and had to acquiesce. He, with a smile, asked me to drive him to Lahore, where he was boarding a train to Karachi. While driving, we had a chance to talk, and after I showed him his sister-in-law's picture and informed him that she was a certified nurse, his demeanor changed. He agreed to my request for a loan to pay for her travel. Immediately after that, I contacted the Thomas Cook Travel Agency to arrange for Reinhild to take the next available passage. I was happy and looked forward to her arrival on October 14, 1956.

The weaving department at the mill was a recent addition, while the yarn spinning had existed for at least two years. The first task was to establish standards for anticipated production against which I could determine the efficiency of the daily output. At the beginning, the efficiency was poor, mostly because of poor training of the workers. I had explained this situation to the management and had informed them of my goal to achieve 95 percent efficiency by the sixth month. The managing director could not understand why I did not aim for the 115 percent efficiency that Yusuf Khan, the spinning master, was achieving. I, self-assured because of my education, explained tactlessly that there was no such thing as 115 percent efficiency because it was practically impossible to exceed the theoretical production. In another meeting I suggested that we might recalculate the efficiency standards in order to assure real progress, but the young director, with no formal technical training, objected to it because he had been grounded in misinformation and, by following my suggestion, he would be acknowledging his ignorance. Later it appeared that I had created an adversary in the person of Mr. Khan, who immediately began his plotting against me.

As I was getting to know all my charges, I met a young man named Dastoor Ali, and when I asked him what he did in my department, he became belligerent and outright insulting, leaving me no choice but to fire him. What I did not know at that moment was that he was employed in order to gain the favors of his father, who was the head of the local dominant tribe. He did whatever he pleased while the management and supervisory staff looked the other way. Later I discovered that he was planted in my department by Mr. Khan, who expected me to discharge Dastoor Ali, who advised me that I would regret my decision. Mr. Khan reinforced the threat when he told me, "The tribe is very protective of their own and has been known to get violent."

My attempts to shake his statement during the rest of the day bore no fruits, and when, at the end of the day, I stepped out of the building, there were about ten armed men threateningly facing the door. It was a fearful moment, and I expected the worst when an elderly man with a graying beard broke from the group and began to approach me. I heaved a sigh of relief when I saw his extended right hand, a nonthreatening gesture. I responded by shaking his hand as he said, "*As-Salaam-Alaaikum*," and continued, "I am told that you are the one who discharged my son."

I responded, "Yes, I had to do it."

"Dastoor is a spoiled child who is catered to by everybody and needed to be taught a lesson. I thank you for doing that. My brothers and I invite you to honor us with your presence at our family dinner on Friday."

I could see Khan, observing the unfolding drama through the window of his office, displaying an expression of disappointment. After that, I began to feel that my position at the mill was becoming tenable, although the works manager assured me that there was nothing to worry about. The job was far from my mind as I was counting the days till Reinhild's arrival on the SS *Batory*, a Polish ship on its last voyage.

I arrived at the Karachi harbor on October 14 just in time to see the first passenger stepping off the stairs of the ship. There were moments of concern because Egypt, after having nationalized the canal and in response to the military threats, had begun a strict freight inspection regimen that had slowed the traffic. The SS *Batory* was the last ship that safely crossed the canal before Egypt blocked its entrance by sinking forty ships in retaliation to the attack on Port Said by Britain, France, and Israel. My anxiety was getting the best of me when I saw the familiar face that my eyes had been longing for. She was carefully descending the stairs with a cigarette in her hand and, stepping forward, I put my arms around her and whispered, "I missed you."

When I informed her that there was a taboo on smoking in our family, she immediately discarded the cigarette along with the packet into the sea and never asked for one again. This was not the first adjustment she would be called upon to make. When I decided to return to Pakistan, I had not realized how many cultural and lifestyle changes would be imposed upon her. While waiting for the luggage in the customs area, she introduced me to some of the Pakistani cricket team members who had been looking after her throughout her voyage.

We traveled by train in the second class from Karachi to Gujranwala, arriving in the afternoon, and left the following morning after the introductions. The works manager had promised to send the company car to meet us in Rawalpindi, but no one was there as we stepped out of the railway station. We had to impose upon a friend to spend the night at his house before leaving for Jahengira in the morning. The lack of funds forced us to travel in the third class, where Reinhild had to ride in the car set aside for women. I got off the train at each stop and walked up to her compartment to make sure that she had not been bothered by other passengers, knowing that it might have been the most harrowing experience for her, but she did not complain, and we made it to our destination.

Our two-bedroom house, provided by the company, suffered from furniture famine. There were no modern conveniences in the kitchen, and for cooking one had to make a wood fire in an improvised brick fireplace that could support a pot. Most management personnel had hired cooks, but being the junior member of the team, I could not afford one. Reinhild quickly got used to it, except that she did not know how to cook the local food, and fried beef patties and potatoes became our daily dinner menu. All these inconveniences did not matter much as long as we were together. At the office I began to feel the pressures of Mr. Khan's attempts at discrediting me, and by early December the new young director, a son of the owner, decided that I was not a team player. I should have foreseen these events when the company car did not show up in Rawalpindi. It was the first week of December when we left Jahengira and ended up back at Gujranwala. Reinhild offered to assist *Bhaijee Manzoor* in his clinic, and at one time she assisted him in resetting a broken arm. I had to travel in search of a job, but whenever I was home, Reinhild and I took evening walks to the new house that *Bhaijee* was building in the suburb of Gujranwala. We were always followed by a few curious people who had never seen a European woman before.

Standing: Masood; Maqbool; Bhaijee Manzoor, d 2004
Seated: Apa Anwari, d 2008; Bayjee, d 1983; Bhabijee
1954 before departure for Bolton

Reinhild & Maqbool: 1955

Reinhild, Ronnie, Maqbool
1958 at Müller Farm

Maqbool, Ronnie, Reinhild
1960 SS America, Captain's dinner

Mutti,
mother-in-law, d 1969
Photo: 1956

Renate,
sister-in-law
Photo: 1972

Reinhart,
brother-in-law
Photo: 1959

Abbajee, d 1947
Photo: 1946

Apa Asghari, d 1948
Photo: 1948

Michelle, d 1984
Photo: 1983

Reinhild, Ronnie, Ruby
1962, back of apartment

Ronnie 10, Michele 3 M, Ruby 7 in first house

Family, 1970

Receiving check from the underwriter

Standing: Late Governor Shapp; Attorney; Attorney; Staff; Staff; Late Lee Zemnick; Late Charlie Gantz; Late John Richardson; Attorney; Attorney.

Seated: Administrative Assistant; Masood Qurashi; Maqbool Qurashi; Steve Fuller, the Underwriter; Late Ralph Fratkin

16

It was the middle of January when I finally landed a job with a textile mill in Lyallpur, presently known as Faisalabad. The bad news was that the mills could not provide family quarters till March, which meant that I had to leave Reinhild behind in Gujranwala for at least three months. I lived in the company guesthouse with three other Pakistani middle management personnel and Mr. Yamato, a Japanese engineer who was supervising the installation of looms in the weaving department. Our meals were provided by the mill and served in the dining room. One day Mr. Yamato received a package from his home and was humming a Japanese tune as he sat down for dinner. I asked him, "You seem to be very happy today. Is it your birthday?"

"I received a package from home with one of my favorite delicacies. Would you like some?" he replied. I inquired about its contents, which turned out to be pickled earthworms, which I had to decline.

Frequently, Mian Iqbal, the young managing director, joined us for dinner to discuss the day's progress. Finally I had a job in the spinning room as assistant spinning master. My immediate boss,

Sharif Ali, always wore a worried look and had no sense of humor. Without any formal training, he had acquired his knowledge over many years working in the trenches, and while his practical knowledge was sufficient to maintain the status quo, his lack of technical knowhow had become a hurdle to further improvements. But I had learned my lesson from Mr. Khan in Jahengira and this time decided not to challenge Mr. Ali. Instead, I made him look good to Mian Iqbal while implementing some mechanical modifications to improve the operations.

It made me feel uncomfortable to think that I was not alongside Reinhild in her difficult task of adapting to a strange culture, and the thought of my inability to offer companionship to her during her ordeal of delivering our first baby was all consuming. I was not worried about the process of delivery itself because of the presence of *Bhaijee* and *Apajee*, both doctors. As customary, the babies are delivered at home, and a midwife prepares the expectant mother for the day by special massages and exercises. A midwife was available when Reinhild delivered our son, Ronnie Naeem Qurashi, on February 7, 1957, but it would be three days later when I received the news of this very important event of my life. *Bhaijee,* in his excitement, had sent the first telegram without a street address. In the absence of any response, he sent the second telegram but forgot to give the name of the recipient. Reinhild was worrying when I did not show up to see our son. Finally, he provided the telegraph office with the proper information, and all three telegrams were delivered to me on February 10. I could not contain my excitement as I ran out of the factory floor to the manager's office to inform him that I would be going to Gujranwala for few days. Along the way I kept shouting, "I am a father. I have a son."

I took the first available bus to Gujranwala, arriving there at noon, and ran from the *Tonga* directly home without stopping at the clinic. As I entered the room, I saw Reinhild holding this little person with dark hair and tiny hands. He was fast asleep. I took him in my arms and wondered about the miracle of life. He weighed six pounds and had brown hair and was the consequence of our love, and I knew that we would do anything to protect and nurture him. I was overwhelmed by a sudden sense of responsibility that I had never known before. Somebody said that he was my exact copy, while others felt that he resembled Reinhild. It was customary to shave a newborn's head with the expectation that the new hair would grow in denser. Ronnie's head was shaved when he was five days old, and later we were surprised when the color of his new hairs turned out to be blond. It was difficult for me to leave my family behind and when I returned to Lyallpur on the fourteenth of February. I promised Reinhild that before my next visit, I would make some arrangements so we could all be together. I requested of Mian Iqbal that I be allowed to have two corner rooms of the guesthouse so I could have my wife and son with me, and he was gracious enough to not only approve my plan but informed me that the kitchen would provide our meals, and he promised that the schedule to complete our future house would be accelerated. I returned to Gujranwala on February 16. The following day, accompanied by Reinhild and Ronnie, I boarded a bus to Lyallpur. My friend Hanif came to see us off. *Bayjee* had cooked my favorite traveling food, *Parathas* (fried flat breads) stuffed with ground meat.

Part of the guesthouse became our home for the coming months as Reinhild kept busy taking care of Ronnie while I began to build my career. Finally the day arrived when we could move into our new home, and with only one person remaining at the guesthouse, we were allowed to take whatever furniture we needed. One day we noticed a rat racing from the kitchen area towards the sofa. Nothing had led us to suspect during our stay at the guesthouse that we were sharing the sofa with a small four-legged tenant. In order to send it packing, we tightly closed all the doors and windows to block its exit. It was a sight to see how Reinhild was balancing herself on the window sill while holding Ronnie tightly in her arms. A broom in hand, I began the chase, and each time I thought the intruder had been pinned down under the broom, the interloper would appear, fearlessly standing up on its hind legs with its beady eyes mockingly focused on me. Its defiant stare appeared to be a challenge, and each failed attempt intensified my determination to win the battle. As the number of failures mounted, the conflict took on a new significance. I felt that I had to win this match in order to prove the superiority of the human race. The battle continued for about a half hour when the rat suddenly decided to make its escape through the front door, probably to return another day. By this time either it had become tired or my senses could anticipate its moves. I managed to get to the door before it could reach there and kept it slightly open to facilitate its plan. As the little mammal scanned the space behind it to ensure that no one was chasing, it sprang towards the door to make a clean break. That is when I shut the door hard enough to squeeze its slender body. Its last squeal bore witness to my triumph.

Mian Iqbal made us very welcome, and he supported me in my work. In the absence of a son in his young family, he frequently visited us to play with Ronnie. Friday is the Muslim Sabbath day, and Muslims all over the world make it a point to hear the sermons that are a part of the afternoon prayers. Mian Iqbal was all bathed and wearing clean clothes when he stopped by to invite me to accompany him to the mosque. He picked up Ronnie high in his stretched arms, and as I turned to go to the bedroom to change, I noticed Ronnie, who was between diaper changes, peeing on Iqbal's clean clothes. At the same moment Iqbal let out a scream followed by a laugh. Reinhild and I were embarrassed, but he made nothing of it, although the poor man had to go home and take another bath.

It was during the spring of 1957 when I was summoned by Mian Iqbal to his office and was introduced to a constable from the local police department who, holding Reinhild's passport and pointing to her picture, asked, "Do you know this German national?"

I informed him that I was her husband and inquired, "How did you get her passport?"

"We keep the passport of aliens who enter the country without a valid visa, and she would have gotten it back upon her departure after thirty days' courtesy stay," he informed me.

"She is staying here with me and our son. What do I have to do to fix the problem?"

Before leaving, he informed me that he was not from the immigration office and that he would have to turn the matter over to the deputy commissioner's office for further action. I asked, "Who is the deputy commissioner here?"

He informed me that the new DC was Masoor Sahib and that he had come from Gujranwala. Mr. Masoor was a friend of *Bhaijee,* and I once had attended a party at his house. One could not pick up a telephone and call, so I had to go to his office. Without a prior appointment, his assistants would not allow me to see him but allowed me to wait till there was a break in his schedule. Once he peeked through his door and, finding me, rebuked his secretary for not letting him know earlier about my arrival. After exchanging the usual salutations, when I explained the problem of my wife's passport, he assured me that all would be taken care of as soon as he had located the passport.

One week later, he, accompanied by a younger man, arrived at the mill to visit us. He introduced the young man as Magistrate Zaman Mahmood, who would be hearing Reinhild's case. Two days later Zaman Mahmood sent his personal car to pick up Reinhild and Ronnie for a hearing. When I came home from work that evening, Reinhild showed me her passport and related what took place at the court. She was ushered into the chambers of the magistrate while waiting for the proceedings to begin, and when she had to change Ronnie's diaper, she had the assistance of the magistrate's c*haprasee,* the errand person. Finally Zaman Mahmood entered the room carrying her passport and told her that she had been fined twenty rupees, which he had already paid. Zaman became a friend of the family.

Consumption of alcohol is prohibited for Pakistanis by law. Zaman, as most people in other parts of the world, believed that the majority of Westerners were alcoholics and that their beliefs were further reinforced by the Western movie characters that were very often shown holding glasses of the intoxicating beverage. Once a week he would visit us and bring a bottle of scotch whiskey with him. I had never tasted alcohol before, not even when I lived in Britain, and Reinhild was not a habitual drinker, but we would sip some while he satisfied his desire for companionship.

During one of his visits, he explained, "In my position I have many enemies, and if the news of my drinking here got out, it could create problems for you and me." He suggested we get a license for alcohol. I asked him how I could acquire such a document, but he had already arranged with a doctor to certify that I needed alcohol for medicinal reasons. The doctor, who was waiting for me when I visited him, asked, "How did you pick up this habit?"

"My wife is from Germany..." I began to answer, but I did not have to complete the sentence before he stated, "I understand."

So the next time Zaman visited us, I gave him the medical certificate allowing me to have six whiskey bottles per month. Reinhild and I became "certified alcoholics", and Zaman found a place where he could satisfy his addiction.

Although I had developed a trusting relationship with my employer, the mill was not large enough to offer social opportunities for Reinhild. Employees at the mill provided me with some human interaction, which was missing in her life, and I felt responsible for her isolation. There were other mills in the area, and I was constantly searching for a better environment, and it was by chance that, while visiting a local hospital that was run by an order of nuns, Reinhild ran into a German woman who lived in the area. Her husband, Ernst Büxenstein, was the works manager at a larger textile mill. When I met him, he informed me that they had just hired a new weaving master who might be reorganizing the department and recommended that I should pay him a visit. Although the weaving room, with a high level of noise, was not where I wished to spend rest of my life, it offered me a career path and also some companionship for Reinhild in the person of Mrs. Büxenstein.

My interview with Mr. Desai, an Indian expatriate, went very well. By the time I left, he gave me the indication that I would be receiving an offer, which came within a few days. He invited Reinhild and me along with Ronnie for a delicious vegetarian dinner when he named me his assistant weaving master in charge of production. I was to be responsible for 950 workers tending 1,200 looms, twenty-four hours a day, seven days a week. Our living quarters were spacious and now I could manage to hire a live-in cook. Imam Din was in his fifties, a good cook, loved children, and Ronnie bonded with him almost immediately. I began to see some variety in the dinner menu, which had been missing, and we could leave Ronnie with Imam Din and explore the city. One evening we borrowed two bicycles and rode to the local cinema to see *Lisbon* with Ray Milland and Maureen O'Hara. Reinhild had quite a following, because a European woman wearing a skirt and riding a bike was a rarity in the fifties in Pakistan. We watched the film about four more times as my colleagues invited us to the movies as their display of hospitality. When Ronnie's feeding had to be switched from breast milk to a formula, Reinhild substituted the water with carrot and meat juices. These were obtained by grating carrots and, in the absence of mechanical juicers, straining them through a muslin cloth and having Imam Din boil the meat and save the broth before preparing the main meals. No wonder he grew up to be six feet two inches tall.

Every Monday morning, as a routine, I met Mr. Desai in his office to plan the week's production schedule. One Monday I could not find him in his office, and when he failed to show up all day, I decided to stop by his residence and, to my surprise, found it empty. Even his cook was gone. Mr. and Mrs. Büxenstein had gone to Germany for a vacation, leaving me no choice but to approach the managing director's office for the needed information. I had never met him before and suspected that he probably did not know who I was, but was surprised when I found him waiting for me. Before I could speak, he said, "You are wondering what happened to Mr. Desai. He had some immigration problems and will not be available for some time. In the meantime I want you to continue the operations you have been doing. My office will provide you the weekly schedules."

I stated that my wife also had an immigration problem and that I knew the magistrate who handled her hearing. He did not respond to my attempt to offer any assistance. Instead he advised me to let Mr. Desai work it out.

That evening Zaman, the magistrate, came for a visit and asked, "Was there any excitement at the mill last night?" I told him that I did not know about any problem, and he continued, "Yesterday I had issued a warrant for the arrest of an Indian national named Desai on suspicion of espionage. He is in jail as we speak."

I was surprised and wanted to know how they found out when he explained that the security agency had been watching some people, including Desai, for some time, and that they had indisputable evidence. I stated, "He appeared to be a very nice person and a good boss."

In the absence of Desai, I wondered aloud about the kind of boss I might end up reporting to. The answer came within a few days when I went to the managing director's office to pick up the production schedule. Mian Rafique, the director, invited me into his office and said, "If you are wondering what happened to Desai, all I know is that he has been deported. You should continue as acting weaving master till the return of Mr. Büxenstein from Germany."

Struggling to hide my excitement, I asked, "Should I hold up on the changes in the supervisory staff that I had proposed to Mr. Desai?"

He looked into my eyes and held my gaze for what seemed to be a long time and then said, "Do what you think is right." Then he stood up, indicating that the meeting was over. He shook my hand and wished me good luck.

17

Around the end of 1956, Renate, my sister-in-law, had moved to the United States and, while working as a nurse, was living with her uncle. As my mother-in-law wanted to see her first grandchild, Renate offered Reinhild and Ronnie a round trip to Germany for Christmas of 1957. We began preparing for her trip and, with the help of our magistrate friend, it was not difficult to get a passport for Ronnie. Western-style women's clothes were not readily available, so we purchased a few yards of printed cloth and cut the panels to size and shape by using one of Reinhild's skirts as a template. She sewed the pieces together by hand to make the skirt. We could not afford to have her hair done professionally. Instead we purchased a home perm kit and, during the night of December 20, I rolled her hair into curlers. The procedure required applying various chemicals during the drying cycle, and, lacking a hair dryer, it took most of the night to complete the process.

On December 21, Zaman provided us with his chauffeur-driven car for the ride to Lahore. *Bhaijee* came from Gujranwala to see her off as Reinhild boarded the evening flight of Pakistan Airlines to Karachi, where she would catch a Pan Am flight to Frankfurt.

She and Ronnie were the last ones to board the plane as we stood there in a long embrace. I could not face another separation, and I was concerned about her long trip. I stood there as the plane taxied to the runway and took off into the night sky. There was no way for me to know how she managed a ten-month-old baby during a five-hour layover in Karachi, as land-line phones were rare and cell phones had not been invented yet. I had to wait for six days for her letter to learn that the airline representative stayed with her at the airport during the layover and took care of her needs.

The one-and-a-half-hour drive back from Lahore to Lyallpur, although depressing, offered me an opportunity to analyze the present and contemplate the future. When I had left for Bolton, the growing textile industry had led me to believe that a well-paying job would be waiting upon my return, but the ever-increasing number of returning graduates from England had depressed the wages. My salary could not support the lifestyle I had envisioned, but, in view of my responsibilities at the mill, I expected that to improve by the time Reinhild returned. These thoughts improved my disposition by the time I reached home.

I began to implement my planned changes, and it took about four months before a sustained 20 percent gain in production could be quantified. In order to present my request for an increase in salary, I documented the weekly production numbers and prepared a graph showing the upward trend of the output. When I stood at the open door of the director's office, he acknowledged me by waiving me in. He appeared preoccupied, giving me an anxious look when I said, "I have some reports to show you about how we have increased the production."

He did not seem to be interested and instructed me to leave the papers on his desk and he would call me after he had read the report. His demeanor discouraged any further communication. I was disappointed because I had expected an energetic discussion. It is not every day that a department improves production by 20 percent, and I wondered whether he had guessed that I would be asking for a raise and his behavior was just an act.

The following day I wrote a letter to the U.S. consulate in Lahore, and it was late in June when they informed me that my quota number for immigration to the United States had arrived and that I was advised to meet with one of the vice consuls in Lahore to discuss the procedure, which I did. I brought Vice Consul Robert P. Smith up to date with respect to my status in life since I had made my application in 1946, and he indicated that there was always a need for middle management personnel in the States. He suggested that the visa application process would be more expeditious in Germany. Reinhild had already shipped her belongings from Germany by sea and was planning to arrive back in Pakistan in early August. I had to make a decision fast, and it came easy. My dream had been flickering again, and I had been feeling that the textiles industry was not offering much of a challenge. I sent a cablegram (telegram across the countries) to Reinhild telling her not to come and that we would be going to the United States. That was followed by a letter that asked her to send me a cablegram requiring my presence in Germany, which would allow me to get the proper currency exchange to buy an airline ticket.

While waiting for the cablegram from Germany, I began to accumulate money that I would need for my travel. I sold my camera and some other belongings to get the needed cash to buy a one-way ticket to Frankfurt, and, immediately after receiving the cablegram, I paid a visit to the Pakistan National Bank, the currency exchange controlling authority. Even Pakistani nationals were required to pay in hard currency in order to buy a ticket for travel on Pakistan International Airlines. The response was not encouraging. I had to bribe a clerk with ten yards of a special print cloth to get the piece of paper that I would take to the airline office. I could only buy a $5 bill on the black market. It did not occur to me how my great dream of immigrating to the United

States would be financed; my faith in its positive outcome became the driving force that could not be resisted. Maybe *Allah's* timing that *Abbajee* always spoke about was at hand.

With the $5 bill in my pocket and a dream bigger than the Hoover Dam and no apparent means to fulfill it, I boarded the Pakistan International Airlines on August 7, 1958. I had visited *Apa Anwari* and *Bayjee* in Hafizabad and *Bhaijee Manzoor* in Gujranwala before taking the night train to Karachi. I told them that I was needed in Germany, and I believe they had some inkling that I would not be returning. Before boarding the plane in Karachi, I purchased a book titled *German by Pictures* so I could learn the language during the long journey. It was my first time aboard a commercial airliner, and I was enjoying the view of the city of Karachi as the plane circled before heading towards Iran and Turkey. The gold and gray shades of the eastern sky began to foretell the impending rising of the sun as we crossed the Turkish coastline. The Greek Islands below appeared as black dots in the shimmering water of the Aegean Sea. The changing of the colors as the sun came up from behind the horizon and brushed the city of Athens with coats of yellow and orange was mesmerizing. My concentration was interrupted by the click of the intercom: "Ladies and gentlemen, this is the captain speaking. We are sorry to announce that this flight will have to be terminated in Rome due to a technical problem. The ground crews will be on hand to arrange for the connections to your destinations." It was disturbing in view of the fact that Reinhild was on her way to Frankfurt to meet me.

The only arranging that the Pakistan Airlines crew did was to direct the passengers to the Lufthansa counter, where the attendant at the desk, after distributing vouchers for lunch, announced that she would call the name of each passenger when a connecting flight became available. Already displeased with her added burden, she did not show any desire to assist me in any manner to inform Reinhild about the delay. There were vacationers crowding every empty space, and I had to stand in a long line at the small café that accepted the vouchers. It was late in the evening when I boarded a Lufthansa flight to Frankfurt as the storms began to gather in the upper levels and the lightning between the high clouds appeared like shining silver strings that I called God's fireworks. Instead of arriving in Frankfurt at 3:00 p.m., I cleared immigration at 10:00 at night and found all areas of the airport deserted. Reinhild had no way to know what had happened, and I was sure that the representatives of the Pakistan Airlines would have been of no help as demonstrated by them in Rome. That led me to believe that after a long wait, she was most probably on her way back to Sattenhausen. Not having enough money to pay for a room at a hotel, I decided to get to the railway station and take a train to Göttingen.

The exchange rate at the time was four German marks to a dollar. After paying two marks for a bus ride to the train station, I was left with eighteen marks, hoping that this would be more than enough for the price of a ticket to Göttingen. I used my *German by Pictures* book to make up a sentence inquiring about the price of a ticket, but the attendant at the window, appearing to be in his fifties, did not seem to understand my repeated request, "*Göttingen, Wie viel, bitte?*"

I was sure I was asking him, "How much to Göttingen?" Other passengers began to line up behind me, and my pleading looks at the persons behind me produced no results. I decided to move to another window or find someone who could help me, and as I turned to my left, my eye caught a door to an office. With hesitation, I opened it hoping to find a supervisor or someone who spoke English. The person sitting behind the desk, younger than the man at the ticket window, lifted his head when I said, "*Bitte, Hilfe*" ("Please, help").

Wearing a broad smile, he asked, with a heavy German accent, "You speak English?"

I, listening to those few words, heaved a sigh of relief and asked, "Where did you learn English?"

Martin Schmidt told me that he was a prisoner of war near Manchester in England during the war. I informed him that I lived in Bolton and related to him what had transpired since my landing in Rome. After I showed him the picture of Ronnie, he told me that he had two children. While getting up from his chair he said, "We go get ticket, ja?"

I followed him to the ticket window, where he explained to the attendant what I wanted. After paying the fare I still had eight marks. While I was shaking his hand in appreciation for his assistance, he looked at his watch and said, "One hour before the train go and you look tired and hungry. We go have a meal, ja?"

I could not refuse such an invitation and was hoping that he would be generous enough to pay for it, which he did. Mr. Schmidt escorted me to the train that was just pulling up to the platform, and, before boarding, once more I thanked him for his hospitality. He wished me good luck during my stay in Germany, as the train pulled away and my thoughts turned to my next hurdle: how to get to the village from Göttingen.

My first experience with a stranger in Germany left a pleasant and lasting impression. It was around 7:00 in the morning when I stepped into the lobby of the Göttingen station and located the Left Luggage counter on the right of the main entrance, where I surrendered my trunk in exchange for a receipt. I asked the clerk, "Post?"

He pointed his finger to the entrance and then gestured for me to make a left turn. As directed, I walked out of the door and looked to the left and found a building with a large sign declaring it to be the *Deutsche Post.* After entering the building and while turning the pages of my book to find the German word for "telegram," I spotted a telegram form on one of the wall shelves. With the assistance from the book I filled the form, and in the message space I wrote, "*Ich in Göttingen Bahnhof*" ("I am at the Göttingen railway station"), and signed it with my middle name, Ashraf. It was easy for Reinhild to call me by my middle name instead of my first, which was a little difficult to pronounce. All my German relatives and their friends addressed me as "Ashraf."

An hour had passed as I walked back and forth in front of the railway station in order to kill time when I saw *Mutti*, my mother-in-law, alighting from a car driven by Erich Müller, the son of the farmer on whose property my in-laws lived. He helped me put my luggage in the car and *Mutti* communicated that Reinhild was still in Frankfurt waiting for me and that she would be coming in a day or so. I was disappointed, but it was nobody's fault. Instead I looked forward to seeing Ronnie, who was eighteen months old by then, and wondered whether he would recognize me. Anxiety was getting the best of me.

18

It was midday by the time we reached Sattenhausen and I carried my luggage up the stairs into the apartment, feeling awkward about intruding in the lives of my in-laws. The only asset I had was a dream that had no present cash value. On top of it, I could not speak German, which made conversation difficult. Ronnie was fast asleep in a crib that was placed in the small sitting room where the couch could be made into a bed for *Mutti.* I took a peek at Ronnie while she made something to eat. Reinhart felt obliged to accept my presence, although his indifference towards me was visible. That was understandable, because I was disrupting his routine and he had to spend the nights at his friend's house till Reinhild returned and permanent sleeping arrangements could be made. As I was engaged in these thoughts, we heard some movement in the next room, signifying that Ronnie was waking up. I followed *Mutti* into the sitting room, where I found him standing up in his crib. Ronnie had learned to speak while in Sattenhausen and spoke only German. When *Mutti,* pointing to me, said, "*Ronnie, hier ist dein Vati*" ("Ronnie, here is your daddy"), he shook his head and then, looking at my picture on the shelf, said, "*Nein, da ist mein*

Vati" ("No, there is my father"). However, it did not take him long to connect me with the picture.

We moved the crib to the main room because *Mutti* would be sleeping there while I slept on the couch/bed. I had been resisting sleep for the past thirty-six hours, and it did not take long for me to enter the dream world. After fourteen hours it was very refreshing when I woke up, but Reinhild's absence made me feel like a stranger. By the time we finished breakfast, Ronnie was getting more communicative, and his mastery of the language was impressive. When I searched for words in an attempt to ask *Mutti* about the bus schedule, he provided the proper vocabulary and expression. It made me proud of my eighteen-month-old son. The bus from Göttingen stopped in the village twice a day, and at each scheduled time Ronnie and I would walk to the bus stop. Along the way whenever we came across a villager he would bow his head and say, "*Guten Morgen.*" And if the person was known to him, his eyes would light up as he introduced me by saying, "*Hier ist mein Vati.*"

I could only smile with pride. Reinhild had done a great job of teaching him good manners. My first day there, Ronnie and I waited at the bus stop in the morning and were disappointed not seeing Reinhild. We took long strolls on the country road while I attempted to communicate in German. He was always quick to fill in the blanks whenever he noticed that I was lost for words. From then on he took me under his wing and taught me German vocabulary. We went to the bus stop in the evening and once again were disappointed. It was difficult to communicate across the land in those days. Some villagers stopped by the bus stop to see what I looked like because I was sure that many of the locals had not seen a Pakistani before. There were all kinds of speculations about our son's complexion before his arrival in Sattenhausen, and some who wanted to know if Ronnie was dark were surprised to see a Pakistani boy with blond hair and fair skin.

It was in the afternoon of the third day that I finally saw the face I had been longing for when Reinhild stepped off the bus. Ronnie jumped into his mother's arms while I embraced both of them.

~

The Müller farm had a large barn in the back of the compound facing the entrance. The living quarters for the farmer and his family lay on the left, with their bedrooms above the horse stables. In the winter, the animals provided the warmth for the rooms above. On the right were the pig sties and the outhouse. *Mutti* and Reinhart lived above the laundry that was situated on the left of the main entrance. I was introduced to the Müller family, whose head was Ludwig Müller, known as Lui, and his wife, who was called Oma Erna by everybody. I always called them Herr and Frau Müller. They had two sons. Erich, with his wife, Trude, and their two sons, named Erich junior and Reinhold, lived and worked on the farm, while the younger son, Walter, had an outside job. There was an older man who, after losing his family in East Prussia, was a full-time live-in farm hand. He had adopted my in-laws as his family, and he was addressed as Uncle Kurt. He spent most of his evenings with us, and many times he would bring us some food that he had swiped from the farmer's dinner table. Ronnie and Reinhold were almost the same age and spent most of their time playing together. Herr Müller, in his late sixties, had an insatiable hunger for information about the outside world and, amazingly, was fully aware of the India-Pakistan conflict. I had many questions about life in Germany under Hitler, but our meaningful discussions would have to wait till I acquired more language skills. In the meantime it did not stop him from attempting to communicate with me, as I could get the sense of his conversation because of the local dialect, many words sounding like their English counterparts.

~

As soon as I located the address of the American embassy, I wrote a letter referring to my Pakistani quota number and requesting the necessary application forms. In the meantime, Reinhild had begun working for the farmer again as she had done for many years before she left for Bolton in 1953. The farm was busy at the time preparing for the harvest season and by working she could contribute to the meager financial resources of the family. The only income was *Mutti*'s pension and a stipend for Reinhart, as he had not finished school yet, and now here I was, another mouth to feed. Each day while Reinhild went to work in the fields, I stayed home to take care of Ronnie, which allowed me to watch him grow and acquire new skills. The family was very supportive of each other and of me by extension. After school Reinhart relieved his sister in the field so she could come home and take care of Ronnie, because *Mutti*'s condition of severe asthma prevented her from doing anything stressful.

My inability to do any work was giving me a feeling of helplessness and uselessness, many times leading me to question my hasty departure from Pakistan. But the uncertainty was always short lived and would quickly be replaced by optimism about the outcome. One slow day, I caught Herr Müller in front of the barn and told him, "*Ich muss arbeiten*" ("I must work").

He squeezed my arm muscles and said, "*Keine Muskeln*" ("No muscles").

At the time I weighed 116 pounds and stood at five feet seven inches tall, a far cry from the build of a farmhand, as I had never done manual work before and hoped that my stay there would be short. One day I saw Uncle Kurt attempting to install a two-way switch at the bottom of the stairs; they were steep, and there was only one switch at the top of the stairs, making it inconvenient in the evening. No matter how he tried, the connections failed to work, and his face began to exhibit frustration. I felt that I could resolve the problem, and when I offered him my assistance, he gladly accepted it. After a few attempts, I had a working schematic on the paper followed by a successful installation. It did not take long before Herr Müller became aware of my talent and asked me to fix the lighting in the pig sties, followed by some electrical work in the barn. Finally I was doing something productive and felt needed, which was great for my psyche and pocketbook. Human beings have an inherent desire to be needed, and it was fulfilling when I overhauled two rusty bicycles, hoping that it would lead to fixing other farm machines so I could make some money.

A few weeks later, I received a reply to my letter to the U.S. consulate in Hamburg that informed me that although my Pakistani quota number had arrived, the whole family could immigrate under Reinhild's German quota. In order to complete the process leading to immigration, I needed to prove availability of financial support in the States that could be in the form of cash, an employment contract for at least two years, or someone guaranteeing that we would not become wards of the state. Those were tall orders and would take time to accomplish, but in the meantime I needed work. I decided to apply with the state employment office, hoping to find a job in the textile industry, but the man at the office did not hold much hope as the unemployment was high and he was not sure if I could get a working visa. That left me discouraged and at a loss to decide my next course of action. Although Reinhild informed Renate in the United States about the situation, I began seriously to entertain the idea of returning to Pakistan, but the thought of possible separation from my family again was saddening. This was the state of my mind when one night *Abbajee* appeared in my dream and guided me to put my faith in God, and I heard him say, "Everything happens according to his timing." These words rang in my ears for many days and lifted my spirits, although Renate's letter was not encouraging. Their Uncle Alfred, who had sponsored her, refused to do so for us because he did not like Reinhild marrying a non-European. She assured us that she would attempt to find someone else.

A few days later Herr Müller asked me if I could drive. When I informed him that not only could I drive but I could also fix cars, he pointed to his big tractor and said, "You think you can drive that?"

The Bulldog tractor was equipped with a single-cylinder engine having eight forward and four reverse gears. He cautioned me by disclosing, "There are only two men in the village that can drive it, my son and the mechanic." He told me, "You get three tries, and if successful I will hire you."

Erich showed me how to start it and demonstrated the gear shifting. I had to rotate a large fly wheel to create a spark and compression in order to start the engine, which I managed to do with ease, as it was still warm. As I stepped in the cabin, all the members of the farmer's family and some farmhands had gathered to see my performance. When I released the clutch pedal after shifting the gear, the rear wheels pushed forward with a jerk, the front of the tractor jumped three feet in the air, and the spectators let out an "Aw." Not having the feel of the clutch, I had expected something like that. As Herr Müller watched in anticipation, my second attempt bore fruit, and I got myself a job. Although this did not offer me a career path, my sight on our ultimate goal lightened the present burdens.

A typical farm in the States contains thousands of acres of contiguous land surrounding the owner's house and other farm buildings where the hired help lived, and neighbors are miles away. In Germany, the farmhouses are clustered in a village around a church and a school. The farmers owned or leased plots of land that were sometimes separated by a few miles, away from their residences. The Müller farm grew wheat, rye, barley, and oats. It also produced sugar beets, feeding beets, and potatoes. There were fruit trees providing pears, apples, and plums for canning and making jellies, jams, and juice. Pigs were bred for personal use and also for sale, and milk from the cows was delivered to the dairies for processing. Each morning I drove the tractor to the designated field, where I would hitch a cropping machine that was operated by Herr Müller to cut the grain stalks while the farmhands tied the stalks into bundles, eight or nine of which were leaned against each other in order to dry. This was repeated till the entire crop had been harvested, by which time the first crop would have dried and would be ready to be hauled to the barn. Herr Müller had this process well organized. The bundles of crop were spaced strategically so that the farmhands could efficiently load the dried bundles onto the wagons that were being pulled by horses. The horses knew exactly when and where to turn without any commands. My job was to pull the loaded wagons with the tractor and bring them to the barn, where Erich and his team unloaded the bundles and stacked them on each side, leaving the middle open for traffic. One day Herr Müller told me to take Ewald, one of the horses, and the wagon home, and when I asked him what I needed to do to drive the horse, he said, "You just sit on the wagon and the horse will know what to do." As soon as I climbed on the wagon and picked up the reins, Ewald started to walk, and when we came to the main road, he stopped at the stop sign and then looked to the left and to the right. When there was no traffic, he made the right turn and continued until he pulled in front of the stalls after making another right turn. When I hesitated to get off the wagon, he looked back and began neighing as if to tell me, "Get off and unhitch me."

As soon as Uncle Kurt unhitched him, Ewald walked into his stall. I did not take him home; it was he who took *me* there. I never knew horses were so intelligent.

19

The harvesting season was coming to an end. The farmhands riding the last wagon sang songs while holding up a straw wreath on a pitchfork. It was customary for the villagers to line up along the street carrying buckets of water that were splashed on the wagon as it made its way to the barn. It was a kind of celebration for a successful crop season. Untimely rain could have easily destroyed the crop. It was near the end of October that the last load came in, and that evening the dinner was special. Mrs. Müller prepared stuffed cabbage just for me.

Each year the village held a *Kirmes* celebration after all the farmers in the village had brought in their crops. It was a festive affair arranged in one of the large dance halls where everybody dressed in his or her finery and danced to the music of a live band. Couples were doing the waltz, tango, fox trot, and some other dances indigenous to the area that I did not know. Reinhild taught me how to polka. Frankfurters (hot dogs), beer, and Schnapps were available. Everybody was enjoying the well-deserved relaxation after months of hard work. Although my monetary rewards were meager, my sense of accomplishment was far greater than I had ever experienced before. I met other men from the village, and they jokingly informed me that I was setting a bad example for manhood. That came about because once I had ironed my own shirt and somehow the word got out. Men were not supposed to do any ironing.

I had never seen such a sense of community as permeated this village. They maintained large tracts of woods that provided them with firewood, and every winter, a team representing each farm would clean the underbrush to prevent fires. Mature trees were marked for cutting and new seedlings were planted to maintain the tree population. The farmers cooperatively owned large farming equipment such as threshing machines, electric saws, etc., each farm taking turns in the use. One day the threshing machine was hauled by the last user and parked in the middle of the barn because it was Müller's turn to use it. Threshing separated the grain from the husk, and the farmhands, including Reinhild, delivered the bundles to the side of the machine while I, standing on top of it, fed them into the hopper. Herr Müller, while supervising the operation, would rub a handful of the grains in his palms and then take a whiff, bringing a contented smile to his face, as his way of determining the quality of the grains. By the end of the day I could not stand the itching from the layers of dust that had settled on my body, and although it was very cold in November, I did not mind taking a shower with cold water in order to feel clean.

Nothing was wasted at the farm. The leftover straw after threshing was used for the bedding of the cows, horse stalls, and the pig sties. After the straw was saturated with animal excrement, it was piled high in a circular area in the middle of the compound. Over time it would emanate a sour odor, but I got used to it just like the other residents of the farm. The *Mist,* as it was called, was the organic fertilizer and was spread in the fields before the plowing. An outhouse served as a latrine for the residents; to catch the human waste, there was a deep well on top of which was built a bench with two holes. I always wondered about the two holes next to each other with only one entry door. Could it be that in the old days a couple sat there together reading newspapers, which then served as a substitute for the toilet paper? Twice a year the farmer would pump the waste, called *Jauche,* into a tank wagon to spray it on the fields. On that day we had to close our windows to prevent the odor from penetrating everywhere into the apartment.

The sugar beets grew just below the surface with approximately one foot of green leaves protruding above the ground. The first step in harvesting the beets was to crop the leaves by the use of a machine that I pulled behind the tractor. The leaves were collected and mixed with other green waste to make compost. The second step was to bring the beets to the surface, and that too was done by the means of a machine that was operated by Herr Müller and pulled behind the tractor. During those days it was only the two of us within miles, and the noise of the tractor was loud enough to drown out my singing Indian songs, which he either enjoyed or could not hear. One day just before noon, the chain on the machine came off and we had to stop, upsetting the farmer because of the interruption it caused. Just then Erich came by to bring our lunch, and I was told to take my lunch break while they proceeded to restring the chain. Father and son argued as their attempts were not yielding any results, and I was waved off each time I offered to fix the problem. Finally they decided to ride the wagon to the village to fetch the mechanic. As soon as they left, after a few attempts, I was successful in rethreading the chain. Forty minutes later when they returned without the mechanic, who was on another call, Herr Müller was really upset and was about to tell me that I should call it a day when I said, "Herr Müller, you should try it, the chain is fixed."

First he was suspicious, but after a thorough inspection, he instructed me to drive the tractor slowly to see if the machine really worked. Finally he was satisfied and gave me the signal to go full speed. I became the talk of the village, and that evening Frau Müller served up my perceived favorite, stuffed cabbage.

The beets had to be loaded on the wagon that was pulled by one of the horses and in order to prompt the horse, Herr Müller would constantly shout, "*Geh doch, du Schweinehund*" ("Go, you swine dog"). It was just an expression and did not make any sense but sounded better than uttering four-letter words.

Reinhild and I teamed up to load the beets, and to overcome the boredom we counted as we picked them out of the loose dirt and tossed them into the wagon. Two loaded wagons, ready for delivery to the sugar mill in Nörten about twenty miles away, were hitched on to the tractor like a train. Erich drove the tractor while I sat on the last wagon with a hand on the brake as required by the traffic regulations. It was a very cold day in December, and although I was wearing thermal under garments and a woolen suit, of course without the tie, I had to wrap myself in blankets, on the urging of Frau Müller, in order to protect myself from the elements. We were driving on the main road, and the cold draft created by the passing vehicles still penetrated my wraps and made me shiver but became more bearable when we had to slow down considerably passing through the city of Göttingen. As soon as I stepped off at the unloading dock, a high-powered hot-water stream was directed at the wagon and washed the beets as they rolled towards a large chute. In the process, the wagons got a free wash and then were loaded with sacks of seeds. It was late evening when we returned to the farm. Usually the job of a break man was entrusted to Erich junior, the grandson of the farmer, but Herr Müller, by asking me to ride the wagon, was complimenting my work. That was what Oma Erna said.

The winter was fast approaching and the work in the fields had come to an end. We all could use some respite. One day when I saw Herr Müller in front of the house, I walked up to him and we engaged in small talk. He wanted to know how our lives were during the British rule of India, and I explained to him how the British maintained their control by encouraging the Hindu Muslim strife. Then I said, "I would like to know what you thought about Hitler." He told me that Germans were very poor after World War I and they had lost their self-esteem when Hitler came on the scene. So they followed him and, after he became a dictator, the SS (Schutzstaffel) violently suppressed all opposition. The government knew everything about everybody, and it took all the production from the village except what it determined the families needed to survive. As far as the Jews were concerned, there were none in the village, although there were some rumors about what was happening, and, he added, "The cunning leaders can charge the emotions of their trusting followers. The people with stirred sentiments are not capable of rational thoughts. This allows leaders to do whatever they want."

After a long pause he said, "As a nation we did not do right."

He walked away with a somber look and drooping shoulders. His statement about leaders holds true even today. We, in the United States, were also led into unwarranted wars by stirring up emotions and fears.

Christmas was upon us and we managed to purchase a goose, turkeys being strictly an American tradition. Reinhart, Reinhild, and I removed the feathers and cleaned out the innards. *Mutti* stuffed it with her delicious stuffing, which she crafted from leftover bread and apples, and the local baker charged two marks to bake the bird. Reinhart got a tree from the woods, and it was decorated with candles and tinsel. Once *Mutti* asked me to go the local grocery store and buy a bottle of "*Lieb Frauen Milch.*" I was puzzled and did not know how I could get a bottle of "Lovely Women's Milk" till Reinhild explained to me that it was a type of wine. Our Christmas presents consisted of oranges, apples, and a few candies. One day we took Ronnie to Göttingen to do some sightseeing. He had never ridden a bus before, although I had taken him for a ride on the tractor. He was taking in the views as the bus made its way. The city was beautifully decorated and Ronnie was excited and amazed to see the many animated figures displayed in the store windows. He would pull us and, pointing to something, would say, *"Mutti! Vati! Guck mal da"* ("Look").

There was a bronze statue in the center square of the city called *Gänseliesel.* A gazebolike structure over a water well elevated from the ground housing the likeness of a young girl carrying a goose in her arm, and a stream of water flowed from the beak of the bird. Ronnie stood there with his mouth open in amazement. We visited Karstadt, a department store, so he could touch and feel some of the toys on the floor, knowing full well that we could not buy any of them. We stayed till dusk when the decorations in the city lit up like fireworks, and I wished I had a camera to capture the expression on Ronnie's face. He wanted to stay, but we needed to catch the last bus home. On New Year's Eve, we went to the local tavern and began the year 1959 with hope and great expectations.

During the first month of the new year, the Müller family slaughtered a pig. That was a very busy day, as other farmers would spend all day assisting the butcher. An inspector would be at hand to test the dead pig for the presence of trichina, a parasite that causes trichinosis among the humans, probably the reason for the prohibition of its consumption in Judaism and Islam. By sunset four hundred pounds of meat were converted into various types of meats and sausages to last the year. That was followed by a *Schlachtefest,* a slaughter feast, where all those who participated were invited for an evening of eating some of the fresh meat and drinking Schnapps and beer.

There was very little work during the winter months, which meant that Reinhild and I could no longer eat at the farmhouse. *Mutti* was great in improvising. She could make a meatloaf that could feed all of us from a quarter pound of ground beef and old bread, and she made sure that Ronnie received his nourishment. Sometimes we managed to buy a frankfurter. Ronnie got the meat and Reinhart and I shared the skin. Once in a while we would have Uncle Kurt babysit for Ronnie so we could go to the local tavern and watch television. I still remember a Perry Como show where a tall Gary Cooper was joking about the short stature of the host. I had never experienced this way of life before, and instead of getting demoralized by it, I felt contented, and the lack of amenities could not undermine my confidence. But I was getting restless, not because of having no work, but because I had this urgent desire to do something productive and, in the absence of any news from the United States of America, it appeared that my dream to immigrate might be getting out of reach. It was time for a change.

Going back to Pakistan was out of the question, as I had burned all my bridges. Reinhild and I decided Bolton would be a better destination. I was sure that I could find a job befitting my education, and, once there, Reinhild could resume her nursing career. I had enough money for a one-way fare and two weeks' sustenance. Ronnie and I had begun to bond, and the thought of another separation from my family was devastating, but the thought that this was necessary provided some solace. On the morning of May 2, 1959, not knowing what awaited me, I boarded the morning bus to Göttingen on the way to England, hoping that my family would soon follow me. But thanks to my time at the farm, I was prepared to face the future with confidence.

20

I arrived in Bolton by noon on the third of May and decided to check out if my old room was available. The landlady still remembered me and, yes, she had a vacancy. She informed me that a couple, Deepak Kumar and his fiancée, Linda, were staying in my old room. I remembered Deepak, who had been one year junior to me at the college and had been thinking of staying in the United Kingdom after graduation. Sammy Bose, who was not a student, was one of the other two residents who had recently arrived from India and was looking for a job. The following morning I visited the student services office at the college and filled out a form that described my experience. Mrs. Murray advised me to check back every few days in case there was a match with an inquiry. Upon my return "home," I ran into Sammy, who said, "I hear you are looking for a job, and I am going to the library to scan the Help Wanted pages of the local newspaper. You can accompany me, if you like."

I had nothing else to do, so I went along, and after one hour of search I spotted an advertisement that held some promise. A new factory was hiring employees to train in the weaving of fiberglass cloth that would be used for window drapes. The following morning, Sammy and I traveled to the address given in the newspaper.

Upon entry into the lobby I was amazed to see the number of prospective applicants. A large card on the back wall instructed the applicants to sign in the book that lay on the table. We added our names to the list and found some place to stand, as all the seats were taken. At 9:00 a young lady entered the lobby from one of the back doors, picked up the book with names, and vanished behind the door. We were settling down for a long wait for our turn when I noticed the same woman reappear and announce, "Bose and Qurashi, please follow me."

While the other applicants appeared puzzled, we were surprised but followed her into a hallway, where she pointed to an office door and said, "The personnel manager will see you now."

I opened the door and a well-dressed young man waved us in and said, "Please be seated." As we took our seats, he continued, "I want to be honest with you and with all the applicants out there; I want to let you know about our pecking order. The born British will get the first call, followed by the Western Europeans, and then the Eastern Europeans, before your names would come up, and we only have very few openings."

We did not have to sit down to listen to the message, as it reminded me of the sign on the front door of a bed-and-breakfast place in London proclaiming that no Indians or dogs were allowed. Attitudes had not changed in the last five years. It was a very disturbing experience and did not bode well for my job prospects.

One week had passed and my funds were fast depleting. Having no success at the college office, I decided to register with the National Employment Office without the mention of my diploma, as any job would be better than working on a farm. The gentleman at the window perused my filled out application and noticed that I had experience in textiles. He said, "I have a request here for a warp knitter and do not know what it entails, but if you want to give it a try I can give you a referral."

"I will try anything."

He added that the company offered training as he handed me the piece of paper and then pointed to the city map on a wall and advised me to look up the address there. It was a short bus ride to the street where the prospective employer was located. I stepped into the lobby of the Warp Knitting Mills at 1:00 and handed the receptionist the referral slip. She asked me to take a seat and said that Mr. Wilson, the personnel manager, would be with me shortly. Half an hour later, a well-dressed man approached me and said, "Mr. Qurashi, please follow me." He explained, "We produce knitted broadcloth. Our machines are the state of the art, and therefore we will provide training if needed. If it interests you, we can further discuss the job description, but first let us go over your application."

I told him that I was interested. After scanning the application, he said, "Looks good. I will need at least one reference in order to proceed further."

I hesitated to mention about my college because the job did not require a technical diploma, and having one could render me overqualified, but he insisted that without a reference he could not offer me the position. Hoping that he would take my word for it, I said, "I did attend the community college for a short period of time."

While getting up from his chair, he stated, "Step in the nurse's office to get your eyes checked while I verify your reference."

I was taken aback, having no choice but to let the chips fall where they might. So I walked into the dispensary.

The nurse told me to look into a optical device while she changed the screens that I was required to read. As she was testing me for color blindness I mentioned, "My wife was a nurse at the Royal Infirmary when I met her."

"What was her last name?"

When I informed her that it was Rümenap, she stopped and asked, "There were two sisters by that name. Which one did you marry?" I told her that it was the younger one. She smiled and nodded her head, signifying that she had met Reinhild while in training.

We had just completed the eye examination when Mr. Wilson, apparently disturbed, entered the dispensary and asked me to follow him to his office, where he demanded, "Why did you lie to me? The records at the college show that you not only completed the course, but you were second in the class and that your instructors were very impressed."

"I need a job and did not want my education to stand in the way."

His anger seemed to dissipate and he asked me to wait till he returned. I was deep in thought, preparing myself for the rejection, when Mr. Wilson entered the room. He was wearing a broad smile as he reached for his chair and said, "A new position of quality control supervisor will be available at the end of July, and you have the qualifications for it. Operating of the machine will provide you the knowledge of warp knitting which will be useful in the new position."

I was elated to hear the news and accepted the offer on the spot. I would begin my new job on the following Monday.

The first payment of my wages would not be available for two weeks after I began working. My funds were depleting fast, and asking the new employer for an advance would not make a good impression. I was trying to come up with some ideas to resolve this problem when I arrived at the National Employment Office, where I had to return the reference slip with the employer's signatures, and I explained to the man behind the counter about my dilemma. He looked at the paper and told me to wait while he consulted someone, and a few minutes later he returned accompanied by a gentleman who said, "My name is Mr. Gledhill. I am a case worker in the monetary assistance section. Please follow me."

He, with a fixed bureaucratic expression and void of humor, perhaps a necessity in his profession, led me into a cubical with low partitions and, while stepping behind his desk, offered me the only other available chair. He pulled out a form from his drawer and began filling in the information that I provided. After completing that process he asked, "For how long would you need the assistance?"

"I begin my job next week and would need help till I get my first wages."

He informed me that he was required to visit the place of my residence the next day between noon and 2:00 p.m.

∽∽

At 1:00 the next afternoon, I heard a knock on the front door. Mr. Gledhill was on time. I led him to my room and offered him the stuffed chair next to the window as I sat on the edge of the bed. Declining my offer of a glass of water, he asked me why I had come back to Bolton. I said, "I got my diploma from the Bolton College and felt that I would have better chances to get a job here. I have accepted a position requiring no technical training because I am waiting for my visa to the United States of America."

He stood up and, while walking to the door, said, "Come to my office tomorrow before noon and I will process a one-time payment of £9."

As I thanked him, I could taste a real dinner that I would have the following day instead of the can of beef and beans with bread that had been my menu since my arrival.

I reported to the mills on Monday morning and was introduced to Kenneth Hill, the shop foreman. After some small talk, he proceeded to instruct me in the use of the machine that could knit broadcloth. It was new to me. Unlike other knitted varieties, warp knitted cloth could be handled almost like a woven material with the added benefit of stretching. As he left me tending a machine, he said, "Call me Ken. Everybody does."

There and then I made up my short name and told him, "Please call me Mac."

He smiled and said, "I was wondering what to call you. Maqbool is a difficult name."

I looked around and noticed that most of the employees were from my part of the world. At noon Ken came by my station and asked me if I wanted to join him for lunch, which I did. I noticed that he did not ask any other machine operator to accompany him except the shop mechanic. That led me to believe that perhaps he had been given special instructions concerning my position at the mill. We had time to spare, so Ken and Rudy, the mechanic, taught me how to play dominoes.

I was enjoying learning the new technology and looking forward to the end of July when the position of the quality control supervisor would become available. It also reminded me that the expiration of my passport was approaching fast. Had I decided to remain in the Great Britain, it would have not mattered, but renewal was needed if I wanted to travel. My ultimate goal still being the United States, letting my passport expire was not an option. I contacted the Pakistani embassy in London to initiate the renewal process, and its response surprised me. In order to do so, I needed to make a security deposit of £187 or an employment contract. I mentioned to Ken about my predicament, and he took it up with the management and informed me that the company had no solution for it. After much deliberation, I came up with the idea to temporarily return to Germany, reasoning that the Pakistani embassy should have no objection to renewing my passport because the German government had already granted me a visa and that my family was residing there. If there was no encouraging news from the United States of America, I could return to Bolton. It was a gamble, but I had gotten used to taking chances in pursuit of my ultimate goal. Mr. Wilson approved my request for a two-week leave of absence, and on Friday, July 17, after receiving two weeks' wages, I headed to Dover in time to board the midnight ferry to Hoek von Holland.

The prevailing practice was for the travelling immigration inspectors to board the train one stop before the border and inspect the passports of the passengers. My passport had expired by the time the train entered the German border, and I was playing hide and seek with the inspectors by staying in the lavatory. They were used to these games and, thinking that they had gone through my compartment, I nonchalantly walked to my seat and was startled by a tap on my shoulder and an authoritative voice saying, "*Reisepass, bitte*"("Passport, please").

I reached in my pocket and handed over my passport to him, and, after examining it, he said, "This is expired."

I acted surprised and asked him to please let me see that. After looking at it, I said, "I am sorry. I did not realize that it was expiring. I assure you that I will renew it as soon as I reach home."

When he wanted to know where home was, I told him that it was in Sattenhausen and that my wife was from there. As he was digesting the information, I whipped out my wallet and showed him Ronnie's picture. He looked at it and called his colleague and, showing him, he said, "Walter, look here! This Pakistani is married to one of our German girls. They have a handsome blond son." He stated that he had two sons, but both of them had dark hair. In addition, my fluent German must have convinced him, because he stamped my passport, wished me good luck, and advised me not to travel across the borders with an expired passport.

21

I was glad to see my family again. I had brought a pair of shoes for Ronnie and a knitted dress for Reinhild. Knowing that I had a job to go back to, my spirits were high. On Monday I dispatched a letter to the Pakistani embassy inquiring about the passport renewal process, hoping that there was no security requirement. While waiting for their response, Reinhild, Ronnie, and I went to the meadows very early in the mornings to pick mushrooms for dinner. The letter from the Pakistani embassy arrived containing an application form for the renewal of my passport and, to my delight, there was no security requirement. I immediately mailed my passport and enclosed a money order for five German marks, the required fee. I could not leave for Bolton on the first of August because the renewed passport had not been received yet. A few days later I got a letter from Mr. Wilson, written in German, informing me that if I returned, they were willing to provide the necessary guarantees. It made me feel wanted. My passport would not arrive till August 14, but on August 7 the mailman delivered a letter from the United States that changed everything. Renate had found someone who would provide us with the evidence of support.

There was one catch. We would be working as a housekeeper and a butler for a period of two years. We would have our own living quarters, including meals, and a compensation of $25 per week. The sponsor would pay the fare for Reinhild and me, and we would have to pay for Ronnie. It did not take long for us to say yes. So I did not return to Bolton.

Reinhild and I filled out the necessary forms required by the United States consulate to process for immigration. I had to get my police records from Gujranwala, Pakistan, and Reinhild needed the same from Bolton. I was advised by the consulate that I should contact the proper officials in Pakistan immediately because they are very tardy in these matters. Unlike the U.S. passport that only warns the bearer about dangerous regions, a Pakistani passport at the time listed the countries that a bearer was permitted to enter. In order to add the United States to the list of permitted countries in my passport, I had to make a lengthy plea in a letter to the vice consul at the Pakistani embassy in Bonn, then the capital of Germany. Reinhild also had to request the police record from Bolton for the period she lived there. I was getting nervous, as one missing document could delay our departure.

In the meantime, I resumed driving the tractor, and when the crops had been harvested, the potato-picking season began. The potatoes were dug up by means of a machine pulled by a horse.

As soon as one row of potatoes had been turned up, Reinhild and I would begin our work from the opposite ends. While crawling on our knees, we would sort the potatoes according to size and toss them into two baskets that we pushed along. As soon as the baskets were filled, they were replaced by empty ones. Counting had become our instrument against boredom, and now it also led to a friendly competition. If we had been paid by the piece, we would have been the richest farmhands in the village. Although it was the beginning of fall, the daylight remained long enough for a ten-hour day. Ronnie had to accompany us on days when *Mutti*'s asthma acted up, and on those days Reinhart, upon his return from school, relieved Reinhild so she could go home with Ronnie. It was hard work, but Reinhild and I did not mind as our ultimate goal was in sight. We became known as the fastest potato-picking team in the village and were in great demand by other farmers. One day Herr Müller walked up to me and said, "Reinhild and you are working too hard. If you keep this up you won't make it to the United States."

"We need all the money we can get. I do not know what awaits us there."

He surprised me when he said, "If you need money that bad, ask me and I will give it to you." He was known to be very tight with his finances. I took his gesture to be a compliment, further lifting my confidence.

A letter from the U.S. consulate dated September 28, 1959, confirmed that we could immigrate as a family by forwarding the necessary documents. My passport arrived on October 15 with proper endorsement for the United States, and we received a letter from the British consulate in Düsseldorf informing Reinhild that UK Immigration did not issue police reports. I was still waiting for my report from Gujranwala when, on November 20, the much-awaited package from the United States was delivered. I held the large envelope in my hands while Reinhild looked over my shoulder and *Mutti* and Reinhart waited expectantly. It contained the affidavit of support, a letter from a bank substantiating the financial claims, and a small note from our employer that read:

> My dear Reinhild and Ashraf –
> I enclose the papers I made out for you here. I hope you have no further delay and will have a happy trip with the little boy. I am looking forward to meeting you and hope we will have a pleasant and successful time together. With every good wish for your prosperity and happiness in my country.
> Sincerely,
> Dorothy Eli Helme

The note, although brief, conveyed to me that Mrs. Helme was a kind and caring person and we needed to have no apprehensions. Included in the package were tickets for the USS *America,* sailing from Bremerhaven on January 2, 1960. Holding the package in my hand, I offered a silent prayer and said to myself, "My name must have come up on God's calendar, and I am ready to face what lies ahead."

The affidavit of support and the letter from the bank had to be authenticated by the German equivalent of a notary public. That was done on the seventh of December, and all the required documents were sent to Hamburg with an apology that the police report from Pakistan had not been received. In reply, the United States consulate in Hamburg asked that the three of us be at the consulate on December 16 by 9:00 a.m. in order to process the visa application.

The best way would have been to spend the night before the appointment in Hamburg. But we could not afford such a luxury. Instead, we spent the night at Reinhild's Uncle Harry's house in Göttingen and took the 3:30 morning train, arriving in Hamburg at 7:30 a.m., giving us enough time to walk to the consulate, which was approximately two miles away. We ate part of the sandwiches that Tante Martchen, Reinhild's aunt, had made for the journey. We had to take a street north on the eastern bank of the River Alster and then south on the other side of the river to our destination. It was bitter cold, and the freezing wind, penetrating our inadequate garbs, crawled on the skin like snakes, and the body heat from walking was not enough to stop the shivering. The surface of the river was all iced up and the cold became more intense as we crossed the bridge. Reinhild and I took turns in carrying Ronnie and holding him tightly to warm his little body. I wondered if he knew why he was being exposed to such severe conditions. He was not even three years old then, and his complaints were nothing more than statements of discomfort.

We entered the large lobby of the consulate and were shocked to see the number of people. It seemed that most of the German population wanted to immigrate to the United States. We had to consent to a complete physical examination that included chest x-rays, urinalysis, blood tests, and more. Ronnie was exempt but became angry when the technicians took my blood, as he did not want anybody hurting his father. It was touching. We had to wait for the results before the processing could proceed any further. Ronnie had not seen so many people in one place, having lived in the country all his life. He did not appear to be intimidated and waited patiently. At noon we were told that we could go to the cafeteria in the basement for a quick lunch. We could only afford one hamburger, which we shared. There was no place to sit, and Ronnie could not keep his hold on a cup of hot chocolate as someone bumped into him. It was about 4:00 p.m. when our names were called and we were ushered into the office of a vice consul, who asked us to take seats. He confirmed our answers to the previously asked questions and decided to forego the English test when he noticed that we had lived in the United Kingdom. He appeared ill at ease when he said, "Mrs. Qurashi, I am sorry, but I am required to ask this question."

Reinhild looked at him with apprehension. Then he asked, "Have you ever been engaged in prostitution?"

"Definitely not," she answered, and commented in jest, "but if I had, do you think that I would admit it in front of my husband?"

While laughing at the joke, he asked us to raise our right hands and repeat after him, "I swear that the above answers are true to the best of my knowledge, so help me God."

After that he stood up, shook our hands, and said, "Welcome to the United States of America. I wish you the best of luck."

We left the building with smiling faces and great anticipation.

We began making our way back to the station, and as soon as I picked up Ronnie, he put his head on my shoulder and fell asleep out of exhaustion. There was a two-hour delay before we could board our train to Göttingen, and we took turns holding Ronnie. It had been a long, tiring day, and we sat there in silence as all kinds of thoughts were invading my mind now that it appeared that our dream was within reach. Reinhild's faith in me was admirable, and she had become a partner in my dream, as it had now become our dream. Immediately after boarding the train, the rhythmic sound of the tracks lulled us to sleep till I heard the conductor announcing, "Next stop, Göttingen."

It was midnight when we arrived at Uncle Harry's house. My body was longing to be in a horizontal position, and I was lost in the dream world as soon as my head touched the pillow on the couch. Tante Martchen prepared a hearty breakfast before our departure on the morning bus to Sattenhausen. I was feeling confident about the future and the year on the farm in Germany had taught me many lessons that would stand me in good stead in my new country.

We kept working and saving as much money as we could. January 2 was fast approaching, and I was impatiently waiting for the visa documents from Hamburg. A suit, which I had purchased in Bolton in 1954, needed cleaning because I had worn it in the field. Everybody in the village knew about our impending departure. Christmas was approaching, and we had no word from the U.S. consulate. Our apprehension was growing with each passing day, and at chance meetings our close acquaintances inquired if we had received the letter from the Americans. Although not for Christmas, our present arrived two days later when the mailman delivered a large envelope from the U.S. consulate in Hamburg. Inside the package were two large, sealed, brown envelopes addressed to the United States Immigration and Naturalization Administration. The accompanying letter informed us that we were to surrender the enclosed envelopes to the immigration inspector in New York, and it further stated that the final decision about our entry into the United States rested with the immigration authorities at the port of entry. This was a little disheartening but not discouraging.

We celebrated New Year's Eve at the tavern, joined by the Müller family. Herr Müller recounted some of our experiences, and his remarks were very complimentary. On January 2, accompanied by Reinhart and *Mutti*, we boarded the morning bus to Göttingen. Herr Müller came to the bus stop to bid us farewell, and he pressed a fifty-mark bill in my hand. When I thanked him, he said, "You have earned it, but do not tell Oma Erna about it."

Uncle Harry and Tante Marchen joined us at the railway station, and after saying our farewells we boarded the noon train that would take us to Bremerhaven by 4:00 p.m., just in time to embark on our journey to the next adventure.

22

We approached the docks of Bremerhaven with excitement and great anticipation as two shiny red smokestacks with white and blue stripes, those of the USS *America*, rose above the horizon. The ship, launched on August 31, 1939, by First Lady Eleanor Roosevelt, was 723 feet long, the largest and the most luxurious liner of its time, outfitted to carry 1,202 passengers and a crew of 643. The war interrupted its original mission of sailing between New York and Bremerhaven, as the ship was called into service by the United States Navy to transport troops instead. The vessel was returned to its intended mission in 1946, the year when my dream took on a life. Here it was fourteen years later on the very cold day of January 2, 1960, to carry us closer to the fulfillment of that dream. Was it a coincidence?

The lobby of the ship was decorated with red and gold velvet drapes and a thick red carpet with a large USS *America* emblem occupying its center. The members of the staff, dressed in white uniforms, were examining the documents and directing the passengers to their cabins. Our cabin was four decks below in the third class, the others being the first and the tourist classes. Our cabin door opened into a small room with three berths, two of them one above the other against the left wall, and a clothes closet in the back corner. A single berth on the right side was wedged between a small desk that faced the closet and a sink with running hot and cold water in the front right corner. The outer wall supported a porthole that was just above the waterline. The shower stall and toilet were situated outside the cabin and were shared by an adjoining cabin. The ship would be our home for the next nine days. Although the dining room was large, it required two sittings to serve all the passengers. Our assigned table allowed us to dine during the first seating, where we had three other dinner companions, an older German woman with two adolescent children. She was escorting her grandchildren to Austin, Texas, where the children's parents already lived. She wanted to own a hot dog concession there. The recreational area was enclosed with glass doors that opened to the main deck, and there was a bar and a dais set in one corner with large speakers and room for a band that played music during the evenings for the dancing pleasure of the passengers. There also was a play area for the children, where they could build things with Legos, view cartoon movies, and occupy themselves with other playthings. Ronnie, one month and five days shy of his third birthday, made friends with the other children who shared our dining table.

The ship pushed off from the docks before sunset and headed to the North Sea, and that night I ate my first hearty dinner of steak and baked potatoes. The third class was separated from the other classes, and the passengers were not allowed to enter the areas of the other classes. After taking a quick walk through our part of the ship, we retired to our cabin, and it did not take long for the hum of the engines to lull us to a deep sleep. The following day began with a buffet breakfast, followed by a sit-down lunch. Ronnie was very excited and had many questions. Around noon on the third day, the North Atlantic Ocean welcomed us with its notorious high winds and unstable seas. Mild in the beginning, the pitching became progressively violent, and by the dinner time, the ship's bow was riding on the crest of twenty-foot gales like a roller coaster and then momentarily disappearing into the next wave. The captain ordered all the glass doors to be closed and warned the passengers to remain indoors. We did not sleep well during the night as the ship continued to pitch and roll and we could see the water line appearing and disappearing above our porthole. Reinhild became seasick and could not go for breakfast. Ronnie, although not sick, stayed with his mother in the cabin, where they would be served their meals during the stormy days. Once a sailor advised me that in order to avoid seasickness, one needed to keep the stomach full at all times, which I followed religiously and therefore did not suffer.

The following morning I entered a deserted dining room, as most of the passengers decided to confine themselves to their cabins. Even our steward was absent. The substitute waiter asked me if I wanted the buffet or an order from the menu, suggesting an American breakfast that consisted of a steak with eggs and pancakes. He informed me that I could order as many steaks as I wanted because there were not too many people eating that day. After breakfast, I walked wherever I was allowed to and watched the violent waves covering the sea as far as the eye could see. A U.S. Navy ship a few miles away caught my attention as it steered through the stormy sea. When it rode the crest of a wave, it appeared to be high above my position, and when we were riding a wave I could only see the top of the mast of the naval vessel. The storm lasted for three days in varying intensity and finally began to ease on the morning of the sixth day, and more of the passengers began to come out of their cabins. As customary, the captain's dinner, held on the night before reaching New York, was very formal. The members of the crew were wearing their dress uniforms with shining bands of their ranks decorating the sleeves. The stewards carrying dessert trays came in marching to Sousa's music. The festivities ended with a short speech by the captain welcoming the passengers to the country where dreams had the potential of becoming realities.

I wondered how Ronnie would adjust to his new circumstances. He was the center of attention in Germany, and suddenly he would have to take a second place to our employer. How would he cope with a totally strange language and customs? These were the thoughts that occupied my mind as we neared New York and our new country. We were informed that we would be docking on pier two on the morning of January 11, 1960, and disembarkation would begin immediately after an early breakfast. At 6:00 in the morning, it was announced that we were passing the Statue of Liberty on our port (left) side. The passengers, mostly immigrants, rushed to the main deck to view the giant lady, as it represented what many were seeking in their new home. The ship had docked by the time the sun began to outline the silhouette of the Manhattan skyline. I had never seen such a collection of buildings except in pictures. There were short ones next to the tall ones with lights in the windows still burning, and the lit-up Empire State Building, the tallest in the world at the time, was reaching for the sky.

All the immigrants were required to gather in the enclosed areas of the main deck while the U.S. citizens passed through a separate exit. We had to wait for over an hour before I handed the large envelope to the immigration officer, who methodically opened the seal of each brown envelope and spread the papers on his desk. After examining the documents, he wanted to see our passports and then, in jest, asked Ronnie, "Are you going to take care of your parents?" Ronnie could only smile as he did not understand the question. He stamped our passports and, with a broad smile, stated, "Welcome to the United States of America. I wish you a prosperous life." He explained that we would receive a communication from the Immigration and Naturalization Administration explaining our further obligations.

It was around ten in the morning by the time we stepped into the customs building to collect our luggage. The place was crowded with not only the passengers but also those who had come to meet their arriving relatives. Reinhild and I did not have to look for long to find Renate. She introduced us to her husband, Henry Schelter, who had also immigrated to the United States from Germany. We carried our luggage to their 1956 Ford. We also had brought along a large crate full of china for Renate, and I assisted Henry to secure the crate on the roof carriers of his car before beginning the next leg of our journey. The tall buildings made the streets appear narrow, blocking the clear sky. We were in Manhattan for a short time before entering a tunnel. Renate explained that the tunnel was under the River Hudson and that the State of New Jersey lay on the other side.

Immediately after the exit from the tunnel there was an attendant in a small booth collecting a toll. We had traveled a few miles when Henry turned onto a divided highway where a large sign announced that it was the New Jersey Turnpike and an attendant handed out tickets that displayed the charges for each of the exits. I had never paid for the use of a road before, and I later discovered that in the old days the owners allowed passage through their private property for a fee and controlled the entrance by the use of removable pikes. We stopped at the first rest area, where there were toilet facilities and a restaurant. While in Germany, I had read an article in the *Reader's Digest* about the Howard Johnson rest areas along the major highways in the United States, and now I was in one of them. Instead of chairs and tables, there were booths with benches and tables where we sat to have lunch. Later we drove by a smelly refinery and entered the open country, where the highway was divided but the clutter of billboards on both sides of the road blocked the otherwise pleasing landscape. Even the sides of the single-lane roads were crowded with billboards. By midafternoon we arrived at Renate and Henry's rented house in Camden, New Jersey, and met their daughter, Ursula, who was over one year younger than Ronnie. In bed that night we still felt as if the room was pitching and rolling. By the time we woke up, Henry had left for work. The last leg of our journey took place that afternoon, when Renate drove us to the house of our future employer.

As we turned into an opening through a line of dense trees and bushes, a three-story sandstone mansion came into our view like magic. Our new address was an eighty-year-old house in the Chestnut Hills area of the historic city of Philadelphia. A tall maple tree, surrounded by neatly trimmed bushes, majestically stood in the center of a circular driveway. Renate parked her car in front of the door and rang the bell, which was answered after a few minutes by a tall, stately woman in her fifties. She invited us into a very spacious hall and said, "Hello, I am Mrs. Helme, and you must be Ashraf and Reinhild."

Renate left after the introductions had been completed.

"Nice to meet you," Reinhild and I said in unison and then, pointing to Ronnie, said, "This is Ronnie."

"Hello, Ronnie," she said with a smile and directed us to follow her to our quarters. We walked through a very large dining room into a narrow passageway that was lined with cabinets to store silverware, china, and other dining accessories. It connected to a kitchen, where an old, out-of-service wood stove stood in the far right corner. Daylight streamed in through a large front window, under which a sink with running hot and cold water was supported by a countertop over a set of cabinets that extended to the end of the room on the right and about five feet to the left, ending against a modern gas range and oven. A large refrigerator and a freezer stood against the opposite wall next to the entrance to a stair well. We followed her up the steep staircase to a landing where it reversed its direction and the door at the top opened into the sitting area of the servants' quarters, which had two bedrooms and a bathroom. It would be our home for the next one year and ten months. A door from the sitting area opened into a second-story balcony of the main house, with three bedrooms, two baths, and a master suite. There was a one-bedroom apartment on the third level. She explained about the bell system in the house by which she could call us when needed and informed us that we would receive a weekly wage of $25, and room and board. Addressing us, she asked, "Where did you learn English?"

"I went to college in England, and Reinhild trained there in nursing," I replied.

"Reinhild, you do not have to wear a uniform," she said. While looking at me, she continued, "You can look for a suitable job and help here in your spare time."

"That is very generous of you. Be assured that we will not let you down."

She told us that she would be going to her son's house in Paoli for a few nights to give us time to settle in and said, "There is food in the refrigerator, and if there is any problem you can walk to the house on the left of the property, and the lady of the house there can contact my son."

She warned us that the woman was blind and we should be careful in approaching her. A few minutes later we saw her green Cadillac vanish behind the trees at the end of the driveway as the sun was ending its day's journey behind the horizon.

Finally I was in the country of my choice, where we had a place to live with some privacy. I had been mentally prepared for it, but to know that I did not have to wear a tuxedo and walk erectly with deliberate steps to answer the front door was a great relief. We decided to explore the property. Attached to the kitchen on the right side of the building was a mud room with a back door that opened onto a covered porch and a few descending steps to a large, paved area, which was in front of two garages behind the house. There was a short, steep climb to the main driveway on the right. We stepped from the mud room onto the porch to view the open landscape, but the cold air compelled us to retrace our steps. When I turned the knob of the door and it refused to open, I realized that a gust of wind had pushed the door shut and we were locked out. Huddled together, we trekked to the house at the end of the driveway and rang the door bell. A few minutes later I heard cautious footsteps, and an elderly lady appeared holding the door open and wanted to know, "Who is there?"

"We just arrived at Mrs. Helme's house, and she had directed us to contact you if we encountered any problem so you could reach her son," I explained.

She seemed alarmed and inquired, "What kind of problem?"

I assured her, "It is nothing serious. We are locked out of the house."

Before I could explain the cause of our problem, she said that she did not have any keys for the house but she could call Jay, her son, and he would take care of it. She invited us in and sat down on her chair and dialed the phone that was nearby on the side table. I was impressed with her awareness of the surroundings and her self-reliance. A blind person in Pakistan would have sat on a cot and expected to be served. She hung up the phone after a short conversation and assured us that someone was on the way. She asked about Ronnie's age and informed us that her daughter's son, Malcolm, was about the same age. She allowed us to stay in her house out of the cold till Reese, a relation of Mrs. Helme's daughter-in-law, arrived. I told Reese how embarrassed I was about the incident on the first day of our employment. He gave me a quick tutorial about the locking system in the United States and then climbed on the outside ledge of a window and slid a card in the gap between the two parts of the window and slid the latch open. He climbed in through the window and opened the front door for us. He noticed my enquiring look and explained, "These old houses have windows that do not fit tightly, making it easy to unlatch them. By the way, the door in the back is self-closing, and you should unlock it before going out. Feel free to call me if you have any problem."

He wrote down his telephone number before leaving.

23

Mrs. Helme returned after a few days and drove us down Germantown Avenue for about a mile while pointing out various local shops, and then stopped at Acme markets to purchase food. She wanted us to pick up what we needed for the "little man." I was happy to know that I did not have to do any yard work, as there was a part-time gardener. She explained what she expected of us, and it did not take long before a routine set in and I began sending my handwritten resumes to various textile enterprises. In the meantime, the winter was moving in with all its fury. By the middle of February, the snowfall began to coat the landscape with layers of fine powder, and by the end of the month it had gathered the intensity of a full-blown storm. Mrs. Helme, as in every winter, traveled to Florida to spend the cold months with her other son, George. I had experienced heavy snowfall in the city of Srinagar as a child, but never had I encountered such a quantity that greeted us during our first year in Philadelphia. We were housebound without any means of transportation. Although it was tough treading through the back streets, I had to travel by foot to the market in order to replenish our food supplies. It became easier to walk once I reached the main road that had been cleared. The snow had begun to fall by the time I came out of Acme carrying four bags of groceries, so I decided to hire a taxi cab for my return journey. The driver made three attempts to reach the house but failed to advance through the high drifts. He drove me within two blocks of the house before abandoning the quest, and once he knew that I was an immigrant, he refused to charge me for the ride. When I insisted that he take some compensation for his trouble, he said, "I can't accept this because I failed to deliver you to your destination."

I had been waiting for some response to my letters that I had sent in an attempt to find a job, but none came. I attended a gathering of foreign students meeting in Philadelphia and followed up on some leads without success. I needed to be engaged in some productive enterprise and was ready to accept any job because I was confident that eventually I would reach my goal. While scanning the Help Wanted column of the Sunday edition of the *Philadelphia Inquirer*, an advertisement caught my eye. A textile mill in the northern part of the city had an opening for a "loom fixer" and required that the applicant apply in person. The following Monday I walked to the Chestnut Hill trolley station and, forty-five minutes and a change of bus later, I arrived at Windsor Textile Mills. It was 11:00 in the morning. I met Mr. John Kendrick, the works manager, for an interview. Fearing that I would be overqualified, I purposely omitted my education and management experience but informed him that I had supervised a weaving shift. He explained to me that it was a small specialty mill that produced high-quality woolen cloth. He could initially offer me the job as a weaver with a chance for promotion to a supervisory position. The starting wage was $1.10 per hour for the first forty hours of the week, but there was a chance for ten hours of overtime per week that would be paid at time and a half. He informed me that I could earn approximately $64.90 per week and, after taxes and other deductions, could take home around $51.00. It was a beginning.

I received a quick training and was assigned to tend four looms producing fine worsted cloth. A week later one of the workers, a tall man with heavy polish accent, handed me a card and said,

"Fill this out and return it to me by the end of the week."

"What is this for?"

"It is a union membership card."

"I do not wish to join a union," I told him

"Then you do not work here. Think about it and make sure I get the card back, properly signed, in time," he said threateningly.

I reluctantly took the card, and as he walked away he informed me that there would be a deduction of 50¢ per week for the union dues. At lunch I caught up with Jack, as John Kendrick preferred to be called, showed him the card, and related my conversation. He explained that the closed shop is the law of the state and that the workers at the Windsor Mills were unionized. I had no choice but to return the signed card to Sam, the shop steward.

This was my first exposure to Americans in a working setting. We were allowed two ten-minute breaks in addition to the half hour for lunch. The only place available to sit during the break was a bench beneath an opaque window in the men's room opposite three urinals and five lavatory stalls, three of which had no doors. Most of the younger workers congregated in that room. My stays there were brief because of the concentration of the blue suffocating smoke emanating from the cigarettes. So I would return to my station earlier than the end of the break and would start up the looms. I had noticed Sam's suspicious looks, and one day he appeared from nowhere and, in a threatening tone, said, "You are working too hard and making us all look bad. You need to slow down."

Although this warning was at odds with my perception about American work ethics, I dismissed it as an anomaly.

What really disturbed me was the verbal harassment by young men against anybody over fifty. This behavior was contrary to my upbringing, where age was revered no matter what station in life one held. But although Russell, in his early twenties, tormented the elder employees, he reached out to me with many questions about my culture and would later demonstrate his kinder side by assisting me in changing the brake pads of my car so it could pass the state inspection. He refused to accept any compensation for his time. I would meet many kind and compassionate young and old Americans along my journey. Even Reinhild's Uncle Alfred changed his attitudes towards me, a non-German, once he had met me.

Renate convinced Aunt Marie, the wife of Uncle Alfred, to invite us for a visit. It was arranged for Uncle Alfred to meet us at the train station in Camden. We took the trolley and changed to the Broadway Subway to Market Street, where another change of train delivered us to Camden. While waiting for a train at an underground station, Ronnie had to go to the bathroom, and my search for one was unsuccessful. Unlike underground train stations in European countries where lavatories were readily available, the Philadelphia station had no such facilities. Somebody suggested we go to a restaurant at the street level, but before we could do that I saw Ronnie relieving himself in a corner of the platform. When he saw my disturbed expression, he told me that he could not hold any longer, and the strong smell emanating from the corner left no doubt that the area had already been used as a lavatory. I would find similar corners at many platforms.

I registered with the National Draft Board as required by the INS, and while I waited for their classification, we discovered that Reinhild was pregnant. We were excited but concerned with the reactions of our employer, fearing that our services may be terminated, and the other concern was that the army might decide to order me into the service. Reinhild had tears in her eyes when she delivered the news of her pregnancy to Mrs. Helme, who, after a pause, told her not to worry and that everything would be all right. I am ever grateful for her generosity. A few weeks later the much-awaited good news arrived in the form of a 4F classification by the National Draft Board. It meant that I did not have to worry about military service. We also opened a bank account at the local branch of the Pennsylvania Banking and Trust company and purchased health insurance from Mutual of Omaha at a cost of $17.50 per month that covered 80 percent of our medical bills. We were required to pay the doctors and then submit a claim to the insurance company. It would not cover the birth of our baby because of a preexisting condition. With negligible household expenses, it was easy to save the needed $400 for the delivery of our baby by November.

We also decided to purchase a television, as there was none in the servants' quarters, and we felt that it could hasten Ronnie's language transition to English. One day after work I stopped at Silo, an appliance store, to get an idea of the prices and found a black and white seventeen-inch TV on sale for $159. After discussing it with Reinhild and carefully calculating our finances, I returned to the store and informed a salesman about my intended purchase. He asked, "How do you want to pay for it?"

"I can pay by a check," I said, wondering what other ways there could be to make a purchase.

"If you finance it and pay it off in ninety days, there is no interest," he informed me.

"I do not need to finance it," I told him, not knowing the financing system.

"Son, the most important asset that one can own in this country is his credit rating. By financing this purchase, you will establish a credit record that will be valuable when you are ready to buy a car or a house."

His advice was beneficial then and is pertinent today and would stand me in good stead in my future life. We also decided to purchase Renate's old 1952 Ford, and Reese assisted me in getting my driver's license.

Reinhild and Ronnie accompanied Mrs. Helme to her Shelter Island home for the summer, joining her daughter-in-law and two granddaughters, who also spent their summer there. The first time, I accompanied Jay, her son, and Reese to the island for a weekend but drove myself during the later visits. The end of Long Island in the Atlantic Ocean bifurcates into northern and southern land masses, appearing like an open mouth of a giant creature, ready to swallow Shelter Island, which was situated between the two prongs. Two ferries connected the island to the northern and the southern extensions of the mainland. The residents of the island were mostly sailing enthusiasts and held boat races during the summer months. The end of the summer brought everyone back home and I was reunited with my family. After that, the time passed quickly and we waited for the arrival of the new member of our family.

It was the evening of November 29 when Reinhild, against the doctor's prediction, warned that the baby would be arriving by the thirtieth. As the waves of pain came closer, I left Reinhild at the Chestnut Hill Hospital and then drove to Henry and Renate's new home in Pennsauken, New Jersey, to leave Ronnie there for a few days. I returned to the hospital around 11:30 p.m. with a paperback edition of *War and Peace* in preparation to spend a long night. I settled down with a cup of coffee and had just opened the book when the doctor entered the waiting room and announced, "Your wife just delivered a healthy baby girl. You will be able to see her in the hallway as the nurse takes her to the nursery."

"Already!" I exclaimed and rushed to the hallway.

I had missed the opportunity to see Ronnie immediately after he was born, and I was determined to see my second child, a beautiful girl with dark hair and a peaceful expression. I was led to the room where Reinhild was resting and still groggy. Ruby, the name we had decided upon earlier, was born at 12:01on November 30, 1960. Three days later I picked up Ronnie from New Jersey, and on the way we stopped to collect the rest of our family from the hospital. Ronnie was fascinated with his little sister and was always eager to help in taking care of her whenever we got busy with our work at the house. Mrs. Helme was kind enough to hire additional help for a few weeks and engaged a diaper service. Disposable diapers had not been invented yet.

The addition of a new member to our family heightened my urgency to find a sustaining career. The fact that the textiles industry was shrinking was reinforced when Jack at the Mills informed me that, because I was the last one to be hired, there was high probability that my job was in jeopardy. While we had a roof over our head, I decided to try my hand at sales and took a job as a Fuller Brush man where I had to make cold calls to sell house-cleaning chemicals, brooms, hairbrushes, and makeup accessories. It offered me a great opportunity to understand the complex American culture. I was given a territory, comprised mostly of row homes, stretching from Tioga Street south to Alleghany Avenue and from Fifth Street west to Broad Street. During my afternoon and evening calls, I would find children playing games in the streets while their parents, drinks in their hands, lounged around on the front steps of their homes. This was just like the movies I had seen. A sense of community pervaded the air. My trainer used to get upset if I spent more than five minutes at one house. I discovered that although I was gaining great insight into the American psyche, door-to-door cold-call sales was not my cup of tea. I could not, as directed, sell the idea that a hairbrush made with the bristles of a wild boar would prevent baldness and could not always satisfy the desires of some customers. The manager had warned me about it. One woman always answered the door in her open dressing gown with nothing underneath. So I decided to seek some other trade or profession.

24

My next job began as an electrician's helper, and within a few months I was leading a team of electricians wiring homes, apartment buildings, and factories with a take-home wage of $64.50 per week. There were some challenging projects that alleviated the otherwise boring routine work of pulling wires through the framed walls. Not being afraid of heights, I was the only employee in the company who was responsible for maintaining the lighting of five billboards that were about twenty feet above the roofs on the edge of ten- to twelve-story buildings. Once it was scary when, with high winds, I had to change the floodlights on a billboard late in the evening. But it was during the renovation of the Broad Street Theater that I experienced the destructive tactics of the unionized labor. The conduits, through which the wires would be pulled for the lighting of the theatre, were placed in the walls awaiting the completion of wall plastering. When my crews arrived to pull the wires, they encountered two major problems. The pull strings that we had left in the conduits were missing in many places, and in others the pipes were filled with plastering material. The cost of rectifying these problems ran into thousands, jeopardizing the financial health of my employer.

By this time Reinhild and I felt that the time had come for us to be on our own. Ruby was almost a year old and needed more attention, while Ronnie was over four years old and soon would be ready for school. Reinhild and I spent many days analyzing our resources and making plans that would allow us to be on our own. We knew that it would not be easy but were prepared to face the challenge. We discussed the matter with Mrs. Helme, who agreed with us, with the condition that we allow her time to find a replacement. We set the time for our move around the middle of October and went apartment hunting.

A second-story apartment was available in the same building where Elvira, one of Renate's friends, lived. It was in the Yorkship Square in the city of Camden in the state of New Jersey, just across the Delaware River. During the war years the complex was built around a landscaped square in order to provide housing for the well-paid employees of the Camden Shipyard. The second-story landing had two apartments. Our front door opened into a very small vestibule connected to the large living room, with a window overlooking the square. A small kitchen and a spacious dining room, attached to the living room, faced the back of the building and provided the access to the fire escape. A narrow hallway extending from the far end of the living room led to a bathroom on the right and two bedrooms on the left. The rent of $75 per month included water and heating. It appeared that the neighborhood had seen prosperous times but seemed to be in decline, as ship building had nearly come to a close, but it offered us a convenient location for the coming few years. The dining room served as our master bedroom so Ronnie and Ruby could have their own rooms. Although tall trees lined the streets, the summer months could become unbearable, and, in the absence of air conditioning, the window fans were the only relief from the high heat and humidity.

In the middle of October 1961, we moved from Mrs. Helme's stately home to our humble abode. Uncle Alfred gave us his very old sofa that was stored in his chicken shed for years, where the feathered residents had made full use of it—nothing that could not be rectified with thorough cleaning and a cover of new tapestry. It was without any arm rests, but it filled the space against the wall and offered somewhat uncomfortable seating for the family. Used furniture that included a double bed with mattress and box spring, a dresser, two twin beds complete with mattresses, and a metal dinette set with four chairs cost us $40. Another $20 was spent to buy a toaster, pots and pans, and other kitchen utensils, all made in the United States of America, at the W. T. Grant store, since defunct. The television found its place on a stack of cinderblocks covered with the leftover tapestry, later replaced by a handmade bookshelf-cum-TV-stand.

It was late afternoon on Saturday, October 14, 1961, when we completed setting up our household and decided to take a stroll around the square to explore the neighborhood. Alabama Avenue emanating from the lower eastern corner connected to State Route 130, while Kearsarge Road, from the lower western corner, provided connection to Interstate 76, which led to the Walt Whitman Bridge to Philadelphia. Yorkship Road, a divided street, proceeded northeast from the top center of the square to Broadway, the main street of the city of Camden. The place was ideally located within a short distance of a Laundromat and a food market where we purchased supplies for the evening dinner. Yorkship Elementary School, which Ronnie would soon attend, was a few blocks away on South Octagon Road. It was Sunday, and I decided to get a copy of the *Philadelphia Inquirer* from a newspaper dispenser near the Laundromat. Ronnie volunteered to fetch it and, after taking the change from my hand, took off shouting, "I know where it is." We became concerned when he failed to return in a reasonable time. Reinhild, pushing Ruby in a stroller, went one way while I, driving the car, began my search the other way. We felt that he became confused with all the streets entering the square and made a wrong turn. Driving back on Alabama Avenue, I noticed a woman walking towards the square holding the hand of a boy who looked like Ronnie. Stopping the car, I yelled out his name and, recognizing my voice, he turned around and then began to run towards me. I jumped out and caught him in my arms as he kept repeating, "I am sorry." The woman informed me that he had stopped her car and told her that he was lost and that his family had just moved from Philadelphia to a big building. She explained that she was taking him to the square to find a car with Pennsylvania tags. Pointing to her parked car, she said he would not get in it because he was not allowed to ride in a stranger's car. I thanked her and felt proud of my little son, who acted with courage when he found himself in a scary situation.

Three bridges, Walt Whitman, Benjamin Franklin, and Tacony-Palmyra, provided easy access to various sections of the city of Philadelphia. Leaving the apartment at 6:30 in the morning, I would take the appropriate bridge to get to wherever my project took me. Reinhild, ever so budget minded, cooked up great recipes with 33¢-cents-per-pound ground beef, purchased when on sale at the local market. Since our first meeting with Uncle Alfred, we visited him often to get a hearty meal that Aunt Marie happily provided. In order to wash clothes, Reinhild would start the morning by loading the washing machines at the Laundromat and then return to prepare breakfast before my departure for work. By the time the children were served their breakfast, it would be time for the clothes to be transferred to a dryer. Later the children would accompany her to the Laundromat to help fold the laundry, a team effort.

At that time interracial marriages were rare, and Reinhild and I were not only racially diverse but had been brought up with different faiths. I owe it to *Abbajee*, who helped me to develop my liberal views in the practice of Islam. Lucky for me, Reinhild had similar thoughts concerning her faith. So we have always strived to be charitable and fair while ignoring the man-made rigors of organized religions. These beliefs made it easy for us to have an enduring relationship, adapting to the culture of our new country as we followed the old axiom of "doing what Romans would do when in Rome." I discovered that, unlike the English, the Americans were outgoing, respected hard work, and were generous to lend a helping hand when and if needed, but their discriminatory attitude towards the African Americans puzzled me. The Vietnam War and the civil rights protests made up the bulk of daily news, and I had difficulty reconciling the behavior of some of the officials and persons with respect to the African Americans in the Southern states.

In December of 1961, *Mutti*, Reinhild's mother, came for a visit from Germany. She took care of the children while Reinhild began to work the 3:00 p.m. to 11:30 p.m. shift as a nurse's aide at Our Lady of Lourdes Hospital in Camden, earning $1.05 per hour. In the afternoon she took a bus to the hospital, and I would pick her up when her shift ended. *Mutti* always liked to maintain a clean house, and one day, upon my arrival, I noticed that the brass knob of the door was polished, and as soon as I entered the vestibule my feet went from under me and I landed on my rear with my head in the door way. The wooden floor was shiny clean. Not knowing the language, she had picked up the bottle of furniture polish instead of the floor polish.

At work, my next project would be like a road sign pointing me to the path of my dream. My employer took on a job to install a security system to protect an expensive mansion. The electronic security industry was practically nonexistent then, because crime was rare and people did not feel threatened. One of the shop owners had to design the control panel using low voltage electric relays, and I got the job to install the system. As we worked together to resolve the technical problems, which were numerous because of the complexity of the system, I felt confident that I could earn better wages by working in an electronics company. In order to accomplish that I enrolled in a home study course in basic electronics offered by the International Correspondence Schools, the same school that taught me all about cotton spinning.

I studied during each and every available moment and completed the course just in time, because my work hours at the shop had been greatly reduced. With the ICS certificate in hand, I began the search for a job in the electronics industry.

Scanning the Help Wanted classifieds in the *Philadelphia Inquirer*, I came upon an advertisement by Snelling and Snelling, an employment agency, searching for an electronics technician. Lisa, an agent responding to my call the following morning, informed me that she would find a position if I was willing to sign a contract to pay a fee of $362 once I had accepted the job. In response to my offer of paying the fee over a period of six months, she advised that once employed I could borrow the required amount from the Household Finance Corporation. Reinhild and I concluded that we had to take the chance, and a day after the contract was signed, Lisa informed me that she had set up an interview at Jerrold Electronics Corporation located in Hatboro, Pennsylvania, in the northeastern suburb of the city. It was a forty-five minute drive over the Tacony-Palmyra Bridge. My apprehension was climbing off the charts when, at 8:30 a.m., I presented myself to the receptionist in the lobby and handed her the referral letter from the agency. Without looking up, she gave me an application form and, pointing to a chair, said, "Make sure all the questions are answered. Mr. Scott Fry will be with you shortly."

She appeared very detached, which led me to believe that there might be other applicants. That thought made me a little nervous, but by the time Mr. Fry stepped into the lobby I had calmed myself by looking at this interview as a learning experience.

"I am Scott Fry," he said, spelling his last name. After taking my filled-out application from my hands, he asked, "How do you pronounce your last name?"

After I told him, he led me to a conference room, where I had to write some of the basic formulae used in electronics. Then he drew a few schematics and wanted to know if I could recognize any of the circuits, which I did. He then directed me to follow him to the laboratory in the back and take a practical test. Before that day I had not seen or touched electronics components, such as capacitors or coils, except in black and white pictures.

While walking to the back of the building and scanning my application, he said, "I see you also speak German. I have never heard it spoken."

"I lived in Germany for over a year."

We entered the model shop on the left at the end of the hallway. The walls were lined with technicians' benches, sheet metal machines, and a desk with a telephone. He directed me to one of the benches and, while handing me a schematic and a small chassis, he said, "You study this while I get Jim, who also speaks German. I want to hear the language as you converse." All eyes were upon me.

A few minutes later he returned, accompanied by a gentleman who said, "*Ich bin James Herman.*"

"Sie können mich Mac nennen ("You can call me Mac)," I continued in German. "Where did you learn the language?"

"I was in the service there for two years, and my wife is from Germany."

"My wife is also German, and I lived there before coming to the United States," I replied. Still speaking in German, I asked him if he could help me with this assembly.

"As soon as he leaves, I will come back and show you what to do," he said while looking at Mr. Fry. Then he left.

"Now I know what German sounds like," Mr. Fry said. Pointing to the wall shelves, he continued, "You will find what you need for the assembly in those jars. Take your time, and I will be back to check on you later."

Immediately after Mr. Fry left, Jim Herman returned and assisted me with the components I needed. The rest was easy, although my soldering was not quite up to par. Mr. Fry returned after approximately half an hour and, taking his time examining my finished work, asked me to follow him across the hall to an office. I was introduced to a man in his forties who was comfortably seated behind a wooden desk. He stood up and extended his hand, which I hesitantly shook. He asked me to sit in the only empty chair at the side of the desk. He was reading my application while I made myself comfortable and after a pause he said, "I am Len Ecker, and I see you want to be called Mac."

"Yes sir. I do not like to be called Joe or Charlie so I gave myself my own nickname."

"There are no sirs here. You can call me Len. Scott says that you are a quick learner. As far as I am concerned, you can start as a wireman in our model shop at $1.76 per hour and, depending on how fast you learn, you can make as much as $9.00 per hour," he said

"When can I start?" I asked.

"Is Monday too soon?"

"Monday would be fine." I told him while attempting to suppress my excitement.

He called Scott and told him that I would be starting on Monday. I was led back into the model shop, where Scott announced, "This is Mac, and he will be joining our team on Monday. Give him all the assistance he needs."

After shaking hands with the seven technicians and wiremen, I filled out some more paperwork for the Internal Revenue Service, company health insurance, etc. The work hours were from 7:30 a.m. to 4:30 p.m., with two ten-minute breaks, one in the morning and one in the afternoon, and a half hour for lunch. It was just before noon when I left the building, and in my excitement I did not take time to ask what kind of business the company conducted. I hurried home and shared the good news with Reinhild, and then arranged a loan from the Household Finance Corporation.

25

I began my new job at 7:30 a.m. on Monday, March 19, 1962, and discovered that the model shop was part of a large product development laboratory with the main office and the production facility in the city of Philadelphia. The building consisted of many areas where engineers did their work, a drafting room, a mechanical testing lab, and a fully equipped machine shop. The chief engineer and the vice president of engineering each had his own electronics testing facilities. I then learned that Jerrold Electronics was the manufacturer and installer of cable television systems, an industry in its infancy.

Initially my job was to wind precision coils, assemble circuit boards, and modify large pieces of equipment, and later I learned how to test some of what I built. My workbench was equipped with the standard testing instruments, and one day after I returned from a break, I noticed that each time I reached for the knob of an instrument, smoke would come pouring out of it. Obviously it was a prank, because it smelled of cigarettes. I quietly observed and found the culprit, Bud, who had rigged a tube from his bench to the back of mine and used it to blow his cigarette smoke each time I reached for a knob on the testing meter. During his break, I reversed the tube arrangement and borrowed a cigarette from one of the technicians. When Bud returned and reached for a knob he received the same treatment that he had given me. This was the turning point for my acceptance by the group.

During the morning break, an elderly gentleman sold donuts and took orders for the lunch. That was when I was introduced to the Philly cheese steak. When I took my first bite of the roll, which was larger than the opening of my mouth, a good portion of the contents fell in my lap, eliciting a laugh from my co-workers.

One Friday, Scott asked me if I would be willing to work long hours over the weekend with Frank Ragone, a senior engineer, and his assistants to complete a project that was fast approaching a deadline. This was a chance for me to make extra money and help pay off the loan, with an additional benefit of working directly with the engineers. A chassis had to be assembled that required 520 rivets no more than a quarter-inch apart, a tedious job. Just as in Germany when I counted sugar beets to overcome boredom, I counted each rivet as I pushed the pedal of the machine. The task was completed in time, and after that I became the one who was called upon for all the challenging prototype work.

Reinhild continued to work at the hospital although *Mutti* had returned to Germany. A teenager who lived with her parents in our complex babysat each day until my return from work. After dinner, which had been prepared earlier, the children and I would watch cartoons, *Flipper*, and *Sea Hunt* on television before their bedtime. At 11:15 p.m., after informing Elvira, our downstairs neighbor, I would leave to pick up Reinhild. We moved in the same social circles as Renate and Henry and joined the local German club, where we attended monthly dance parties.

My beliefs are based on the teachings of the Quran that directs Muslims to respect the earlier scriptures and confers the highest honor upon Jesus. So I had no problem to accompany our friends to the German church and did not mind when they suggested that on July 1, 1962, we should have Ronnie and Ruby baptized along with their children. We maintained open minds towards the teachings of all religions and wanted our children to find their own belief systems.

My overtime pay and Reinhild's earnings enabled us to pay off the loan, and when Reinhild wrote the check for the outstanding balance, the folks at HFC wanted to know from her if we had borrowed the money from some other lender to discharge our liability to them. The first pay increase of fourteen cents was in my paycheck at the end of six months, as promised by Len, who was later transferred to manage the production facility of a newly acquired company. Scott, before moving into Len's old office, created a prototype fabrication group that became my responsibility, and another ten-cents-per-hour increase appeared in my paycheck. A few months later Mike Jeffers, the vice president of engineering, asked me personally to assemble a circuit board that he was working on. This recognition was a great confidence builder but also made me realize that I lacked the appropriate skills and knowledge to be an engineer. That thought slowly grew into an obsession and led to the search for some affordable institution that offered training after work hours.

A few days later I saw Mike leading a group of company officials, who I had not seen before, towards the back of the building. I backed up to allow them to pass when one of the visitors, breaking away from the group, walked towards me with extended hand and said, "I am Milton Shapp. Who are you?"

I recognized his name and for a split second froze because I had never met the president of the company, any company, before. After a quick recovery, I shook his hand and replied, "My name is Mac and I am honored to meet you, sir."

"Where are you from?" he asked.

"I emigrated from Pakistan via Germany after attending college in England."

"What do you do here?"

Before I could answer, Mike said, "Mac is the best prototype technician we have."

"Are you attending any college now?" Mr. Shapp asked, and then, without waiting for my answer, he continued, "If you do, the company pays for the tuition and the books."

While looking at Mike, I told him that I was thinking of doing so and that I was not aware of this benefit. He instructed Mike to get the proper paperwork for me.

I said, "Thank you, sir."

Walking away, he shouted, "Call me Milt, everyone does."

I could not believe what had happened, and then remembered my father's words: "God has his timing." It seemed that my timing had arrived, and I found it difficult to suppress my excitement. When I went to pick up Reinhild from work, I gave her the good news. A few days later Mike's secretary called and explained the Education Subsidy Program. The company paid full tuition for the semester if I earned an average grade of A, 60 percent in the case of a B, and 40 percent if I received only a C. This program was available to those attending evening classes leading to bachelor's or master's degrees. She gave me a list of colleges and informed me that there were four employees who were already participating in this program and that the labs closed at 4:30 p.m. to facilitate those students. What a company!

Reinhild and I studied the catalogs from LaSalle University and Drexel Institute of Technology, both located in Philadelphia. If I followed the recommended schedule, it would take eight years to accumulate enough credits for a bachelor's degree. According to the counselor at Drexel, very few attendees finished in eight years, the average being ten. This meant that I would be an absentee father and Reinhild would be having most of the responsibility of raising the children. We agreed that in order to provide our children with proper educational opportunities, I needed to educate myself first. With that in mind, I began to prepare for the entrance exams. Two days after the tests, the counselor informed me that I had qualified for admission to the college and that I possessed the aptitude to pursue a career in engineering, administration, and even in politics. I received acceptance from both colleges.

The job of managing the weaving department in Pakistan was very satisfying, and I felt confident that a degree in manufacturing engineering could one day lead me to such a position. I chose Drexel Institute of Technology because the curriculum met my needs and I could add business administration as my second major. Once college started, I would no longer be able to work overtime on weekdays, but I could make myself available on Saturdays. Sometimes when I had to work for only a few hours over the weekends, Ronnie would accompany me.

One day in July, Scott told me that Eric Winston, an engineer across the hall, had asked to see me. He was known to be an intellectual type who I thought was probably interested to learn about Pakistan. At 3:00 p.m. I walked into his office, a large room with a drafting table against the hallway wall, a desk under the window, and a chair tucked in the far left corner. A large heating and cooling test chamber stood against the right wall. Eric was in his middle forties and wore a very inviting smile as he inquired, "You must be Mac. It is not your real name, is it?"

"No, it is Maqbool Qurashi."

"We will go with Mac. I wanted to meet you because I have an opening for a technician in this lab and you come highly recommended. So tell me about yourself."

I gave him the short version of my story, adding that I had been accepted at Drexel. When asked about the kind of work done in his lab, he explained that he was responsible for the mechanical development and testing the reliability of the equipment that was developed in the labs. He informed me that there was another candidate for the job and he would decide within the following week. I thanked him and walked back to my work station, amazed at the opportunities that were being presented to me. It reinforced my belief that the United States was the land where dreams could come true.

I learned that cable television systems were needed in the rural areas where the TV signal could not reach because of distance or mountainous terrain. A typical cable system required a tall tower with TV antennae erected on a location where the signals were strong enough to allow further amplification. A coaxial cable from the antennae delivers the TV channels to the homes. Just as the voltage drops across the electric wire, so the TV signal weakens as it travels over the coaxial cable. Jerrold, being the innovator of cable TV systems, had to invent each and every piece of equipment, including the testing meters that were necessary to make a system work. We had to design amplifiers to boost the TV signals every few thousand feet. As the equipment had to work in the outdoors, Eric's lab tested every prototype in the heating and cooling chamber to ensure its proper function in a wide range of environments.

The year 1963 was turning out to be very fruitful except for the fact that we would miss the income from my overtime work. Life at home would be affected when I began my second career as a student, and Reinhild's work schedule would have to change from weekdays to weekends only. These were the thoughts occupying my mind when Eric stopped me in the hallway on the Tuesday following the interview and led me to his office, where he said, "I have decided to offer you the job on a three-month trial. If it works out there will be an increase of 30¢ per hour followed by a review at the end of six months. If you agree about your transfer, I will work it out with Scott."

How could I refuse a job that appeared to be very interesting with a chance to learn and also be a contributor?

Beginning in late August, Reinhild changed her work schedule: 6:00 p.m. to 11:30 p.m. on Fridays and 3:00 p.m. to 11:30 p.m. during weekends and holidays. When my classes began, instead of going directly to college from work, I took an extra thirty minutes to drive home and have dinner with the family before dashing off to school, not wanting to be a weekend dad only. Ronnie and I began our first grades in 1963.

One evening, while watching TV, we were startled by a loud crashing noise, followed by the screeching sound of tires. Upon investigation, we discovered that someone, unable to negotiate the corner of the square, had slammed into the back of our station wagon, moving it about twenty yards. The perpetrator had fled the scene. The tailgate of our vehicle was smashed in, and the impact had dislodged the radiator. We could drive the car, but instead of getting the car repaired, we traded it in for a brand new green-colored 1963 Ford Falcon with automatic transmission but without radio and air-conditioning, saving about $800. The monthly payment came to $43, which we eked out of our budget.

26

The nation was in turmoil because of the civil rights movement, and the protests, while peaceful, elicited violent responses from the officials who used dogs and fire hoses to disperse the crowds. The arrest and later release of the Reverend Martin Luther King Jr. and the murder of Medgar Evers culminated into a gathering of 250,000 people in Washington, D.C., where, on August 28, 1963, Reverend King delivered his famous “I Have a Dream” speech. I had firsthand experience of discriminatory practices in India that had led to violent racial strife, although not to the extent found in some parts of the United States. I feared the same could happen here.

On November 22, 1963, I was standing in the sheet metal shop when Charlie Woods, the metal fabricator, looking distraught, announced that President Kennedy had been assassinated. No one believed him. Our building was made of metal as a shield against radio interference and could not receive AM radio signals, and the FM stations did not broadcast news. We stuck the antenna of a portable radio through an open window to confirm the news. It was devastating for me, because I had experienced the murder of the first prime minister of the then newly established country of Pakistan and could not believe that an assassination could take place in the United States in the 1960s. I would miss the president's sincere expression and wit at news conferences. It was the first time in many decades that Drexel canceled all classes, and I sat in front of the television for many days, watching the coverage of all the events leading up to the time when President Kennedy was laid to rest.

In 1964, the cable show was held in Philadelphia. Jerrold, having its headquarters in the city, arranged a day of bus tours of the labs for the attendees of the convention. We set up many props to demonstrate the reliability of our equipment, and I was assigned the task to lead the tours in our department. This provided a great opportunity to meet the customers, who I encouraged to call me if they needed any assistance. The following day I accompanied Eric to the show. A local hotel had converted its roof into a recreation area with a swimming pool and attractive landscapes. The cable show occupied the whole roof, where all the competitive hardware was on display. Jerrold, occupying one quarter of the space, offered me a glimpse of the industry which would be part of my professional life. We visited each of our competitors' booths to gather information about their products, and it quickly became clear that new manufacturers were entering the market and utilizing transistors, making their equipment smaller. It was the first time that I met the sales and field engineering personnel; I did not know they existed. On the way back we had stopped for lunch when Eric informed me that we would be developing new products using solid state technology and that there would be an opening for a mechanical engineer, and he thought that I could do the job. He would give me small projects and see how it worked out. I had just completed my course in mechanical drafting at the college. What timing!

The F connector, which is an integral part of video hardware today, was developed and tested in our lab. I had just completed testing one of the connectors, designed to connect the new aluminum sheathed cables (the shiny cables hanging on the electric and telephone poles), when Vick Nicholson, the director of field engineering, picked it up and wanted to know what that was. After I explained, he commented, "It is a very sexy fitting. What is its model name?"

Without much thought I declared, "VSF."

He wanted to know what the letters meant, and when I informed him that it was "Very Sexy Fitting," we had a good laugh, and I wrote down the name on the drawings. Eric thought that it was a great idea. VSF connectors became an industrywide standard for many years. Who says engineers do not have a sense of humor?

In order to study at home, I required a desk and a chair, which I purchased at a local flea market. The sofa we had gotten from Uncle Alfred was very uncomfortable, and now that we could afford it, we acquired a new, more comfortable one along with an armchair. I taught Reinhild to drive our new car so she could use it to go to work on Fridays when I did not have to attend any classes. In the interest of saving time, I would keep the car running in front of the apartment, and we would pass each other on the stairs as she took the car to go to work. On weekends we would all drive her to the hospital after midday dinner, a German tradition, and on the way back the children and I would stop at the playground in the Cooper River Park. After evening snacks we would watch TV, and once they were in bed, I studied till it was time to pick up Reinhild.

By 1965 I was earning more than a junior engineer although officially I was still a technician. The review of our finances led us to believe that it was time to move into a house of our own. Renate's real estate friend informed us that there was a nice home with four bedrooms and one-and-a-half baths that had just come on the market and was only a few blocks away from the schools. The price of the house was $15,500, and the Realtor assured us that I could qualify for a thirty-year mortgage with a $500 down payment and $143 per month that included insurance and taxes. It was a split-level home where the front door opened into a small vestibule connecting to a large living room on the right and the dining room on the left, with a kitchen in the back. Seven steps in the back of the living area led up to a small hallway with two bedrooms, one on each side, with a bathroom in the middle. Across from the bathroom, another set of ascending stairs connected to a landing accessing a bedroom on each side. Next to the kitchen in the back of the living room, seven descending stairs led to a partially sunken family room attached to a small powder room and a utility area, with enough space for a washer and a dryer, leading to the back door. A nice fenced backyard offered a play area for the children, and part of it would later be occupied by an above-ground pool, twelve feet across. Sparky, a rescue dog, completed our family. Reinhild began working in a small, private, residential, clinical facility during the weekends from 7:00 a.m. till 3:30 p.m., a time when I could be with the children.

The cable TV industry was growing rapidly, and requests for small ancillary products from the sales department poured in daily. One of the products needed urgently was a wall connector modified so that when not in use it could prevent radio waves from interfering with the cable TV systems. Eric assigned its development to me, and the project was completed by the end of the week. The following week we received an initial order for five thousand pieces to be delivered within fifteen days, which was not possible at our busy factory. I was given the responsibility to get them made at the company's smaller production facility in Sherburne, New York. As it was put together without written direction, I felt that I needed to inspect every piece. The schools were closed, and therefore Ronnie was able to accompany me when I traveled to test the products. We had to stay overnight in a nearby motel, where one could hear every sound from adjoining rooms, and a young couple had checked into one of them. At night, although not needed, I had to run the fan of the room air conditioning at the highest speed available so I would not have to explain to Ronnie, if asked, about the noises emanating from next door due to their "activities." With his assistance, we managed to deliver the shipment of the fi product on time to the warehouse in Philadelphia. The product was a success, and the higher management took notice of my capabilities when it was decided to apply for a patent. It would take six years before Patent Number 3525056 for the invention of STO-75 was granted by the United States Patent Office in my name.

The year 1967 was full of milestones, career advancement, and family changes. Our attempts to have another child bore fruit, and Reinhild became pregnant, expecting our third child in August. On March 17 in the Federal District Court of New Jersey, I took an oath to become a naturalized citizen of the United States. Frank Ragone and Jim Herman were my sponsors, and in the evening Reinhild arranged for a surprise party to celebrate the event.

On May 21, 1967, at an assembly of the student body and guests in the main auditorium of the Drexel Institute of Technology, I was awarded the Academic Achievement Award. *Mutti*, who was visiting for a few weeks, and Reinhild were present when Professor Montgomery announced, "The next award goes to Maqbool Qurashi, and I am going to make an exception to let you all know that Qurashi has just returned from an illness, and he is one of the few students who will complete the degree program within the recommended time of eight years."

I walked on the stage and received my certificate and a scholarship of $250. On the way home, *Mutti* finally expressed her confidence in my ability to take care of my family. As August approached, Reinhild looked very pregnant, and we began preparation for the arrival of our third child.

Monday, August 7, 1967, began with usual fervor, but just before I was ready to walk out of the front door, Reinhild informed me that her labor pains had begun and it was time to go. We dropped off the children at their schools and continued to the hospital, where a volunteer wheeled her past the double doors while I took a seat in the waiting room. An hour later the doctor suggested that I could go home or even to work because he did not expect the baby for many hours and that they would inform me as soon as there was some progress. During that time, the husbands were not allowed to accompany their wives in the labor or delivery rooms. Before driving to work, I called Renate and asked her if she could be at our home when the kids returned from school. From work, my repeated calls to the hospital were answered by the same statement, "There is no change."

My anxiety grew with each passing hour, and when Eric noticed that I was suffering from an expectant father's jitters, he recommended that I should be with Reinhild. I drove to the hospital, where I was advised to take her home because she was not ready to deliver. Unlike today, when the birth of a baby can be scheduled for the convenience of the mother-to-be or the doctor, induced labor deliveries were rare at the time.

Once at home, Reinhild prepared the evening meal, and immediately after that the labor pains returned. Ronnie sat at the kitchen table with a watch, timing the intervals between the contractions. I heard him shout, "Mom, they are coming every seven minutes. You better hurry up."

By the time we left the house, the interval had diminished to five minutes. Something prompted her to take a bath towel on her way out, and once she had settled in the back seat of the car, I took off like a rabbit with flashing hazard lights and blaring horn, but policemen are never available when one needs them. In the event of an emergency, one was supposed to hang a white handkerchief out of the window while flashing the lights. All of those signals went unheeded, even when I drove by the police department building. Reinhild would let out a wail each time the pain returned, and after it was over, she would calmly advise me, "Don't pay any attention."

No matter how I tried, each moan, piercing my body like a bolt of lightning, was difficult to ignore. As I made a right turn on Chapel Street, Reinhild declared that the baby was coming. Pulling the car in the back of a gas station, I flung open the driver's side door and entered the back of the car. Reaching in, I noticed that the baby had already begun its journey into the world and all I had to do was catch her. Reinhild urged me to check her fingers and toes, which I did, and then held the baby upside down by her feet as I had seen in the movies. But before I could do anything, she sneezed and cleared her nose. Because the hospital was nearby, I rejected the urge to tie the cord with my shoelace. Instead I wrapped the baby in the towel and placed her on her mother's tummy.

The doctor had been informed by Renate about our return trip to the hospital, and when I pulled in front of the emergency room a doctor and nurse rushed to the car. The doctor handed the baby to the nurse after tying and cutting the cord and then moved Reinhild to a stretcher. While making the phone call home to inform Renate and the kids about the arrival of our little girl, Michelle, I felt that my hands were covered with a sticky coating, probably transferred from the baby when I held her after her birth. Michelle's sneeze had cleared her nostrils, which were plugged to prevent drowning while her body was protected from the salinity of the water in the womb. Reflecting on the whole incident, I could not help but marvel at the complexity of life's creation, a miracle. My admiration for Reinhild and mothers in general took on a new meaning. Those who think that women are the weaker gender should experience delivering a baby. Dr. Warren, our family doctor, remarked, "You wanted to be there at the time of your baby's delivery and you did it."

That evening, the local radio announcer called and asked about my experience. Many of my colleagues heard my voice on the radio, because when I returned to the labs the following afternoon to hand out the cigars, everyone knew what had happened.

As Mike Jeffers, accompanied by two other company officials, came down the hallway, I pulled out three cigars, but before I could hand them out, Mike, addressing the others, stated, "I just want to let you know that Mac delivered his daughter in the car."

"I believe in carrying the project all the way through, Mike," I quickly added, following up on our earlier discussion about consolidating the project management. He retorted, "I got the message."

When I went to pick up Reinhild and our daughter, I was informed that Michelle had to remain there a little longer because she was jaundiced and also had dropped below the required discharge weight. It was difficult for us to come home to Ronnie and Ruby without our baby, as they had prepared a little banner welcoming her. But Michelle began to improve rapidly, and we picked her up after three days.

27

Although still a technician, I represented Jerrold in front of the cable and equipment standards committees of the national electronics associations. Eric and I developed the first pluggable modular package for the new amplifier, and Patent Number 3479633 was granted jointly in our names. Around that time, in order to pursue his political goals, Milton Shapp sold Jerrold Electronics to General Instrument, and the new owners of the company decided to discontinue the profit-sharing plan. My share of the disbursement was more than enough to purchase three window air conditioners for our home. There were enough funds left over to pay for a trip for Ronnie and me to visit Pakistan. It had been ten years since I had left the country, and I was looking forward to see all my relatives, and Ronnie would have the chance to see the city where he was born. Uncle Saleem, who had by this time given up his pursuit of medical education, owned a movie theater and had requested me to bring along an audio booster that he needed.

On January 14, 1968, Ronnie and I boarded the evening Pan Am flight from Kennedy Airport, arriving in Karachi at 4:00 a.m.

on the sixteenth. We were tired, and as we passed through immigration, I noticed that the customs inspector, while not paying attention to our luggage, was curious about us. When he also checked the heavy transformer box without asking for the import license, I asked him why he was so attentive to us. He informed me that he had not before seen a blond boy carrying a Pakistani passport and a Pakistani-looking man who carried a U.S. passport. His mind eased when I informed him that Ronnie was born in Pakistan. As we stepped out of the airport, I found Uncle Afzal waiting for us with an import license for the transformer. He stayed with us as we waited for our two-hour flight to Lahore. *Bayjee, Apa Anwari,* her daughter Waseema with her husband, Hameed, Masood, and my nephew Shaukat were waiting for us. It was an emotional reunion. My nephews and nieces had all grown up. While Ronnie went with the others, I accompanied *Bayjee* in Hameed's car. On the way she had a thousand questions, and when I attempted to answer her in Punjabi, my native language, I found it difficult to communicate. In frustration, I asked my niece to translate as I spoke in English. That moment *Bayjee,* in clear English, reminded me, "Have you forgotten who taught you how to speak in English?" She had. *Bhai Manzoor* had not been communicating with me since I lived in Germany. He was touring Europe and wanted to visit me in Sattenhausen. My circumstances did not allow me to invite him, and I wrote him that it was not a good time for him to come. In order to mend fences with him, I told my niece's husband to drop me off at the clinic. He understood once I explained to him about my situation in Germany, and we embraced to make up.

Ronnie was disturbed to see so many children begging on the street, and within the first hour he gave away all his change. He had difficulty in adjusting to the local cuisine and was not eating very well. We became very concerned, and one night *Bhaijee* called a friend who distributed canned food imported from the United States. It was 10:00 p.m. by the time we stepped into a large warehouse full of Campbell's Soup products. Ronnie picked up half a dozen cans of SpaghettiOs that the cook prepared for him. One of the family friends invited us for a dinner, and Ronnie took one of the cans along. As we sat down at the table, he asked the host if he could use the kitchen, where, with the help of the cook, he heated the contents of the can and joined us just in time to begin the meals.

I borrowed *Bhai Manzoor's* car, a Citroen that had been assembled from a kit. Named as the "Junkmobile" by Ronnie, we drove it to visit Uncle Nazir in Daska and my niece at the site of the Mangla Dam, where Hameed worked as a consulting engineer. He informed us that there were many American expats who had their own community with bowling alleys and a McDonald's franchise. That was music to Ronnie's ears. Once at the American recreation center, he found himself in paradise and devoured a few cheeseburgers and some french fries, a change from the canned food that had been sustaining him so far. Upon our return to Gujranwala, we had many family dinners and reminisced about the past. Ronnie received an air rifle as an early birthday present, which occupied his time when we were not visiting some relative. On January 27 all my family from Gujranwala drove us to Lahore, where I had invited them for a dinner at the Intercontinental Hotel. It was difficult to say our farewells before boarding the afternoon flight to Karachi. We arrived at Kennedy Airport on the evening of the twenty-eighth.

The new management at the company hired Arthur from the telephone industry to head up the Jerrold Labs, and he attempted to transform the culture of a group of freewheeling engineers and technicians into the image of the company he had left. This created tension in our highly productive environment. On Friday, April 29, while driving from work and only a few miles from home, I began to experience difficulty in breathing. By the time I pulled in our driveway, I was in distress and, with extreme difficulty, went in the house long enough to ask Reinhild to drive me to the hospital. One and a half weeks later, I was released without really knowing the cause of my ailment. My family doctor suspected that I had walking pneumonia due to the stress at work and carrying a full study schedule at the college, and he advised, "If you keep burning the candle at both ends, we will pin your degree on your gravestone."

That prompted me to seek a change in my situation. During one of my earlier visits to the factory in Philadelphia, the plant manager had offered me the position of senior manufacturing engineer. When contacted, he informed me that such a position was not available any longer but asked me to wait so he could attempt to get permission from the management. A few hours later he called and informed me that he had sent a request to the labs for my transfer. Later in the afternoon, I received a call from Eric, who sounded disturbed, wanting to know what led me to seek the transfer. I explained to him that the promised promotion had been delayed since 1964, making it difficult for me as a technician to deal with some of the engineers who had master's degrees. After a pause, he asked me not to do anything till he had time to discuss it with Mike. The following day he delivered the good news of my promotion, which was reluctantly approved by Arthur, who had instituted a strict requirement of a degree from an American college for the position of an engineer. The plant manager deserved an explanation about my return to the labs, which I did in person, as I did not want him to get the impression that I had used him for the sake of my promotion. He was very gracious about the whole incident. As I was preparing to leave his office, he stated that if I desired the job, it would still be available after the project was completed

The labs had been without a conference room since Arthur had converted it into his personal office. I required a room with a large table that afternoon, so I approached Irene, who, although officially only Mike's secretary, did much more to keep the lab at even keel. "I need a room with a large table where I could spread the drawings for a meeting with a visitor."

"You can use the old conference room," she replied.

"That is Arthur's office, and the way he feels about me, he will kill me."

"He was fired last Saturday and he cleared out his office yesterday."

I stood there amazed. "What happened to his executive assistant?"

"Gone," she remarked.

On Wednesday that week we had a new manager of the labs. Caywood Cooley was transferred from the city office, where he had been in charge of administrating the installation and technical services. Engineers spend most of their time and skills in manipulating inanimate objects and therefore generally lack the skills for dealing with humans, who react with emotions. Caywood possessed the genius to understand the complexities of a cable TV network, but had no clue how to deal with the disparate personalities of creative people. Eric was a gentleman's gentleman, an engineer full of ideas, and a person who avoided conflict, and therefore, each time he had a meeting with Caywood, he appeared shaken and stressed. He and his wife had become our family friends, and many times I deferred to him for personal advice. His patience exhausted, he resigned a few months after the completion of the project he and I had worked on and recommended me to take his place. After a farewell luncheon, while collecting his personal belongings, he opened the desk drawer and, pointing to the two small pill boxes, said, "You will need them. Take the pill in the silver box before your meeting with Caywood and the aspirin from the gold box after the meeting to get rid of the headache. After a few weeks, you probably will hate me for recommending you for this job."

The following day Caywood informed me about my new position as the manager on a six-month trial, and he was confident that I would do well. My first encounter took place when, without my knowledge, he proceeded to make contact with the same candidate who I had been considering to fill my old position. As soon as I discovered this, I confronted him.

"Caywood, you must have enough confidence in my abilities to give me the manager's job, so why are you hiring my replacement?"

He assured me that he would not interfere again, and therefore I did not have to take any of those pills. A few months later, the management came to the conclusion that Mike Jeffers was the right person at the helm of the lab and we all heaved a sigh of relief at Caywood's departure.

~

On March 21, 1968, Reinhild took her oath of citizenship in the presence of Ronnie, Ruby, and Michelle. Shortly after that, the process was repeated when Ronnie took his citizenship oath while the family watched. All the members of the family were now proud citizens of the United States of America, Ruby and Michelle by birth.

I was earning a comfortable salary, and because of the need to travel between the two labs, the main office, and the factory, we decided to acquire a second car, a used 1960 Buick Special. It was burgundy red with bucket seats, automatic transmission, and air conditioning, a blessing because one extremely hot day I was stuck in traffic for five hours when the Tacony-Palmyra Bridge got stuck in the open position.

The manufacturing engineer at the factory required my assistance in writing the assembly procedures for the newly released amplifier. In order to demonstrate the pressure testing device, I picked up a screwdriver and, at that moment I heard someone loudly announcing, "This is the shop steward ordering you to stop work immediately because a nonunion member is working with a tool."

I was shocked. The steel industry had ceded its dominance to the Japanese in recent years, mostly because of union work rules, and now I was experiencing it firsthand. The engineer asked the union leader to file the complaint in writing as required by the contract and ordered all others to go back to work, and I proceeded to complete the training session. Reflecting about what had happened, I felt that although at one time unionization had been a necessary and beneficial movement, the unions' archaic work rules would one day drive businesses away.

28

My first encounter with Bill Lambert was a little testy because I was a mere technician then and he was an accomplished engineer, but later we began to respect each other's professional acumen. We were very much alike in speaking out when necessary, but with a difference in our approach. While he was direct, I had learned to be diplomatic. Together we would lay the foundation for two-way communication on the cable TV networks that later would facilitate high-speed Internet. As a manger, I was required to attend the cable shows, and my first such show was in San Francisco, where we had an irate customer. Now that I was in charge of system reliability, the sales department had scheduled for me to meet the customer's engineer. Joe was six feet tall, weighing about 280 to 300 pounds, with a neck like a football linebacker. Immediately after introducing me, the regional sales manager quietly slipped away, leaving me to assuage his tirade. I sat there passively holding my fists in my pocket and once he had exhausted all his vituperations, I calmly informed him that I had taken over the department only a few months ago and that I would like to visit his system to learn the problem first hand. We set up a time for me to visit his South San

Francisco office. My examination determined that there was a flaw in our connectors, and I promised to find a solution as soon as I returned to Hatboro. Before I left he said, "If you fix this problem, I will invite you to a party where you will swim in female flesh." The problem was resolved, although I never accepted his invitation but wondered about his promise.

While still at the show, one evening somebody asked that I join the other managers to have dinner and see some sights afterwards. I followed the group to a street that was lined with nude dancing clubs. As we entered one of the clubs, Bill picked up a copy of the *Berkeley Barb*, the university paper, and was intrigued with all the classified ads where gay men and women were looking for company. While still absorbed in the paper, he took a seat immediately in front of the stage and did not pay any attention to the hard-working dancer. She, annoyed by his behavior, bent as far towards him as she could and asked, "Is the paper more interesting than what I am showing?"

Pausing to look her over from top to bottom, he answered, "Yes."

The manager politely asked us to leave, as we were distracting his customers. Before that day, I did not know that such places existed.

At one time Bill invited me to join him in an equipment manufacturing venture that he desired to establish. Although I readily agreed, the idea never proceeded any further, but it encouraged me to look for any opportunity that came my way. That chance came when John Watts, a manufacturer's representative, approached me for an advice in putting together a very intricate mechanical assembly that needed to be filled with nitrogen gas. This was my first venture into the business world, and "Dynatech Engineering" took on the task of assembling this gadget. Reinhild and a neighbor, after filling the assembly with nitrogen, would crimp the end of the tube, dip it in molten solder, and then submerge it in a pail of water to check for leaks. We produced over one thousand of the assemblies before our customer discontinued the product line. As the work at Jerrold and studies at college did not leave enough time for my business venture, I closed the enterprise, but only temporarily.

In order to investigate cable breakages at a system, I had arranged to meet the chief engineer of the cable manufacturer at a restaurant outside of the town of Thibodaux, sixty miles from the city of New Orleans. Upon entering the restaurant I found myself surrounded by the early lunch crowd, mostly local men, each one bigger than I, holding bottles of beer. When most of them turned their inquiring gaze towards me, a brown-complexioned person in a Southern state, I felt a momentary shiver down my spine. Recovering my composure, I declared, "I am looking for Jack Arbuthnott." Two of the men came towards me and one of them said, "We are looking for him, too. We work for the local cable TV company and we brought a bucket truck because we were told that some guys want to go up to see the cable at the pole."

"I am one of the guys, and I am from Jerrold," I responded. They offered me a bottle of beer, which I declined, and at that moment Jack walked in.

Back at the labs, I simulated the conditions that caused the failure and made recommendations that changed the method of construction, extending my professional sphere beyond the equipment development. Unlike the telephone cable that consists of bundles of thin copper wires, the cable television cable is a solid aluminum sheath needing special handling. The cable manufacturers, the construction experts, and I developed the construction standards for the industry and spoke at the first System Reliability Conference.

General Instrument hired a consulting company to advise it on how to manage its new acquisition. In 1970, Dr. John Malone, the consultant who wrote the final report, was appointed group vice president overseeing Jerrold. On the last day of March of 1971, Mike informed me that Eric would be returning to a newly created position of director overseeing my department and the group that developed passive devices. My position did not change much, but I received an increase in my pay. In a way I was happy about Eric's return because I had missed our lunchtime intellectual discussions. On Friday, April 9, 1971, I was halfway to the front door when the phone in my office rang. My first reaction was to ignore it, but my inner voice compelled me to answer it. I picked up the phone and said, "Mac speaking."

"This is John Malone. I want you to go to Akron, Ohio, and estimate the time needed to take down the amplifiers that are there and replace them with one of ours. Call me by 1:00 p.m. at the telephone number I will give you later."

"Sir, I am sure the guys in the construction department can give you that information more accurately, because I do not know very much about cable construction," I protested.

"Call me John. Everybody I have spoken with tells me that you are capable and reliable to do this, and, by the way, the construction managers do not want to commit themselves. So you are it, and make sure you call me no later than 1:00." Before hanging up, he gave me the telephone number where he would be waiting for my call.

At the time I had no clue who John was. I immediately called Mike at his home and informed him about the call. After explaining what John's position was, he directed me to do whatever was required. The Sunday evening flight to Cleveland and a thirty-nine-mile car ride brought me to a Holiday Inn in Akron, Ohio. In the morning I met with the local Jerrold supervisor of construction, who went by the name of Gander. He was given this name because he was a skinny, tall man with long legs and once made gander-like steps while crossing a stream, and since that day Gander had been his nickname. Using a stopwatch, we came up with an average time, and I called John Malone in New York at the appointed time. On the way home on the plane, I thought about my meeting with Gander, and his information about the cable TV systems construction business led me to consider a career in the turnkey division, responsible for the design, installation, and certification of the networks. The Akron contract, later signed by Jerrold, would play a gainful role in my future.

It was in May 1971 when a representative of an employment agency called and said, "I represent a large corporation who is interested in your services." I told him that I was not available, but he was very persistent and kept calling every week, sometimes at the office and sometimes at home. He even called Reinhild and attempted to lure her to a nice Southern city. He would not divulge the name of the company he represented until I agreed to an interview. Finally one day, I told him that I was not willing to make any move and that he should not phone again.

Traditionally, every year sales training meetings were held a few weeks before the cable show and usually lasted for three days. We had developed a new line of two-way equipment, and the company, in anticipation of a successful launch at the show, held the 1971 sales meeting at Mount Airy Lodge, a famous resort in the Poconos Mountains in Pennsylvania. During my presentation to the assembled sales and top management personnel, Eric, who had returned after three years' absence, instead of highlighting the features for the benefits of the salesmen as we used to do in the past, began a critique of my design concepts. It alarmed me because that was not the place for such discussions. Even Lee Zemnick, the executive vice president, appeared disturbed and had to step in to divert the salesmen's attention. Eric and I had become family friends and remained so even after this incident, although I never understood his motives on that day. This was the first time John Malone had attended a Jerrold preshow sales conference, and as we strolled along the lawns, he had many questions, one of which concerned my presentation and what followed. That was my opportunity to tell him that I had reached my highest level at the labs and would like to transfer to some management position at the company's main office. He advised me to stay where I was for a few more months and things would turn out in my favor.

❧

On June 5, 1971, at the fourth commencement exercise held at the Convention Hall in Philadelphia, I received my bachelor of science degree from Drexel University. Reinhild also received a PHT, or "Putting Him Through" certificate. While it was a moment of great feelings of accomplishment, looking back at the past eight years saddened me for being absent from my family and the realization that suddenly Ronnie, Ruby, and Michelle had all grown up. The only solace came from knowing that the first-generation immigrants had always been called upon to make sacrifices.

❧

The incident at the sales conference was nagging at me, and I could not decide whether to be proactive in my desire to make a change or wait, as John had advised. The headhunter's timing could have not been better, because a few days after the show, when he called again, I told him to call me later after I had a chance to discuss it with Reinhild. When he called again, I agreed to the interview. Within days I received a round-trip ticket from Philadelphia to Lynchburg, Virginia, where a meeting with Carmine Dellio had been arranged at General Electric. It was general knowledge that the company owned a few cable TV systems with their offices in Schenectady, New York, and it puzzled me why I was going to Lynchburg, Virginia, for an interview. Carmine had been hired by one of Jerrold's competitors and had attended many of the same cable TV shows that I had, but we never crossed paths. When we met, he informed me that GE had decided to enter the equipment manufacturing business and would very much like to have me as part of its team. He explained all the benefits that the company offered, which were very attractive. The interview was brief, and I promised to call after I had discussed it with Reinhild.

Not hearing from me for a week, the headhunter called again and offered a considerable increase in my salary that was difficult to turn down. Reinhild and I agreed that although our children would have to change schools, it might be a good experience for them. We took an evening flight to Lynchburg and checked in at the Holiday Inn and, after my brief medical test and completion of the paperwork, we went on a city tour conducted by the real estate agent referred by the company. Before I left the GE office, Carmine advised, "In the event Jerrold lets you go earlier than the two weeks, call me if you want to start before the agreed date."

On June 18, 1971, I informed Eric about my decision to resign effective July 2. I explained to Mike and him, later in a meeting, that I needed to experience working in a larger company and that I had an attractive offer. My employment at Jerrold ended the same day after attending a hurriedly arranged farewell luncheon. It was difficult to leave a place that had offered me an opportunity to discover my talent and grow into a profession beyond my expectations. By the time I reached home, I was full of cautious anticipation. Carmine, when informed that I could begin my work at GE on June 28 instead of July 5, was pleased and was looking forward to working with me.

29

On June 27, 1971, after spending a week with my family, during which we took a few day trips to the New Jersey shore, I left for Lynchburg, Virginia, with high hopes and great anticipation. The drive became pleasant once I left the crowded Interstate 95 and took Route 29, which wound through pleasant mountainous terrain that our new sky blue Ford Pinto handled with ease. With no more evening classes to attend, I was looking forward to a nine-to-five job that would allow me to spend more time at home. It was 5:30 p.m., seven hours since I had left home, when I pulled up in front of the Holiday Inn. The following morning I reported to the personnel department to process the paperwork and to receive the information about the company's personnel policies. After getting my identification badge, I was led to a cubical that would be my office, and Carmine introduced me to Paul, the GE manager of the cable TV equipment venture, and Harry, a specialist in electronics.

In a meeting that afternoon, Paul explained his strategy.

"We have long-standing business relationships with the Nippon Electric Company of Japan, and we have contracted with them to develop and manufacture GE's amplifiers in accordance with the specifications which all of you will write. The remaining ancillary equipment will be made by a company in Honk Kong." Welcoming me to the team, he continued, "Mac, you will develop the mechanical packaging design, working with the mechanical department of NEC."

I was given a package of drawings for my review that had been submitted by NEC as part of its proposed amplifier, and, with the assistance of a draftsman, had to complete the other work needed for the company in Hong Kong. All that in ten days before leaving for Tokyo!

We had picked out a house in the wooded suburbs of the city of Lynchburg when Reinhild and I had visited the area. The builder still had to complete some of the items that had been left to the buyer's discretion, but he had promised that the house would be available before school started. We had placed our home in New Jersey on the market while I made the Holiday Inn my temporary residence. Before my first trip to Japan, I took a flight home and, after spending a day with the family, joined up with the team in Baltimore for the flight to Tokyo.

An overnight stay in a city on the West Coast was always part of our itinerary to break up the tiresome, long trip. We arrived in Honolulu in the late afternoon and found the famous Waikiki Beach very disappointing because of the construction of hotels that had crept ever so close to the water line. As planned, we arrived in Tokyo on a Sunday afternoon after crossing the International Date Line and losing a day. After completing the immigration formalities, we hailed a taxi, and as I waited for the driver to open the trunk, it puzzled me when the others jumped into the cabin with their baggage. One of my companions instructed me to bring the luggage inside, as the trunk was occupied by a tank of pressurized natural gas, a requirement for the taxis because of high levels of pollution. There we were, three in the back and one in the front, our luggage on our laps, leaning left and right as the driver continued his slalom race, filling the empty spaces between unending streams of cars and trucks, sometimes only inches away from the passing vehicles on the wrong side of the road. Although I could understand driving on the left in the former British colonies, nobody could credibly explain why the Japanese were doing so. As we entered the heart of the city, many of the pedestrians wore face masks, perhaps to ease their breathing, because I could taste the polluted air. Finally the taxi came to a stop in front of the Okura Hotel, and we peeled ourselves out of the car one by one. I heaved a sigh of relief when the bellhop relieved us of our luggage and we were led to the registration counter.

The hotel had opened in 1962, and its native character was evident by the abundance of Japanese brush art, rice paper screens, and strings of lighted globes decorating the walls of a spacious lobby, further complemented with artfully scattered, delicate furniture. Breakfast and lunch were served in a café in the back right corner, and elevators on the left, tended by young girls, whisked the guests to their rooms. Against the back wall, a teletype machine was clanking away on a roll of paper, and a large cork board then displayed its labors to update guests with the latest news. These machines were the only means of communication and information, as desktop computers, laptops, and the Internet had not yet been in commercial use.. In the right front corner of the lobby, winding stairs with a railing descended to the Benihana Restaurant, where one could find the famous and very expensive Kobe beef and, as I would discover later, a shopping mall with a wide variety of stores lining a maze of intersecting alleyways. After a short ride on an elevator attended by a woman who bowed and uttered "*Arrigato*" each time she received instructions from the guests, I entered my room on the fourth floor. A few minutes later the bellhop knocked on the door to deliver my luggage, and I could not believe when he refused my offer of a tip, a usual practice in the United States but absent in most of the rest of the industrialized world.

After unpacking my clothes and taking a quick shower, it was time to meet the others in the lobby. Paul, having been in Tokyo many times before, knew the right eating places, and after dinner he led us to the Last Penny, a supper club. The Japanese middle managers, as part of their benefits, were encouraged to mingle with the competition at such facilities, where alcohol flowed freely while the band played Western music and Japanese singers mimicked famous American artists. It was late in the evening when I could finally lie flat in bed, and once there, my body succumbed to the overwhelming urge to relent, although the slumber lasted for only a short period. The room, almost sealed and with air conditioning running twenty-four hours a day, was uncomfortably dry. All the nights I stayed there I had to let the shower run with the bathroom door wide open in order to spread some moisture around.

⁂

At 11:00 on Monday morning we arrived at the offices of NEC, located in the Tokyo World Trade Center, where we joined up with our local GE contact, who understood the Japanese customs and language. We were directed to a small conference room with ten chairs, five on each side of a rectangular table. Asian societies in general show great deference to strangers and do not dive into business matters before having a round of tea, which was delivered five minutes after we were directed to take our seats on one side of the table. An elderly woman, wearing a stern face, appeared with a large pot of green tea and ten cups and saucers, and, after meticulously placing each in its place, she quietly retreated. Immediately after that a grey-haired gentleman and a group of four younger men marched into the room in single file like a mother goose leading its goslings. We stood up and shook hands while exchanging our calling cards, English on one side and Japanese on the other. Once the card exchange had been completed, each one of us possessed five calling cards. The grey-haired gentleman, the apparent group leader, nodded at nobody in particular, and one of the men stood up and poured the tea. That ritual was repeated each time we had a meeting. Paul, after the usual greetings, pointed to me and said, “I’d like to introduce the new member of our team, Qurashi San. He comes from Jerrold.”

I heard the group leader saying, “From Jerrold. Great.”

The small talk lasted about fifteen minutes, and then Mr. Okubu, the vice president of international marketing, entered the room and, after welcoming me to the team, invited us to follow him for lunch to a restaurant on the top floor of the building.

He appeared at ease with Western culture and even told us some jokes, unlike other Japanese that we had met so far.

Upon our return, the meeting began in earnest when we presented our specifications and plans, after which the Japanese discussed our documents among themselves in their language while our team sat there like inanimate objects. The group leader then conveyed their position to us in English while his team sat in silence. This was contrary to how we conducted meetings, where any one of us would enter the discussion when deemed appropriate, and it appeared that we had a long way to go before agreeing upon the specifications. While they studied what we had offered, we had free time to explore the city. At night, the billboards wrapped around the tall buildings would light up in colorful displays, and the city seemed to become alive. We took a day trip to Yokohama by bullet train that topped speeds of 147 miles per hour, according to the meter in the dining car.

While Americans in general are very focused on the results, to our consternation, our Japanese hosts paid attention to the smallest of details. It took two more meetings before the final agreement was signed, after which they invited us to a dinner followed by a show at a Kabuki theater. It was surprising to discover during our social meeting that each one of our hosts spoke perfect English. As we sat in the theater, it appeared odd that there was no applause or reaction by the audience as the performers entered or exited the stage. In the absence of any clapping, laughs, or boos, in what other ways could a performer know how his or her act was received?

After concluding the business in Tokyo, the flight to Hong Kong in a Boeing 747 was a treat, although landing there was another matter. The aircraft had to fly between two 1,300-foot-high peaks cluttered with tall apartment buildings. A huge orange and white billboard on top of one of the peaks warned the approaching planes of its location. It was early morning when the Boeing jet made its approach at a low enough altitude so I could see the residents in the tall apartment buildings having breakfast in their dining rooms. A taxi took us to the terminal, where a ferry across the Victoria Harbor brought us to the Island of Hong Kong and the Hilton Hotel, a short walk away.

As a British colony since 1846, with a short period of Japanese occupation during World War II, the English influence was clearly visible. The Peninsula Hotel, on the mainland, still displayed the pomp and splendor of the bygone days of British colonial power. One of the restaurants served a tasty curried chicken, which Harry, an Indian, and I thoroughly enjoyed. Two days later, after meeting Richard, an English transplant who was managing director of the company that would manufacture some of the products, we departed for the long trip home to Lynchburg. I would be making these trips once a month during most of my employment period at GE.

Our house was completed, and Reinhild and the girls flew in for a weekend to finalize the purchasing process. I felt very lonely after they departed and I could not wait until we all could move into the house. Burda Corporation of Germany was in the process of establishing a printing plant in the area, and a few of the families of the German employees of the company were making Holiday Inn their temporary homes, just as I was. One evening, while taking a stroll along the expansive grounds of the hotel, I saw a six-year-old blond boy with blue eyes sitting all alone on a cement bench. Thinking that he probably belonged to one of the German families, I asked, "*Wie gehts?*" ("How are you?").

In the absence of a response I inquired, "Do you speak English?" He shook his head.

"Do you speak French?" He again shook his head, and then I questioned, "What language do you speak?"

To which he replied, "American, sir," with emphasis on "American." He and his family were from the state of Mississippi and on their way to Washington, D.C., for a vacation.

Our moving day was set and Reinhild had been working with the packers and the movers while I had to take another quick trip to Japan. On the morning of August 17, she picked me up at the Philadelphia International Airport, and we arrived at the New Jersey home just as the moving van pulled away. The house had been sold, and after signing some papers we bid farewell to all our neighbors and left for Virginia. Ruby and Ronnie wore long faces of discontent and were not pleased to leave their friends, and probably were apprehensive about the unknown that lay ahead. As a distraction, we decided to take the winding parkway through the Blue Ridge Mountains, stopping often to visit many points of interest along the way as we sang John Denver's famous song "Country Roads." It was a long trip, and Ruby and Ronnie, typical of siblings, picked on each other, because frequently I would hear "He touched me" or "She kicked me." The only contented passengers were Michelle and Sparky, the four-legged member of the family and Maxie in its cage. The sparrow that had been with us for the past nine years was found by Ronnie as a featherless chick lying next to a broken egg on a sidewalk. Upon entering the new house, the dog began his tour by sniffing at each nook and corner. The builder had promised to leave the key under the mat at the front door, and it was late at night by the time we got to bed.

30

Our house was built in a colonial style with a front porch supporting four two-story-high columns. The front door opened into a spacious landing with steps ascending to the upper floor. There were three bedrooms, a dining room, and a living area, and stairs descending to a full basement. Half of the basement was finished as a recreation room, with sliding doors opening into the driveway on the left side of the house. Later on Ronnie and I built his bedroom and my study in the large unfinished part of the basement facing the right front of the house. We quickly made friends by participating in GE gatherings, and Reinhild discovered roller skating with other newly arrived German ladies. The biggest surprise was the high standards in the curriculum and the discipline practiced by the local schools, where the students had to address their teachers by "Ma'am" or "Sir." While traveling in the area, one of our friends from New Jersey phoned and asked, "What happened to Ronnie that he addressed me as 'Ma'am' when I called before?"

This was good news, because the kids were being taught courtesy and respect, which are the glue that binds a society. Another display of Southern courtesy happened when, one day, one of Ruby's classmates, an eleven-year-old boy, showed up at our door with a bouquet of flowers and requested to see her.

While Reinhild and the children were making new friends, I, on the other hand, coming from a small, informal business environment, was having difficulty adjusting to the rigid rules that a company with thousands of employees required. There were areas where employees of my level were not allowed, and then there were protocols that had to be adhered to. I never met the man who ran the division!

Caywood Cooley, my former boss at Jerrold, had left and joined a division of Magnavox that had been created through acquisition of a small cable TV ancillary equipment manufacturer. He wanted me to join his team in Manlius, New York, but I declined each time he called. When Paul asked me to take a trip to Japan and Hong Kong over the Easter holidays, I saw an opportunity to take a few extra days and continue to Pakistan and visit my mother, who I had not seen for four years. When I informed Paul about my plan, his response was very direct: "I would have to dock you for four days." I was upset and advised him, "You do what you have to do, but I will be back on April 10."

My discussion with Paul had been gnawing at me all through my journey, and I decided to visit Caywood if he called again.

Pan Am 002 from Hong Kong landed in Karachi early in the morning, and I was looking forward to a scrumptious lunch with my relatives in Gujranwala. My ballooned excitement suffered a pin prick when the immigration official informed me that I could not enter the country due to lack of a visa. Zulfikar Ali Bhutto, the new prime minister, had imposed visa requirements for U.S. citizens while I was in flight. My explanation that it was not possible to get a visa while in the air did not move the inspector. When informed that the plane was full, he had no choice but to allow twenty-four hours' entry under the watchful eyes of the Pan Am representative, who escorted me to a hotel and left when I assured him that a relative could assist me in getting the visa. Not finding a telephone in my room, I dashed to the front desk and demanded, "There is no telephone in my room."

"There are no phones in the rooms, but I can place a call for you, if you like," he replied.

"I need to call Gujranwala."

"Sir, that will take about two hours."

I walked away disappointed because it was difficult for me to comprehend that, since its inception twenty-five years ago, the country of my birth had made no progress. An elderly taxi driver drove me to the home of Uncle Afzal following the directions that I had vaguely remembered. My uncle was surprised to see me, and after breakfast assisted me to navigate through the bureaucratic jungle to acquire a visa. Before my passport received the stamp that allowed me to enter the country legally, half of my first day there had been wasted, and it would be midnight when I knocked on *Bhaijee Manzoor's* house in Gujranwala. Although the visit was short, it allowed me to spend some time with my family and meet Sultana, Masood's wife.

My trip to Tokyo and Hong Kong was successful, and the work was proceeding according to schedule as we prepared to receive a quantity of amplifiers for final testing before the next cable show, where GE would formally announce its entry into the cable TV equipment business. It was the evening of April 13 when Caywood called again, and that time I promised to call him back after discussing the matter with Reinhild. As soon as I hung up, the phone rang again, and it was Carmine, asking me to join the others at Paul's house for an urgent meeting, where it was announced that GE had decided to abandon the project. The news was disturbing, even though I had already decided to leave in the near future. In a meeting the following morning, the personnel manager, after retrieving our ID cards, informed us about the severance pay and offered placement services, which I declined. The severance pay and other remunerations were enough to sustain us for a sufficient time for me to search for a position that I really wanted. But there was an opportunity in the person of Caywood knocking on my door, and I was being nudged towards it. When I arrived home, Caywood, in the absence of my promised call, had already phoned. Later my conversation with him was brief, and he agreed to arrange for my visit the following day, a Saturday.

The florescence begins early in Virginia, and during the month of April the hills and valleys put on a coat of light green. When I boarded the plane in the early Saturday morning, the dew-laden airport lawns were shimmering in the sunshine, but as the plane progressed north, the ground colors changed to wintery brown and the trees appeared naked without their leaves. By the time the plane landed at Syracuse, I was experiencing a wave of sadness, probably brought on by the change in the scenery. Caywood and Daniel, the division president, were already aware that GE had aborted the project and, from the faxed list, knew the names of the available engineers. The meeting was brief because the absence of my name had led them to believe that I might have other opportunities. The interview became more of a salary negotiation, and once an agreement was reached the discussion turned to schedules and scope of the work. It became clear that in order to complete all the tasks, I would have to assume my duties as soon as possible. The following Monday once again I embarked on a ten-hour journey to another Holiday Inn that would be my home for the coming months.

When the school year was over, we moved into our new house in Manlius, New York. A spacious living room, dining room, kitchen, and a breakfast area were on the first floor, while the second story contained four bedrooms, two baths, and an additional room built above the two-car garage. Later Ronnie and I erected a tool shed at the back of the large yard to house the lawnmower and other garden tools. An attractive landscape lined the space between the walkway and the porch leading to the entrance. Our neighbors were very congenial, and our children found many friends among their children. During the winter months we joined a ski area, where we spent many weekends and evening hours on the lighted trails. We felt that time was right to file the necessary documents to sponsor the immigration of Masood and his family from Pakistan, as I sensed some permanency in my job.

So I thought.

Once the development of the products was completed, the drawings and specifications were turned over to Magnavox for manufacturing at some other facility. After a few meetings with the factory engineers, my role was diminished to one of support only.

Following the veto of my proposal to establish a turnkey group, I found myself left out of the weekly staff meetings, which I did not mind, as those gatherings always ended up in violent arguments between Daniel and his brother-in-law, who was vice president of marketing. But when I found someone else occupying the new office that was originally assigned to me, my instincts sent a warning signal. This was the second time that a large corporation had disrupted my life in order to gain from my experience and then discarded me like an empty can of Coke. While GE was more forthcoming and compensated handily for my inconveniences, the tactics employed by Magnavox's division were humiliating and distasteful. I could easily relate to Iacocca's experience at Ford. This placed me in an awkward situation, as Reinhild and Ruby were visiting Germany and Masood and his family were on their way to the United States from Pakistan. On June 9, 1973, Michelle and I drove nearly six hours to Kennedy International Airport to meet my brother, his wife, Sultana, and their one-year-old son, Ahmed. It was very early on June 10 when we arrived home because the plane was seven hours late.

I had one day to show the newly arrived family the American way of life and acquaint them with Ronnie and Michelle, because on Monday, June 11, I had to drive to Horsham, Pennsylvania, to meet with Lee Zemnick, the executive vice president of Jerrold. I had requested the meeting in order to secure employment at the company I had left less than two years earlier when he had given me his word that there would always be a job for me. I discovered that John Malone had left and joined TCI, a cable TV system operator, Bill Lambert had assumed the position of vice president of sales and marketing, and Eric was planning to retire. Lee informed me that Mike, my old boss, and Bill wanted to discuss what they could do for me, but that he needed my assistance in the turnkey department to resolve some of the system construction problems in the field. Although I had to take a pay cut, the job offered me an opportunity to move away from engineering, where I had reached my potential, into a position that could lead to management. During my journey home, with restored confidence, there was a feeling like never before that my dream of owning a business was nigh.

On June 16, upon their return from Germany, Reinhild and Ruby got the news of our impending move. The house was put on the market and we spent the following week implementing the recommended improvements to make it attractive to the prospective buyers. On Sunday, June 24, I drove our 1968 Ford LTD station wagon to Horsham Inn, which would become my temporary home for the following five weeks. In describing my responsibilities when I reported for the work on June 25, Lee explained that the department had not been able to complete its projects on time and there were millions of dollars outstanding because some of the customers had not accepted the completed projects. He instructed me to meet with the customers and coordinate the efforts to resolve the outstanding issues in order to collect what was owed. That was what I really wanted to do.

Each Friday after work, I drove to Manlius to be with the family and left early Monday morning to be back in my office by 9:00 a.m. One Monday Masood accompanied me for an arranged interview, after which he also began working at Jerrold. This way he could stay with me in the hotel room that was being paid for by Jerrold and also provide me with some company. The homes in the area were selling like hotcakes, and any of the ones I found suitable was sold before I could discuss it with Reinhild. I located a two-story house, under construction on a two-and-a-half-acre lot, that, when completed ,would have four bedrooms and two bathrooms upstairs and a living room, dining room, a recreation room, a powder room, and two-car garage on the first floor. It was one of fifteen homes built on hilly terrain in the village of Spinnerstown, near the city of Quakertown. After quickly describing it to Reinhild, I paid $100 to hold the property under contract. The completion was scheduled for October 1, which created a problem because the schools in the area started on September 1, and we had to have established residency in the district within thirty days.

We had sold our house in Manlius, and the buyer wanted to move in during the last week of August. That left us with no choice but to rent a place near Quakertown for at least a month, but all efforts to find a house for a month bore no fruit, and we were forced to rent a two-bedroom efficiency suite in a motel in Ambler, about a forty-five minute drive to the schools. There we were, eight of us, our dog, Sparky, and our bird Maxie. We registered our three children in three different schools with the condition that in the event we failed to establish an address in the district within the thirty days, we would have to pay a fee each month after that. Reinhild had to drive Ronnie, Ruby, and Michelle to their respective schools each morning and then pick them up at the end of the day. On October 1, 1973, we closed on our new home, but the storage and moving company failed to deliver our belongings in time, so we had to make do with borrowed camping cots and sleeping bags for a few days.

As I closed more of the open projects, I began to feel comfortable in situations that presented problems, contractual or technical. One day a certified letter addressed to me arrived at my office containing a check for $94,000, made out to me personally. This was the amount that one of the customers had agreed to pay before I could authorize the crews to fix the problems. Naturally I endorsed the check to the company.

After a few months on the job, Sam, the new vice president of the turnkey department, asked me to study the organization and the workings of QC Construction, a subsidiary of Jerrold that did the actual construction. Two weeks later I presented my recommendations. Immediately after the monthly senior management meeting, rumors began to circulate about impending layoffs due to company's financial problems. After the meeting, Mike stopped by my office, and said, "Congratulations. Sam announced your appointment as the general manager of QC Construction." It was a surprise to me, because my discussions with Sam had been confined only to my opinion about the personnel at QC, and when I approached him about it, he confided in me that although he had made the announcement, he did not feel that I should take the position, because later he was directed by the company president to liquidate QC Construction, and he did not want me to get stuck with shutting down that group. Once again the warning bells began their concert.

On the way home I came to the conclusion that my job was safe for the near future, as I was engaged in negotiations with a large cable system owner who was holding many millions of dollars pending the resolution of the outstanding issues. I toyed with the idea of purchasing QC Construction, but rejected it not only because of the time and energy it would require, but also because of the lack of finances. The following morning, in a meeting with Sam, I wanted to know Jerrold's position if I started a construction company of my own. He informed me that he was sure that the management would have no objection to it, but there could be some persons here who might have a problem because of mere jealousy.

The company was in a shrinking mode, and employees were being let go each Friday. Lee Zemnick took early retirement, and one Friday in the beginning of March, Masood received his pink slip. The same day I received an IRS refund check for $1,200. That evening I made a cash flow plan for a cable TV construction business. Masood agreed to front the company, and John Richardson, one of the project managers, became our partner. My dream was about to take a tangible shape.

31

AM Communications, Inc., was incorporated by an agent in Delaware in late March 1974 at a cost of $45. By renting a room next to a cold storage facility and opening an account at Quakertown National Bank, Masood, John Richardson, and I became business owners. That part was easy, but giving life to the new venture and then sustaining it would require all my past experiences and, above all, faith in its success. When informed that my brother had joined a cable construction company, Sam consented to place AM on the bidders' list. Masood had been in the country for only a few months and did not yet understand the local idiom. So, in exchange for his physical assistance in the storage facility, the secretary there agreed to answer the phones. AM received its first contract worth $6,000 a few weeks later.

Before any work could begin, we had to submit insurance certificates, which came at a great cost due to the lack of previous business experience. Harry at the local Ford dealer could only sell a panel van to me personally because our business had no credit history. With QC closing its doors, I would have ample choice of experienced employees. Bill Ross, a splicer at one of Jerrold projects, had impressed me with his analytical mind while testing a cable installation tool and was my choice for our first employee of the new company. Our immediate problem came in the form of the gasoline shortage that had spread throughout the country due to the oil embargo, and the job site lay seven hundred miles away to the west. We managed to fill three five-gallon gas containers and drove the new van to Allentown airport to meet our employee. Bill, wearing long, scraggly hair under a baseball cap, cowboy boots, and a large belt buckle, recognized me in the lobby of the airport and, as he approached, I experienced a fleeting sense of doubt, which was quickly replaced by a feeling of trust and faith in the success of the new enterprise. After completing the required employee documents and explaining the contract, I handed him the keys to our new van, cash for expenses, and a stack of forms for reporting his weekly progress. If he had any concerns, he kept them to himself.

Heavy rains at the work site hampered Bill's progress, and although he kept working through the bad weather, we were forced to hire another splicer in order to meet our obligations. The additional expenses severely disrupted our cash flow, and Masood had to beg the local bank for a loan, which eventually was granted only after my personal guarantees. Earlier one of the local churches had offered AM a loan at 15 percent interest, although the going rate was 5 percent to 7 percent, and when he questioned whether the rate might be illegal under the usury laws, Masood was told that the difference would be written as his binding pledge to the church. It reminded me of Shylock from the *Merchant of Venice*; I was not expecting it from a man of the cloth. By now almost everybody at Jerrold knew that my brother was working for a cable construction company, and some of the project managers would call Masood for a bid, which we would prepare in the evening at home, but many times he had to contact me when an adjustment in pricing was required.

At work, the negotiations with one of the top three cable companies, who had acquired the Akron System, had finally come to a conclusion whereby Jerrold had to agree to upgrade all the electronics. One day Robert, who took over the turnkey services after

Sam had left, asked, "Do you think AM, where your brother works, can handle the Akron job?"

I had to suppress my excitement, and before I could answer he continued, "You know what is required, and this way the project will be done right."

"I will discuss it with him and see what he can do," I replied.

"Why don't you set up a meeting with the president of AM?"

I left his office and immediately called Masood about the possibility of a very large project and also informed him about the meeting. While driving home, it became clear that AM needed to hire a president and I decided to discuss it with one of my neighbors, who could easily do the job. Phil, who worked as a sales representative for a large company, agreed to perform the duties without pay in exchange for a 5 percent share of the company and, after a quick coaching, felt comfortable in calling Robert. The meeting went very well and, as planned, Phil assured Robert that AM could handle the work with Jerrold's help in the form of vehicles and lift trucks that he understood were sitting idle in the yard. Harry from the Ford dealership had taken a liking to us and in exchange for a dinner, agreed to act as AM's fleet manager and finalize the renting agreements with Jerrold for the use of their equipment.

AM had just completed the first project that was valued in the thousands without making any profit, and now we were handed a job that could exceed a quarter of a million dollars. As part of the contract, we were required to remove some modules from the amplifiers and replace them after modifying the circuit boards at our facility in Akron. The work had to be done at night in order to minimize the interruption in the delivery of the cable services to the customers. Being the representative of Jerrold, I could direct the operation of AM without any conflict and, in the process, train Bill in managing twenty technicians and two engineers, who were on our payroll. Once the first area was completed, tested, and accepted by the cable TV system owner, Robert informed me that I would be part of the group of Jerrold employees whose services would be terminated. When he volunteered to call the president of AM to find a position for me, I thanked him while thinking, "You are talking to him."

That was a blessing in disguise, as I wanted to take the helm of my company and expand the customer base. The experience I had gained during my recent employment was valuable in developing project management practices, and once it was announced that I was the president of AM Communications, Inc., it was not difficult to find customers. Masood took the responsibilities as the vice president of administration and chief financial officer, and Phil sold his shares back to AM for $3,000. In the meantime our bank displayed more faith in us and financed a bucket truck, also known as a cherry picker, for $14,000. Having not seen a vehicle of this kind before, the president of the bank requested that I bring the truck around before dispatching it to a work site, as he wanted to ride in the bucket. I parked the truck in front of the bank and pushed the switch after he was secured in the bucket, which reached thirty feet up in the air. When he asked me to bring him down, the switch failed to activate the mechanism, and I had to use a manual crank to lower the bucket. Although the incident was embarrassing for me personally, once on the ground he laughed it off by telling me that I should make sure that it works before sending it out.

~

As the Akron project came to a close, we had projects lined up in Connecticut and later in Florida, requiring more employees and vehicles. We purchased new trucks and spent day and night equipping them with hitches. Ruby, at sixteen, and her girlfriend drove two of the vehicles to Fort Lauderdale, Florida, and had a paid vacation for a long weekend at AM's expense. AM ended the first year by making a profit of $63,000; the majority of it was spent to purchase the equipment that we had rented from Jerrold.

The project that provided us with cash for our next growth entailed the completion of the construction of a haphazardly built system that had no continuity. The customer agreed to receive the invoice by fax on Monday and pay on Friday. Each Friday I made a140-mile round trip to pick up the check. Earlier the cable TV systems were only allowed to be built in the suburban towns at least thirty-five miles away from large cities, but once the restrictions had been lifted the demand for construction services grew exponentially. The required expansion taxed our resources, and many times Reinhild had to call me to know if she could cash my paycheck as the customers delayed paying our invoices.

Citizens band radio was the prevalent means of communications before the emergence of the cell phone technology. Truckers used the CB radios, with its own lingo, to warn each other about speed traps and to overcome boredom. With no licensing requirements, the technology found its way into people's homes and cars. The users adopted made-up names called handles to identify themselves, my handle being "Flying Dutchman." Many times I conversed with others on the road while driving home from some project late at night. Once I contacted Masood with the help of a home-based CB user so he could inform the bank that I was going to be late bringing the check because I was delayed due to the weather. It was necessary in order to prevent the bank from returning the payroll checks.

My compensation was just enough to provide the necessities; not suitable for a business owner, but the eye on the bigger picture made it easy to face the sacrifices needed to establish a new business. In order to supplement our finances, Reinhild enrolled as a distributor for a home sales company and received many awards for her efforts, and the monthly motivational gatherings, which I also attended, were very enlightening. There I learned to build on the faith and the magic of thinking big. I began to act as if AM was already a nationwide turnkey services contractor. Till then I consulted with manufacturers in order to supplement my income. I charged $550 per day for my advice and one company, in exchange for reducing their product cost, paid enough for us to build an in-ground swimming pool at our house. At one time it became necessary to use our house as collateral with the bank in order to finance the expansion of the business.

Since the Pakistan Air Force rejected my efforts to become a pilot, I had been waiting for the right time to learn flying, a fact well known to one of my neighbors. One day he informed me that he had paid $20 on my behalf for an evening class being held at the local school to learn the ground part of flying. After passing the test administered by the Federal Aviation Administration, I received a learner's card allowing me to take flying lessons, and, after forty hours of flying instructions and solo trips to three airports at least one hundred miles away, a federal examiner tested me for my flying proficiency and awarded me a license to fly a single-engine plane and carry invited passengers. In partnership with our insurance agent, we purchased a Cessna 172 airplane that made it easy for me to visit the job sites and be home in time for dinner. Ronnie graduated from high school and headed to college in his car, an MG that often needed mechanical repairs, and I would fly there to fix it, reminding me of my time with the little green Morris.

In the early years, AM had to work as subcontractor to the equipment suppliers, and I was required to attend preconstruction meetings. It was at one of those where I met William, a former NASA contract administrator, who represented the system owner. After the usual introductions, William looked at me and said, "You do not address my team, as you are only a subcontractor, and you must communicate through Dick," the latter being the project manager for the equipment supplier. Most of the system owners knew me from my product development days and felt comfortable with my participation in similar meetings and appreciated my input. I could understand where William was coming from, because such a regiment was necessary when dealing with many contractors. When we broke up for lunch, I approached William and asked, "Is it all right for me to talk to you now that we are no longer in a meeting?" And before he could answer, I gave him my background and AM's capabilities.

One night while we had just gone to bed, the phone rang, and when I heard William on the other end, I panicked, thinking that something had gone wrong at his project. Instead he apologized for calling so late and informed me that one of their other projects was not meeting their expectations and he would like me to take it over. It was music to my ears because it was an endorsement by a system owner who had the reputation for quality. When he also asked me to select the equipment supplier of my choice in the event I found it difficult to work with the one they already had, I was on cloud nine.

Each city or community grants the franchise to the selected system owner to provide cable services to its residents, and applicants are required to present their plans in open council meetings. In order to provide credibility to their construction plans, I was called upon by prospective customers to appear in these meetings. I was not surprised when one Friday afternoon the receptionist—by then we had one—informed me that there was a man named John on the phone.

"This is Mac, how may I help you?"

"Hi Mac, this is John Tatta. I am president of Cablesystems and we would like to buy your company."

"I am very flattered, but why do you want to be in the construction business?"

"We have many projects in the works and feel that we could do with our own construction facility."

"First, AM is not for sale, but if it were, I probably would be in Florida drinking gin and tonics while your work fell behind schedule. Instead, we can agree on a blanket price for all your projects in exchange for us having priority on your work."

He thought for a while and said, "That sounds good. Can you come and see me on Monday and we can discuss it further?"

During the weekend, Bill Ross and I worked up some pricing, and on Monday we met with John to conclude a verbal agreement, which led to the construction of hundreds of miles of networks in many cities using the equipment from Jerrold. By this time we had begun providing turnkey services by sub contracting the mapping and the system design work. By the acquisition of the sub contractor, AM Communications, Inc. became a full turnkey services contractor. This change allowed us to negotiate favorable discounts with the cable and equipment manufacturers. I felt confident enough to promote Bill Ross to the position of vice president overseeing all the projects.

Deregulation spawned many independent channels, such as HBO, Showtime, etc., further placing a burden on equipment manufacturers to increase the bandwidth. The assembly of most of the cable products had been transferred to Mexico or Taiwan, but I had an idea to design the tap, a pole-mounted cable-to-home interface device, in a way that it could competitively be produced in the United States of America. AM purchased a building about fifty miles away, in a community where the unemployment rate had climbed to over 11 percent, and established an assembly plant under AM Electronics, Inc. Although we had created the most employee-friendly environment, the local union decided that there could be no employees in that city without representation. Their planted person proceeded with the organizing efforts, with the officials showing no interest in the fact that the goal of the project was to keep the jobs from going overseas. The union won the election by one vote, and their contract's work classification and restrictions left me with no alternative but to search for an overseas location, the very thing I had avoided doing

Masood and I traveled to the Philippines and found that the government had small factory buildings available in its free zones and offered trained personnel. Later John Richardson accompanied me there to establish our overseas operation after we had completed the lease of a building. While John got busy with getting work benches made, I traveled to Taiwan to establish component suppliers. Ronnie, who had joined the AM organization since his graduation from college, assisted in the worldwide search for the needed parts. Globalization had not become the household word that it is today, but our factory in the city of Cebu was assembling circuit boards and components that came from Taiwan and the United States of America, using solder from Hong Kong in enclosures (die casts) from Japan, and employing over a hundred hardworking persons. This AM tap was used in all our turnkey projects.

In order to expand the market for the tap, I negotiated a distribution agreement with a hardware retail company and we decided to display it at the upcoming cable TV show at his booth. We had set up a live demonstration when one of the officials from Jerrold informed the distributor that it would cancel all outstanding orders unless the AM tap was removed. That prompted me to rent a booth of our own, after which I called Ronnie to make up some signs and bring some old system maps. He arrived just in time before the second day of the show, and we pasted the maps on the partitions and had better traffic than we'd had in the distributor's booth.

One day Albert, an employee, having completed an assignment, stopped by at the office before taking a bus to Bridgeport to spend his two weeks of vacation. As part of my twice-a-week visits to various projects, I happened to be flying to New Haven, Connecticut, that day and offered to give him a ride in the plane. While we were flying, another employee whose first name was also Albert was accidently electrocuted at the New Haven project. When the supervisor at the job site called the office to inform them that Albert was dead, Masood immediately asked, "How is Mac?"

"I do not know," said the person on the other end of the line.

The answer further puzzled and panicked him, not realizing that the caller had no idea that there was another person named Albert traveling with me. As soon as I landed, the supervisor, noticing that my passenger had the same name as the dead person, advised me to call Masood immediately. On the other end of the phone line I could hear his sigh of relief when he heard my voice, and he immediately began offering prayers of thanks.

32

By now our revenue had increased to over $2 million, with a reasonable profit for the year ending 1979. One day Lee Zemnick, my former boss at Jerrold, paid a visit to discuss an idea he had for AM. Masood joined in the meeting. Lee said, "You have all the ingredients needed for a company to raise capital by selling stock to the public." Before I could comment, he continued, "I know people who can assist with the process."

"What will it take to make it happen?" Masood asked.

"Mac, you probably do not remember Ralph, but let me arrange a meeting with him and go from there," Lee said.

Once I discovered that during the early days of Jerrold, Ralph had provided financial advice to Milton Shapp, who I held in high esteem, the decision in favor of the meeting came easy. After Lee left, Masood and I attempted to understand what "going public" would hold for us. As we decided to go with the flow, I reminded myself that although financial security was still in the future, most of my dream had already become a reality. I had not only learned how to fly but owned a plane, had a business in the United States of America, had a beautiful house with pleasant surroundings, a loving family and the love of my life and best friend by my side, and also had earned the respect of the industry and the community we lived in. I had been elected to the position of the president of local chapter of the Rotary Club and vice president of the Upper Bucks Chamber of Commerce where I was called upon to moderate a debate between the congressional candidates. Reinhild had joined the boards of the local YMCA and the Children's Developmental Center, and she also volunteered at the YMCA and the local hospital.

Ralph Fratkin, in his late sixties, was a partner in a very prestigious accounting firm in the area and, after listening to my story, requested that we meet again in two weeks, by which time we should have prepared consolidated financial statements for the past three years. At our next meeting, after looking over the documents, he informed us that our numbers looked very encouraging and that he would contact me as soon as he had consulted an underwriter, who would sell the stock to the public. Those words, as if by magic, uplifted my spirits and confidence, and while driving back I began to fantasize about being a CEO of a publicly held company.

~

There had not been any word from Lee or Ralph for almost two weeks, which had led me to believe that his friend had not shown any interest. I was too busy to think about it, and then one day as I was leaving the office the phone rang and it was Ralph, informing me that Steve, the underwriter, wanted to visit our office on Friday in order to understand the industry and our operation. Steve, at seventy-two years, displayed enormous energy and asked very probing questions, and before he left I had a good feeling and began to think big. He wanted to meet me at one of our projects and asked that I bring my estimates for the year ending March 31, 1980. As Masood and I sat down to develop the revenue and profit estimates for the coming year, we could not believe that we had over a $5 million backlog with expected profits of nearly half a million dollars. I was getting second thoughts about taking the company public, but the rapid growth of the industry demanded that we expand with it to maintain our position. A few weeks after his tour of our project in the Long Island area, he informed me that if, by early next year, it became clear that we were tracking our estimates that I had given him, he would commit to underwrite our IPO, or initial public offering. He wanted to be kept informed at the end of each month about the company's progress. It was in February when we began to negotiate for a letter of commitment that included the details of the offering. Immediately after that we began the formidable task of preparing our enterprises for the public view.

The cable industry was on the threshold of becoming the next economic engine, and therefore the underwriters desired to change the name of the company to AM Cable TV Industries, Inc. It was very gratifying when Milton Shapp, who is considered the father of the cable industry and had just completed his second term as governor of Pennsylvania, agreed to be a member of the board of directors along with Lee Zemnick, Charlie Gantz, a bank official, and Masood, while I assumed the duties of the chairman and president. The company attorney had prepared an eight-page director's questionnaire that each of us had to fill out. As we began merging our various enterprises into the new entity, I was amazed at the complexities of the U.S. tax code, and tax attorneys spent many hours to resolve all the issues. Ralph arranged a million-dollar line of credit with a large Philadelphia bank and also introduced us to attorneys specializing in the work pertaining to the SEC, or Securities and Exchange Commission. From then on it became a game between our lawyers and those of the underwriter while one of the eight largest accounting firms was auditing our accounts and contacting our customers to verify the receivable amounts. Masood was managing this process, and sometimes he had to sternly persuade the team to speed up their efforts as every minute of their time was costing money. At one of the meetings, I was amazed to watch six highly paid lawyers discussing the intentions behind one of the words in a sentence for four hours before agreeing with my interpretations. Masood and I sat through many such meetings before a final draft of the prospectus was completed.

Finally the day came when we filed the draft of our offering, called a red herring, with the SEC, and then the wait began for its response, which came two weeks later. In the meantime Steve cautioned us against divulging this information to anybody. Two weeks had passed when our attorney informed us that he had received one page objecting to some of the language and a list of questions requiring clarifications. He assured us that it was normal and that we should expect this back-and-forth communication a few more times before the approval, which came on the seventh day of October, when the final prospectus for the IPO of AM Cable TV Industries, Inc., became public. Steve had presold the allotted stock, and the closing date was set for October 21, 1980. During those two weeks, I, along with Masood and Bill Ross, who had been promoted to the position of vice president, had to appear before the meetings of stock brokers at multiple locations. The day of closing arrived, and the members of the board, the teams of attorneys, and John Richardson gathered at Steve's office, and I watched as the couriers from the broker firms lined up in the hallway to exchange certified checks for the stock certificates. At 3:00 p.m., on behalf of the company, I received a check for over $3 million, and a much smaller one for the sale of my personal stock.

Driving back from Wall Street, Masood and I offered our prayers of thanks. My office was closed by the time I reached there, but my secretary had a message on my desk from Steve that read, "We opened at $10 and closed at $14, and AM shares were the most traded stock of the day. Congratulations."

During the two weeks from the issue of the prospectus till the closing, I was on an emotional roller coaster and wished that *Abbajee* was there to see how our dream had played out. Many times when I wanted to settle for less, his words gave me the encouragement to continue. Reinhild and I had already purchased a farm in the area and were planning to build a house there. Once during a vacation to the islands, we had taken a day trip aboard a sailboat and found it exhilarating as the keel of the boat cut through the deep blue waters and the waves beat against the hull. The absence of any engine noise calmed me, and the mild hiss of the wind filling the sails was music to my ears. As soon as we could, we purchased a twenty-four-foot sailboat, because that was the limit at the local lake. But before venturing out, we decided to learn sailing, and that brought us to Annapolis, Maryland.

During the month of July in the city of Annapolis, Maryland, it can be balmy as the still warm air, laden with moisture, hangs over the Chesapeake Bay, and frequently the invading cool breeze from the Atlantic Ocean causes stormy winds followed by heavy downpours and lightening. The sudden absence of rainfall shook me out of my deep thoughts, and as I looked towards the bay, the flying flag brought a satisfactory smile to my face. The quest for my dream was complete.

Faith can lead us to our dreams as long as we are prepared to take the detours.

EPILOGUE

The yearly revenues at AM Cable grew from $5 million at the time of going public to over $30 million after three years, showing record profits. By being invited to join the Cable TV Pioneers Club, I was recognized for my contributions in the establishment of the cable industry to what has become a worldwide, multibillion-dollar business.

Reinhild went back to college and received her degree in psychology and sociology. Ronnie, having graduated from college, joined AM, where he managed various projects. A few years later he left to follow his interests in the programming sector of the industry. After having been part of the team that got the Weather Channel off the ground, he joined the E! Entertainment Television channel while it was in its infancy. Later he went on his own as a consultant to the programmers and presently is the founder and CEO of Intelligent Life Productions. He lives in California and has two daughters; one of them is a stepdaughter who is now married with two children. That makes us great-grandparents.

Ruby, after her graduation, began her career in computer networking and specialized in its security. She has a daughter from her first marriage. After remarrying, she and her husband, along with their two adopted children, live in South Carolina. Ruby continues her consulting on a part-time basis while her husband is employed as president of an enterprise that develops network security software.

Michelle had suffered from bouts of depression, and when she found one of her friends after his suicide, her survival became a daily battle. In spite of professional care, on January 26, 1984, at the age of sixteen, her struggle ended when she took her own life. The ordeal dealt a severe blow to us all, and the survival of the family became the single focus of our attention.

All my accomplishments suddenly lost their appeal and appeared to be the cause of her demise. Having become ineffective, I gave up the management of AM Cable, and we walked away from all that we had achieved. In the face of a rash of teenage suicides, I embarked on multiple community awareness projects while Reinhild and two other mothers of suicide victims established a group called Survivors of Suicide, which spawned other chapters and is active to this day. The story of this tragedy is beyond the scope of this book and commands its own narrative. We moved to Florida in 1993, where I continued some consulting work till I retired.

Bayjee, Bhaijee Manzoor, and *Apa Anwari* have since passed away. All my brother's descendents reside in the United States, while the family of my sister's daughter lives in Britain, and her brother remains in Pakistan. In that way, my father's wish that I lead the family out of the Indian subcontinent has been fulfilled.

AM Cable TV Industries, Inc. was the silver cup of my dreams, but the journey leading to it was a learning and growing experience. This exercise allowed me to view the progression of changes that took place not only in my personal life, but also in society at large.

When I stepped on American soil in 1960, there was an air of extreme optimism, as the nation had begun to build its infrastructures after World War II and new industries were making their appearances. Although we could not vote yet, my political leanings were determined by the persona of President Kennedy, and by the 1964 elections, it was the rhetoric of Barry Goldwater about doing away with the social safety nets that pushed me to the Democratic column. The Vietnam War had been escalating since my arrival in the United States of America, and the nation was not only divided, but some groups were resorting to violence. The pictures of the sufferings of the innocent civilian victims that filled the TV screens each evening not only fanned the fires of opposition to the already unpopular war, but it also stirred the deep-seated agnosticism against the prevailing societal values. The widespread protests reminded me of the time I marched for the independence of India, but I had difficulty comprehending the total rejection of the mores and experiences of the over-thirty population. It appeared that a revolution to do away with all the prevailing disciplines was in progress, and the "us," as in a community, was being replaced by "I," and the era of self-aggrandizement had begun to take roots.

The 1968 elections were crucial as the nation yearned for a new approach to end the conflict and the bewildered President Johnson could not find a path out of it. Nixon offered the unique un-American idea of talking to the enemy that influenced my political thought. President Reagan's communicative skills dug the nation out of the postwar depression, and he took a stand against the Russians in Afghanistan. I joined his White House Action Committee and raised funds and successfully campaigned for the local Republican congressional candidate. Although President Clinton's intellect impressed me, I remained a steadfast Republican and supported the invasion of Afghanistan after 9/11, but the unwarranted attack on Iraq without the consideration of its future ramification for the region vis-à-vis Iran made me question the Republican ideology. By the time of the 2008 elections, the exposé of the torture and the cruelty meted out by ideologically driven members of the U.S. armed forces disturbed me. It appeared that the perpetrators did not stop to think that they were violating the founding principles of our nation. But the revelations that the officials who were elected to be guardians over our ideals sanctioned such behavior left me no choice but to become an independent voter.

In the 1960s and the '70s we never locked our doors, but now we need sophisticated security systems to guard our homes. Our children were taught to ask whether we could afford an article they desired before even looking at it, but today the parents slave and borrow in order to satisfy their children's insatiable desires. As a result we have a generation the majority of whom do not understand the responsibilities that come with the right to freedom. I am glad that our children grew up at a time when it was safe to play in the streets without the fear of abduction or molestation. Today I would not feel comfortable allowing my grandchildren to go out of the house alone. It begs the question: did the child molesters always exist in such numbers as today, or is the malady being perpetuated by the easy access to the means of dissipating information, good and bad?

President Kennedy set the moon, literally, as the goal for the nation to rally around, and we watched its progress with excitement and anticipation. When the Apollo 13 astronauts were stranded in the space, the nation united, as never before, in prayers for their safe return. The technologies developed at NASA fired up the inventive spirit of the nation and spawned the high-tech industries that became the envy of the world. We watched in awe when Neil Armstrong set his foot on the moon. The nation's investment in the venture has since been paid back many times by giving birth to the technologies that we experience today. Now we are losing the opportunity to seed the next business frontier, renewable energy.

Although the cable television industry provided me a venue where I could nurture my entrepreneurial spirit and be recognized as one of those who laid the foundations for what the cable communications industry has become today, I cannot say the same for the purveyors of the cable channels who have been dumbing down our ethics and mores by portraying weird and obnoxious behavior as a norm. The twenty-four-hour news outlets, in the guise of delivering accurate information, have instead, by disseminating rumors and innuendoes, divided the nation and raised tempers to a level where calm conversation has become impossible. The people have formed their positions not based on facts, but on emotionally tweaked falsehoods and out-of-context sound bites available on the Internet or cable channels.

Unfortunately these technologies, while opening new frontiers, have also inflicted irreversible harm upon the society. The face-to-face interaction arouses personal emotions and feeling for the parties involved. It has been replaced by anonymous dialogue that creates strangeness and antipathy. Texting and such other means of communications have widened the gulf of separation among members of our communities, corrupting the hitherto generous and forgiving character leading to the hardening of attitudes. We no longer desire to listen to others' ideas or positions and lack the time to know how others live.

Our obsession with sports, reinforced by the sports coverage on cable channels, pervades the national character, giving rise to the aggressiveness of an athlete. This single focus on winning by any means, even at the sacrifice of our ideals, has permeated into our psyche. It has been demonstrated by uncompromising behavior at every level of human interaction, and the last Congress exemplified it by practicing the task in their attempt to demolish a duly elected president. In the absence of referees or judges who monitor a match in a stadium, the politicians and the talk show hosts are free to use unfettered misinformation to undermine the governance of the country. The news commentators frequently borrow from sports lingo to describe a political party's strategy.

The cold war years vitalized our competitive spirits, and Sputnik laid the foundation for an education revolution that since has withered. It is a sad commentary when an athlete, whose talent lies in throwing a ball, enjoys a life that only few can dream of, while a teacher, who shapes the future leaders and sustainers of the society, has to live from hand to mouth. It is not surprising, then, that the United States is ranked twenty-eighth in science and math education in the world.

There is no other country in the world that can match the wisdom of the founding fathers of the United States. We need to teach in our schools and find the means to constantly reinforce the ideals entombed in the Bill of Rights and the Constitution. We need to understand that freedom, which we cherish so much, places heavy responsibility upon the one who claims it. I would leave the burden of discussing how we got here to those with smarter brains than I possess. History stands witness to the fact that great empires of the past withered from within and we must attempt to avoid such a fate. My faith in my country is unshakable because our passions that swing the pendulum of our values will again provide us with the vitality that will keep the United States of America as the beacon of hope for the rest of the world.

ACKNOWLEGEMENTS

English language was not my native tongue although after living in the United States for over a half century, I have begun to think in English. Still there have been instances when, subconsciously, Urdu sentence structure that I learned in my school days came through in my writing. I am indebted to Reinhild for correcting my composition errors. She must have been more attentive in her English 101 class than I was.

Many pages of this book could be filled by those who touched my life and made this story a reality. Without the persistence of my sister-in-law, Renate, we could have not been able to ride the Atlantic to the shores of the United States and the story might have been quite different. I acknowledge her efforts in finding a sponsor who was willing to take the financial responsibility for my family.

Authorship and publishing is new to me and quite different from product design and business management. The team at Create Space made it easy for me to tell my story. My hearty thanks for their assistance. The final word on the success and failure of my new career lies with you, the readers. I hope that you enjoyed reading it and in some way it motivated you to follow your own dreams.